The Women in God's Kitchen

The Women in God's Kitchen

COOKING, EATING, AND SPIRITUAL WRITING

Cristina Mazzoni

continuum

NEW YORK • LONDON

2005
The Continuum International Publishing Group Inc
15 East 26 Street, New York, NY 10010

The Continuum International Publishing Group Ltd
The Tower Building, 11 York Road, SE1 7NX

Library of Congress Cataloging-in-Publication Data

Mazzoni, Cristina, 1965-
    The women in God's kitchen : cooking, eating, and spiritual writing /
Cristina Mazzoni.
        p.   cm.
    Includes bibliographical references and index.
    ISBN-13: 978-0-8264-1760-2 (13-digit hardcover : alk. paper)
    ISBN-10: 0-8264-1760-4 (hardcover : alk. paper)
    1. Christian women—Religious life. 2. Women in Christianity. 3.
Food—Religious aspects—Christianity. 4. Cookery—Religious
aspects—Christianity. I. Title.
BV4527.M36   2005
270'.082—dc22

                                                    2005019641

For John

Contents

Acknowledgments

❧

T HOUGH IT IS SAID that too many cooks spoil the broth, it is not as a lonely chef that I concocted this book. The intellectual, spiritual, and culinary debts incurred during the years it took me to think (but also to cook and eat) through these pages, and of course to write them, are almost too many to recount. Being able to thank people here truly is the icing on the cake of writing. The staff at the Bailey-Howe Library, University of Vermont, provided daily help and a "library kitchen" to work in (the cubicle where most of these pages were written); in particular, the women in the Interlibrary Loans Office promptly found all the essential ingredients of my research—however exotic or obscure. Also at UVM, the people in the Department of Romance Languages include friends and colleagues who sample my work and sweeten my days. Presentations at the Rutgers Center for Historical Analysis, the Institute for Catholic Studies at John Carroll University, and, as a Dean's Lecture, here at the University of Vermont, have helped me bring some chapters out of the kitchen, so to speak, and onto a tasting table. For their generosity in reading and commenting on portions of the manuscript, I am grateful to Rudolph Bell, Catherine Connor, Anne Clark, Madeleine Kamman, Paul Lachance, Vincent Pelletier, Miriam Sheehey, and, above all, to John Cirignano, whose complete reading and numerous comments were essential to the final draft. James Deming, Sarah Curtis, Tina Escaja, Kelley DiDio, Wolfgang Mieder, Irma Valeriano, and John Waldron gave me helpful bibliographic and linguistic tips. A sweet thank you goes to

Elizabeth Johnson, whose groundbreaking work on feminist theology I have long admired, and who first put me in touch with editor Frank Oveis at Continuum; his immediate support of this project made the final stages of the work a delight to complete. Previous drafts of chapters 6 and 7 were published respectively as "Washing Lettuce with Holy Water: Food and Spirituality in Angela of Foligno's *Memorial*," *Rivista di studi italiani* XX.1 (June 2002): 116–28; and "Of Stockfish and Stew: Feasting and Fasting in the *Book* of Margery Kempe," *Food and Foodways* 10 (2003): 171–82. I am grateful to these journals for giving me permission to use my articles as the basis for chapters 6 and 7.

Dulcis in fundo, sweets at the end: It is a treat for me to thank the women who taught me about the secrets of the kitchen and the pleasures of the family table: in childhood and adolescence, my mother, Stefania Mazzoni, and my grandmother Ida Filippi (*in memoriam*), and later, as an adult, my mother-in-law, Ann Cirignano, and my friend Maria Sale Zampini. Equally sweet is my debt to my immediate family, with whom I share meals and so much more: my husband, John Cirignano, eats everything I cook with great gusto—often sampling it at the stove—and indulges my taste for culinary experiments and for literary, cultural, and theological arguments; our children, Paul, Gemma, and Sophia, though not nearly as tolerant of the greens on their plates, and in many ways a bunch of picky eaters, often surprise the adults in their lives with their appetite for spice and novelty—both in food and in conversation.

It seems appropriate to end this thanksgiving and begin my book with a table grace by one of the women in God's kitchen, the German nun Margaret Ebner—a grace as fitting for beginning a meal as for starting a book on food—"I ask you, my Lord, to feed me with your sweet grace, strengthen me with your pure love, surround me with your boundless mercy and embrace me with your pure truth, which encompasses for us all your graces so that they may increase in us and never be taken from us until we enter into eternal life."

Introduction

❧

Learning to Cook, Eat, and Read with Christian Holy Women

KITCHENS ARE HUMBLE PLACES. Other than a handful of celebrity chefs, the people who work in the kitchen are underpaid—when they are paid at all. Most kitchen work is monotonous, tedious, even; much of it goes unappreciated. Some of it is dangerous, involving fire and scalding liquids, sharp knives, and the stinging fumes of onions and hot peppers. It is true that, with their changing shape and evolving functions, kitchens have participated in the history of the family, of women, of social classes, and of entire cultures. But women have fought long battles to get out of the kitchen, and what began as a figure of speech, with the kitchen standing for patriarchal oppression, has now become a sad reality: people cook less and less at home in the West, and it is more and more seldom that families and communities sit down to a meal together.

God is not especially known for spending much time in the kitchen, either. Powerful eaters use dining rooms, kitchens being for those who cook and clean or for quick, ordinary meals. The Last Supper took place in an upper room, not in the kitchen, and when Jesus did cook, he grilled fish and bread by the beach. Nevertheless it is in the kitchen, aware of God's company, that many women in the tradition of European and

1

American Christianity have spent time—to cook, to eat, to pray, to learn. In their writings they tell how, in the kitchen, they cut through meanings and starved for knowledge, they savored union and, at times, burned with pleasure. The women in God's kitchen evoked in the title of this book are saints, mystics, and holy people who, in the difficult retelling of their encounters with the divine, did not hesitate to use culinary terms and images, to compare spiritual flavors with the sensations on their taste buds, to understand their preparation and ingestion of food as continuous with their spiritual training and sacramental gifts. The divine kitchen their writings in turn evoke is both a literal place—where they make and share what they eat—and a figural location, metaphorical and symbolic: here, they meet their loved ones and their loved One, thanks to, and not in spite of, their gender and its most traditional activities; here, those very activities—such as, in the pages that follow, making cheese, washing lettuce, skinning fish, cooking lasagna—acquire new meanings or, just as often, their hidden meanings are finally recognized.

One of the women working in God's metaphorical kitchen was a nun powerful enough that she probably never cooked an actual meal for her community, but not so proud as to shun culinary metaphors: the Benedictine visionary Hildegard of Bingen, who lived and worked in twelfth-century Germany. In one of her letters she tartly wondered, "The voice of life and salvation says: Why will a person chew on a grape and still wish to remain ignorant of the nature of that grape?"[1] How, that is, can we eat and not desire to know more about what it is that we are consuming? How is it possible to choose ignorance over knowledge of that which sustains our very existence?

Of course Hildegard's grape is more than that sugary fruit—green, red, or black, and, in times of envy, sour—so delicious freshly picked and even more delightful when juiced and fermented. Hildegard's biblical grape is a sweet and crispy symbol of the vineyard planted by Noah after the Flood. The first man to plant grapes and to make wine with them, Noah did not know about the intoxicating effects of their fermented juice: he consumed too much of it, got drunk, and lay around naked (Gen. 9:20–21). Knowledge of the grape is essential if we are to make good use of it, and not make fools of ourselves. Hildegard's grape, furthermore, gives her reader a taste of people's frivolity and their inability, or unwillingness, to seek truth and justice, "life and salvation," as she puts it. "A person who acts like this," Hildegard continues, "wants merely to chew and to gratify his own appetite, just as, by nature, he seeks after food." God's grape, instead, grows from the transformed, clean earth. It is neither green and sour as envy nor bitter and livid as greed; much less is it the color of ignorance. God's grape, for Hildegard, flavors discernment and nourishes wisdom, even as it sweetens pleasure.

Discernment of truth, transformative wisdom, and the sweet pleasure of fruit: the gifts of the grape are precious ones. Rather than read without wondering and chew without learning, readers and eaters wishing to see, to grow, to enjoy, are well advised to heed Hildegard's counsel not to chew and eat just in order to gratify our appetites—but to seek, instead, life and salvation. Nowhere is this teaching more apropos than in the stories of food and holiness related in women's writings. They are stories of deprivation, but they are also stories of pleasure and desire, stories full of discernment and wisdom, stories flavored with memories and seasoned by grace. Told by nuns and wives, heretics and widows, hermits and orphans, these stories will strike the reader aesthetically, but hopefully also spiritually, by the subtle connections they evoke, the hidden meanings they reveal, and the pleasure they recount and wish to share—pleasure that is aesthetic, alimentary, restorative, and, ultimately, divine.

The prayerful words of God addressed to, and penned by, the fourteenth-century nun and mystic Margaret Ebner speak of processes of concern to all readers intrigued by Hildegard's warning. God tells Margaret, "You are a knower of truth, a perceiver of my sweet grace, a seeker of my divine delight and a lover of my love." Knowing, perceiving, seeking, and loving are the work of and are rewarded by truth, grace, delight, and—what else?—love. Sweetness, on the taste buds and in the soul, is a divine consolation, a celestial grace, but it is also a means of contact with the deity, a sensation that travels back and forth from its earthly place of birth to its heavenly home. Sweetness is sticky, and the delight, desire, love, and truth experienced by Margaret must return to God, sticking to the divine like crumbs on the sugary hand of a child. God tells Margaret, "Your sweet delight finds me, your inner desire compels me, your burning love binds me, your pure truth holds me, your fiery love keeps me near."[2]

Food: it too delights, compels, binds, holds, keeps. It too conveys meanings, encourages connections, and gives pleasure. Food wants to be read much like a story: the increasingly popular genres of recipes and cookbooks, not to mention culinary mysteries and romances, attest to that. Variable as they may be according to history and geography, menus follow rules that are no less precise than those regulating verbal narratives. And the ingredients, the steps, the serving of each dish tell a unique, often controversial, story: flour tortillas in Mexico speak of the European conquest as the sweet-and-sour flavors of Sicilian cuisine tell of the Arabic presence; the use of butter in northern Italy reflects the climate much like the olive oil of the center and south speaks of the sun.

So another German nun, Elisabeth of Schönau, a contemporary of Hildegard living almost two centuries before Margaret Ebner, proclaimed that her God the Lord is as sweet as cinnamon during a time—the Middle Ages—when spices were essential to the cuisine of the aristocrats. In seventeenth-century France, for Margaret Mary Alacoque the pungent smell of premodern cheese made its revolting ingestion the most burdensome way to prove her love for God. At the close of the nineteenth century, at the height of the bourgeois love affair with sugar, Thérèse Martin, the Little Flower of Lisieux, remembers with relish the sweet foods from her life before the convent; it is only as an ascetic Carmelite that she learns to appreciate condiments that are vinegary sour or, worse, bitter as the criticism of her peers.

Holy women were fed, personally, by God, and that their lives and writings should have in turn nourished generations of Christians is no surprise. That some decidedly secular cultural figures have developed an intense taste for them, a veritable craving, on the other hand, is more likely to catch some people unawares.

Activist Carla Lonzi (1931–1982), widely regarded as one of the mothers of second-wave Italian feminism, was attracted since childhood to the autobiographies of women saints, and it is to Thérèse of Lisieux and Teresa of Avila that she returns at the beginning of her feminist journey: because Thérèse and Teresa entertain fewer self-deceptions about the world and are less compromised with it than other women; because they are stronger in terms of their personal experience; because, Lonzi believes, holy women more than other women possess an indestructible core—a sense of self made unbreakable by their relationship with the divine. Italian philosopher Luisa Muraro (1940–), also a secular thinker and a leading Italian feminist theorist, has dedicated several books to women mystics, referring to them as "theologians in the maternal tongue"; like Lonzi, Muraro turns to Thérèse of Lisieux because Thérèse had no self-deceptions and because of her engagement with philosophy: to do philosophy, for Muraro, is to work on speaking the truth, and self-deceptions are a grave and insidious obstacle in this effort. More grandiosely, in the words of Luce Irigaray (1932–), mysticism is "the only place in the history of the West in which woman speaks and acts so publicly," and "the love of God," the Belgian-French psychoanalyst notes elsewhere, "has often been a haven for women. Certain women mystics have been among those rare women to achieve real social influence, notably in politics."[3]

Journeys toward the other and within the self, liberation from all self-deception, engagement with speaking and writing the truth, the hard work of spiritual, social, and political influence . . . these traits are standard fare for the protagonists of *The Women in God's Kitchen*. Most of them wrote or dictated their ideas, teachings, and experiences, and a few we know about from tradition. Many are mystics, having developed a personal, unmediated relationship with God in a spiritual path that included visions and other supernatural graces. (Mysticism and spirituality can have many definitions: Christian mystics are usually holy men and women who enjoyed extraordinary graces such as visions, ecstasies, and union with God; by the words "spiritual path" and "spirituality" I mean the myriad ways in which human beings experience and practice religion or the sacred in their daily life.) Mystical experiences often exceeded language, and were put down in writing only with much doubt and hesitation on the part of the authors themselves. Several of these women are official saints or blessed, canonized or beatified by the church, acknowledged as having the ability to intercede with God on behalf of the faithful (an unofficial phenomenon in the early church, the recognition of sanctity was not formalized until the thirteenth century, interestingly enough, by the same pope—Gregory IX—who instituted the Inquisition).[4] To some extent, it is thanks to their ecclesiastical recognition that some of these women's writings and stories have been disseminated, and yet they need to be reread because, all too often, as Elizabeth Johnson reminds us, "tales of their holy lives and images of their devout selves make them seem too perfect, too miraculous, too otherworldly, too eccentric to have anything useful to say."[5] A few of our protagonists had to contend with accusations of heresy, and, though many continued to regard them as saints, some of them were never officially rehabilitated by the institutional church. Some were married with or without children, others preferred the company of women in or out of convents, still others lived primarily alone, as hermits. Many embraced changing lifestyles at different stages of their lives: Angela of Foligno, for example, a medieval spiritual follower of

Francis of Assisi, first lived with her family and, after the deaths of her mother, husband, and children, remained in the world as a preacher, living and working with a female companion.

All of the women considered here have something to say to today's reader—about our connections with ourselves and with our loved ones through the meals we make and share; about the struggle to mean what we say and to say what we mean at home and in more public places; about the pleasures found in love and at the kitchen counters, stoves, and tables.

Among the many holy women writers whose texts have come down to us, I have chosen quite a few—but still only a sample—because they dwell on cooking and eating but also because, quite personally, I find them irresistible (those two reasons being more interconnected, maybe, than I am willing to admit). They all, in one way or another, bitingly defy stereotypes of female self-effacement in the pursuit of goodness; they all had personality, behavioral, or lifestyle traits that preclude them from being comfortable models of womanliness, that prevent them from proclaiming the message that there is only one way to love God, only one way to be a good woman.

At a time, the twelfth century, when women were normally barred from formal educational establishments, Hildegard of Bingen became a writer, physician, composer, and theologian. Her contemporary Elisabeth of Schönau saw in a vision the humanity of Christ embodied in a beautiful young woman sitting in the sun. In late medieval England, Margery Kempe bargained with her husband so that she could stop having sex with him, and a century or so earlier, Angela of Foligno, more radically, had successfully prayed for the death of her family so that she could follow God. Teresa of Avila was pursued by the Spanish Inquisition in the period of the Counter-Reformation, and Sor Juana was forced to give up her intellectual pursuits and her library (among the largest in colonial Mexico). In seventeenth-century Venice, Cecilia Ferrazzi, Sor Juana's near contemporary, heard the confessions of, and gave absolution to, her many protégées; two centuries later, in France, Thérèse of Lisieux repeatedly claimed the vocation to be a priest. Gemma Galgani, an Italian contemporary of Thérèse, was repeatedly rejected from the convent but wore a habitlike outfit nevertheless and, like Thérèse, decided early on that she would become a canonized saint. In nineteenth-century America, Elizabeth Ann Seton converted to Catholicism as a single mom and became a nun while raising five children aged seven to fourteen.

"To be a female human being trying to fulfill traditional female functions in a traditional way *is* in direct conflict with the subversive function of the imagination," poet and critic Adrienne Rich (1951–1999) famously stated.[6] And subversive, in a variety of ways, these women certainly were.

However one may define "traditional"—the key word in Rich's quotation, for she is quick to point out on the same page that "there must be ways, and we will be finding out more and more about them, in which the energy of creation and the energy of relation can be united"—the stories that the protagonists of *The Women in God's Kitchen* tell of themselves resist being cooked up into a recipe for appropriate womanly personality, behavior, or lifestyle. Their stories grasp at homemaking even as they reject it, for not always can the "energy of relation" and the "energy of creation," as Rich puts it, be reconciled. Angela prays for the death of her family and then wanders around central Italy in search of her lover. Margery wanders much farther away, abandoning home and, for a time, country. Teresa of Avila, though in theory a cloistered nun, never settled anywhere for very long, and she died during her travels in her quest to found more convents. Elizabeth Seton was in practice homeless for much of her life, and if her voyage to Italy eventually gave her a religious dwelling in the Catholic Church, it also deprived her of acceptance in the city—New York—that she had called, until then, her home.

These women's creation of a spiritual home based on the fulfillment of the bodily needs, particularly the eating and drinking needs, of their neighbor, is predicated on the rejection of the permanence of a fixed home, of a set table. Angela gives away everything she owns, even sells her head veils to buy fish for the poor at the hospital and literally and spiritually strips herself naked to follow Christ: this holy woman's Franciscan choice of poverty is amply rewarded by the vision of God as a lavishly set table. Elizabeth Seton's change from American to Tuscan food sounds to us today like a culinary improvement, yet knowledge of the context in which she was forced to endure this change—in a damp and cold lazaretto with a small child and her dying consumptive husband—neutralizes the flavor we might otherwise have imagined.

Admittedly, holy women—including some of the ones mentioned thus far—are better known for their rejection of food than for their embrace of good eats. The work on the subject of religious inedia by historians Caroline Walker Bynum and Rudolph Bell, especially, has been groundbreaking.[7] By working on thirteenth- and fourteenth-century European holy women, Bynum has found in *Holy Feast and Holy Fast* (1987) that food, a significant theme in late medieval spirituality, was more important in women's than in men's piety: women used their own ordinary biological and social experiences as the source of their symbols; for women, food, by preparation or renunciation, was a way of controlling self and world; women, linked to body like men to spirit, found in the humanity, the physicality of Christ a bond to their own flesh—a flesh made bread in the Eucharist, a flesh made milk flowing in blood from Christ's pierced breast. Fasting from ordinary food and feasting on the Eucharist, like Bynum's holy women (who sacrifice ordinary food in favor of the Communion wafer), are the protagonists of Bell's study, *Holy Anorexia* (1985)—though Bell's holy women are all Italian and belong to a wider historical spectrum (from the thirteenth well into the twentieth century). Anorexia, be it holy or *nervosa*, develops mostly (though not exclusively) in young women, creating in them the desire to transcend the body—its drives, its physicality—and to achieve a noncorporeal purity.

Overall, both Bell's and Bynum's works focus on a "negative" view of ordinary food in connection to the spiritual life: this daily food is generally renounced, they both rightly note, in favor of the spiritual nourishment that is the Eucharist. Bell and Bynum are historians, and their work accesses a wide variety of documents in order to understand and explain behaviors and attitudes shared by a group—in the case of *Holy Anorexia* and *Holy Feast and Holy Fast*, religious women. As a literary critic, my objective is primarily to read and understand each text, and—with some exceptions (in the first and fifth chapters)—my book focuses on the writings by the holy women themselves. Historical, religious, and alimentary contexts are necessary to my work; however, I am trained to observe the text in itself, more than as a document from which to learn about a world. And in this process, I have found that, although not as prevalent as the holy anorexia that often destroyed them, not as frequently alluded to as the holy fast broken only by equally holy feasts, not as adored as the Eucharist that fed them body and soul, regular food can still be found in the writings of many Christian holy women, where, though usually a minor element, it can be an immensely useful one for understanding their relationship with God and with others.

Often joyous and life-giving, usually meaningful and binding, sometimes tender as love and tough as rejection, other times soupy as a failing memory or crispy as a well-planned action, examples of food that is *not* refused, food that is *not* Eucharistic bread and wine, also pervade the lives and the writings of many holy women and are to be explored further—in this world where food is all too often either insufficient or excessive, and where its glut is, ironically but typically, accompanied by a loss of connection, of meaning, of pleasure. (Needless to say, food images also appear in the writings of spiritual writers of the male sex; though some of these are occasionally mentioned in the upcoming pages, I leave that study, and a comparison of holy men and women writers on food, for another occasion.)

The Women in God's Kitchen begins with a chapter on bread, starting with images in the New Testament then going on to the very early and the very late medieval period: poverty, chosen or inevitable, hardens the bread of the poor and the bread of the holy women of Byzantium, and, several centuries later, impels Catherine of Genoa to knead bread the way she gives hope to the sick and poor (chapter 1). Back to the twelfth century: for Hildegard of Bingen, an intellectual omnivore and a discriminating palate, food preparation provides a means of explaining dense theological matter, and food ingestion is an excuse to learn more about God and the world; a century later, poet and seer Hadewijch of Antwerp will, like Hildegard, see human beings as food for their ability to be eaten by God (chapter 2). For Elisabeth of Schönau, in the same century as Hildegard, and for Margaret Ebner, in the first half of the fourteenth, sweets are the sensual equivalent of the loving feelings inspired by their divine lover—whether as honey and cinnamon (for Elisabeth in chapter 3) or as honey, sugar, and apples (for Margaret in chapter 4). The subsequent chapter does not focus on particular mystics and embraces a longer historical span: Italian nuns have for centuries confected spiritual delight into candies and baked goods oozing with creamy fillings and symbolic meanings; these candies and baked goods, through their shape and function, insist on the proximity between sweetness, women, and the divine, and connect present pastry making with a martyr of late antiquity, Saint Agatha (chapter 5). Living between the thirteenth century and the fourteenth, Angela of Foligno memorably sets the scene of a fight with the devil at her kitchen sink, or its medieval equivalent, while she washes lettuce (chapter 6). A century later, when she identifies herself with food, English mystic Margery Kempe stays away from eucharistic bread, choosing stockfish and stew instead (chapter 7). The Counter-Reformation kitchen cabinets of Teresa of Avila are known to have seen God walking among their pots and pans thanks to the virtue of obedience, capable of turning a menial job into the most transcendent of tasks (chapter 8). While Hildegard saw in cheese a reflection of human reproduction and a place to learn and teach about the varieties of the human soul, Margaret Mary Alacoque, in seventeenth-century France, used the disgust cheese inspired in her to better test her love of God; during those same years, in colonial Mexico, Sor Juana, who craved cheese as a child, gave it up in favor not of God but of learning; for their Venetian near-contemporary Cecilia Ferrazzi, too, food works as an instrument of divine knowledge, and it is through her manipulation of food that God teaches Cecilia to save a baby with almond oil, heal the sick with roast thrush, and return to wholeness her injured sister by feeding her lasagna with buttered greens (chapter 9). For Elizabeth Seton and Thérèse of Lisieux, the significance of food lies primarily in the workings of memory it embodies and in the memories it recalls. In the first part of the nineteenth century, Elizabeth Seton remembers American food in Italy and Tuscan food in America: both bind her to God and neighbor in preparation and enjoyment (chapter 10). Elizabeth makes healing candies for her family, Gemma Galgani, a few decades later, only consumes them—their sweetness alone among earthly foods being able to compare in intensity of flavor to Christ's passionate embrace (chapter 11). As an ascetic Carmelite, Gemma's contemporary Thérèse remembers the sweet treats of her childhood at a time when sourness and bitterness provide the exclusive flavor of her daily life, but manages to return to sweets—a chocolate éclair, no less—as she approaches death (chapter 12).

Whether they write about making food or ingesting it, preparing it or serving it; whether they identify themselves with food or instead taste in it God; and whether God, in food, bestows knowledge or withholds divine mysteries, shares miracles or exposes a mirage, the women in God's kitchen set in their writings a table adaptable to a variety of uses: it is a spacious kitchen table, where they can cook, eat, and write. At this kitchen table, heavenly food and culinary paradise mix with theological and visionary ingredients, and food is given the words to say when, how, and why it tastes, teaches, and transforms the way it does. At this table, the women in God's kitchen preserve, in writing, their mystical and gustatory pleasure. And, full as their lives are, the women in God's kitchen always, so to speak, save room for dessert—in hopes that, perhaps, in recognition of their cooking, serving, and eating work, God will allow them for once to practice paradox, to share with others and to keep for themselves, and, especially, to write of their divine cake and eat it, too.

With its emphasis on preparing, consuming, and imagining food, *The Women in God's Kitchen* is neither a comprehensive study of Christian holy women, nor an in-depth reading of one or two great mystics. If the former would have been a recipe with too many ingredients leading to a half-baked result, pursuing the latter task would have meant rudely ignoring too many cooks calling me to their table—a table already so full of dishes and so empty of guests. Because positive images of food in mystical writings have been little noticed, much less studied, it seemed right to let readers sample this topic broadly and thus to learn, at a plentiful table, how generous a wide variety of Christian holy women have been with their eating and cooking knowledge and wisdom. At the same time, no one book could include all or even most of them. My selection has been based on a combination of relevance, general interest, personal attraction, and a variety of historical periods—from late antiquity to the very first years of the twentieth century.

Holy women's writings have been read and analyzed by a range of disciplines, each of which has uniquely enriched the field of mystical studies: historians have discovered in mystic writing precious evidence for alternative religious views through the centuries; feminists have perceived in mystic texts the audible presence, in the past, of women's voices; psychoanalysts have recognized in mystic writers kindred spirits, because of their in-depth exploration of the human soul; linguists have identified some veritable masterpieces of rhetoric among mystic books; theologians have been humbled by the intellectual and experiential complexity of these seemingly unlearned writers.

Since my training is that of a literary critic, my primary allegiance is to reading texts, and connections, meanings, and pleasure drive all my work: the connections within each piece of writing and the connections between it and other texts and contexts; the meanings we as readers find in a written work, and the meanings others may have derived from it; the aesthetic pleasure reading gives us, but also the spiritual pleasure thanks to which the mystic was convinced to write. It is important to me, for example (though all these things may not be possible in every text) to read in the original language, to determine the authorship of a text, to discern its aesthetic value, to learn of its reception and influence, to see how it fits in the tradition of its genre, to understand the worldview it represents and helps to construct, and to discover its more subtle connections—the ways in which its meanings are not always what they seem at first sight, its pleasures not necessarily the ones the reader expected.

This book, then, is not interdisciplinary—I remain a literary critic throughout—but the different disciplinary approaches I mentioned above remain essential to what I do. Knowledge of history limits my freedom of interpretation even as it accentuates the need to interpret in order to understand the past and its remains. Feminism encourages me to seek the voice of women, even when that voice is almost inaudible. Psychoanalysis helps me grapple with some of the more bizarre wordings and practices of these mystic writers and, more importantly, with their unrelenting focus on the Other—God, neighbor, words, as well as the otherness within oneself. It is close linguistic analysis that unveiled for me the most literary aspects of the mystic's words, their rhetorical import. Theology provides the tools to grasp the extent of these writers' claims, the novelty of their statements, and their continued relevance in discussions about our relationship with the divine Word: not for nothing have mystic writers been called, as I mentioned, "theologians in the maternal tongue." While acknowledging my debt to these disciplines, I do not directly make historical claims, issue feminist calls to action, psychoanalyze the saints, discover new uses of language, or produce a mystical theology. But hopefully, these tools can reveal each work's connections, clarify its meanings, and let us share in its pleasures.

There are two medieval holy women who, though they are among my very favorites, for reasons that have nothing to do with the value of their written work (mostly because their period, the Middle Ages, was already heavily represented), did not make the final cut as teachers of eating and cooking: the French Marguerite Porete and the English Julian of Norwich. I would like nevertheless to invoke them now, at the inception of our reading, as sources of inspiration and as guiding spirits—as patron saints, perhaps.

Marguerite Porete was born around 1250 and was a beguine, a laywoman who dedicated her life to prayer, poverty, chastity, and service to the poor without, however, taking vows or living in a convent. She was burned at the stake in 1310, charged with being a relapsed heretic. A few years earlier, between 1285 and 1295, Marguerite had written in Old French a book known as *The Mirror of Simple Souls*, claiming that the soul united with the will of God does not need an external law to be saved. Indeed, a soul united with the will of God is incapable of sinning.

Marguerite's statement was interpreted by the Inquisition as an open invitation to hold oneself above the law and thus to sin freely. But this accusation, to the modern reader, is an obvious act of misreading, of reading out of context—and there was a self-serving reason for this on the part of the Inquisition, since Marguerite criticized the church and claimed that those who are pure should have the right and the duty to also expose ecclesiastical abuse. (Ironically, a few centuries later, the name of its author forgotten, *The Mirror of Simple Souls* was taken as an example of the highest stages of mysticism and was in turn used, in all likelihood, to differentiate true mystics from dangerous heretics.) The instrument of Marguerite's condemnation, though, whatever its true motives, was a lopsided reading of her book: bits and pieces of *The Mirror of Simple Souls* were read to mean what it is clear, upon a more holistic reading, Marguerite did not intend to say.

For this, we might elect Marguerite Porete as the protectress of literary critics. More personally, I might ask her not to let me become a sort of counter-Inquisitor, one who reads out of context in order to make words mean what they do not say. In Marguerite's own words, "Grasp the gloss, hearers of this book, for the kernel is there which nourishes the bride. . . . Grasp the gloss, for whatever nourishes is savory, and, as one says often, what nourishes badly is unsavory."[8] The gloss to which Marguerite refers is more than an explanatory note or even an extensive commentary. Her gloss is meaning itself: the author, like Hildegard in the letter about the grape, is pleading with us to seek understanding, for while ignorance is deadly, reading correctly is an activity as life-giving and nourishing as eating kernels of wheat. With the help of Marguerite Porete's memory, may I not read feast where there is famine, hunger where there is satiety, cooking where, in fact, there is only a lot of cleaning up.

Marguerite never claims to be small and unlettered, never refers to her feminine weakness and womanly inadequacy. This might be because she was a woman writing for other women to whom, Marguerite well knew, she had much to teach; perhaps it was a stylistic choice, perhaps a spiritual one. A few decades later, Julian of Norwich (1342–1416), a recluse and the first woman known to have written a book in English, entitled *Showings*, makes a different choice: "I am a woman, unlearned, feeble, and frail," she laments. "But because I am a woman, should I therefore believe that I

should not tell you the goodness of God?"[9] Julian's self-proclaimed ignorance, weakness, and frailty, however, did not prevent her from fulfilling
her calling, nor from elaborating a sophisticated and original theology
that is sweetly summed up in God's repeated assurance to her that "all will
be well, and every kind of thing will be well."

It is Julian's optimistic focus on the importance of the unimportant that
makes her central to those seeking meaning in ordinary food—Julian's
vision of the entirety of creation consisted of a hazelnut. Not a jewel, nor
a gem, gold, or fire, but a small, plain, brown, hard-shelled hazelnut
(hazelnuts may be relatively exotic in the United States, but certainly not
in Europe where they grow by roadsides and flavor a variety of cakes and
confections). As Julian tells her reader, "[God] showed me something
small, no bigger than a hazelnut, lying in the palm of my hand, and I perceived that it was as round as a ball." When Julian wonders about the
hazelnut, not recognizing its significance, God explains to her, "It is everything which is made. I was amazed that it could last, for I thought that it
was so little that it could suddenly fall into nothing. And I was answered
in my understanding: It lasts and always will, because God loves it; and
thus everything has being through the love of God."[10]

"*A littil thing the quantitye of an hesil nutt*," wrote Julian in her Middle
English: the hazelnut emerges from Julian's memory much like lettuce
from Angela of Foligno's, corn pudding and pork fat from Elizabeth Ann
Seton's, coffee, chocolate, and wine from Gemma Galgani's. Founded in
Jesus' invitation to eat the bread that is his body, as he put it, "in memory
of me" (Luke 22:19), the bond between food and memory resonates
through the writings of women like Julian as a way of understanding the
present through the past, but also as a means of recapturing past moments
through the flavors they share with present experiences. Rather than
being imagined or invented, the hazelnut belongs to Julian's past, to that
very experiential knowledge that gave her and other women mystics the
ability to speak, to write, to be listened to and even followed despite their
lack of education and thus of officially recognized credibility.

Borrowing from the vocabulary of rhetoric, we might note that Julian's
hazelnut is not only a symbol (indicating salvation because of its alleged
ability to cure scorpions' stings, and thus to save lives), but especially a
metonymy, that figure of speech in which the part stands for the whole: a
hazelnut for all that is. Metonymy is an especially apt figure in this case,
since, with the metonymy of the hazelnut, Julian underlines for us the fun-

damental unity of creation, that we are all metonymies, parts of a whole, that is, and that metonymic thinking is therefore inescapable. That small-ness causing Julian's surprise, the seeming insignificance of the hazelnut, is actually replete with meaning—for the Christian message heard time and again by women mystics, the message of the hazelnut, we might call it, is that the last shall be first, and that, as Mary's "Magnificat" pro-nounces, "God has thrown down the rulers from their thrones but lifted up the lowly" (Luke 1:46–55).

Through a misreading, Marguerite was condemned to the stake. Through the metonymy of the hazelnut, Julian is shown the salvation of all that is. And so it is in the metonymic spirit of Julian of Norwich's hazel-nut and with the caveats of Marguerite Porete's more than simply rhetor-ical troubles, that I invite you to seek out and to savor with me in the following pages the food concocted, dished out, bitten into, tasted, and swallowed in the writings of holy women: food that may be mundane, unexceptional, and commonplace, but food that may also be delicious, nutritious, indulgent, or healthful. Whether in the form of stockfish and stew or chocolate and jam, whether cooked as lasagna with greens or curdled into a fine or bitter cheese, this food—through metaphors and similes, through anecdotes and memories—leads to mystical connections, underlines the presence of meaning even, or especially, in the midst of seeming meaninglessness and leads us to share in the pleasure of cooking, eating, and learning at a divine table in God's kitchen.

1

How to Bake Wonder Dough into Miracle Bread

BYZANTINE SAINTS

AND

CATHERINE OF GENOA

F OR HIS FIRST MIRACLE, Jesus turned water into wine during the wedding at Cana, because wine is more festive than water, and because a woman got him to do it—despite his initial resistance (John 2:1–11). Also in the Fourth Gospel, though less dramatically, he drinks with an outcast woman at a well—a woman who goes into the city and speaks of Christ, a woman regarded by many as the first apostle to the Gentiles (John 4:6–29). A Gentile woman, as persistent as his mother Mary had been at Cana, obtains from Jesus a healing miracle for her daughter because she is willing to be, in the eyes of Jesus, like a dog content with crumbs fallen from the table (Mark 7:25–30). Women belonged to Jesus' inner circle, women accompany Jesus to Calvary, and it is to women that he first appears after coming back to life on Easter morning. Jesus enjoyed a special relationship with women, a relationship based on his rejection of women's ritual impurity, his affection for the many women in his life, his encouragement of women's full participation in religious practice. The memory of this scriptural connection is surely central to the life and work of Christian holy women. Drawing from this relationship, some feminist biblical scholars believe that the early "Jesus movement" was egalitarian, that it rejected oppressive sexist structures; they observe that even the male-centered tradition that has necessarily influenced the composition and selection of the Christian canonical scriptures has not erased the many instances of female privilege in Jesus' teachings.[1]

Among feminist and liberation theologians' favorite stories is Jesus' parable about the baker who, with flour and a little leaven, prepares to make bread. "The kingdom of heaven is like leaven that a woman took and hid in with three measures of flour until all of it was leavened" (Matt. 13:33; Luke 13:20–21). In the religion of God made man, the religion we might say of kenosis, of the self-emptying of God (Phil. 2:6–8), small things have great significance. So also in the kitchen, and particularly while making bread, something small—such as yeast—can have big effects. (In this we might remember Julian of Norwich's hazelnut, a tiny nut embodying, within its hard and plain brown shell, the entirety of creation.) And though it is the leaven that does the work of puffing up the dough, thus improving its texture, flavor, and digestibility, still the woman's activity is just as clearly emphasized: she is the one who takes the leaven and "hides" it in the flour (*enekrypsen* in Greek, *abscondit* in Latin: a curious choice of verb), with an action both deliberate and covert.

This parable recalls earlier appearances of bread and flour. Three measures was significantly the same amount of flour used in the Hebrew Scriptures by Sarah, when Abraham invited her to make cakes for the three angelic visitors announcing that she was to bear a child (Gen. 18:6), and by Hannah, for the offering at the temple during the presentation of her son Samuel (1 Sam. 1:24). It was a huge amount, enough to feed one hundred people, and unlikely to be prepared at home: in addition to evoking Sarah and Hannah, the amount of flour might have been a comic exaggeration on Jesus' part, or it might be intended to give the woman cooking for a crowd a priestly role: home baking was for women, but the baking for special offerings was done by priests.[2] And though flour was considered as nourishing then as it is now, leaven at the time of Jesus had more negative connotations: it was regarded as contaminating and corrupting. Jesus himself uses it in this sense in his own metaphor against "the yeast of the Pharisees and the Sadducees," meaning their false teachings

(Matt. 16:11). Likewise, Paul enjoins his followers to "cleanse out the old leaven that you may be a new lump, as you really are unleavened. For Christ, our paschal lamb, has been sacrificed. Let us, therefore, celebrate the festival, not with the old leaven, the leaven of malice and evil, but with the unleavened bread of sincerity and truth" (1 Cor. 5:7–8). Jesus is the main course, the sacrificial lamb, and the faithful are, metaphorically, the unleavened bread accompanying him.

Why are the faithful to be "really unleavened"? In biblical times, leaven, like the starter that is used today to make sourdough bread, was made out of old, fermented, basically rotten and smelly dough—though as French mystic and activist Simone Weil (1909–1943) reminds us, "it does not matter if the consecrated host is made of the poorest quality flour, not even if it is three parts rotten"[3] (it does matter, however, at least in the Catholic Church, that it is made of wheat—as my celiac friends know well). Because it is old and reused from one batch to the next, leavened bread ties the present to what has come and gone—but for a lump of dough. Furthermore, liberation is associated in the Jewish tradition with unleavened bread: there was no time to wait for the dough to rise when the Jews fled from Egypt, and, in memory of that hasty departure toward freedom, unleavened bread is prepared to this day for the Passover celebration (Exod. 12:39). In addition to its historical importance, unleavened bread is considered pure because it is made with flour that is not fermented and is thus clean and unblemished. Unleavened bread recalls history and the old days, through its connection with the Jews' flight from Egypt, but, materially, it is a wholly new food, untouched by the contaminations of the past.

Bread can thus be in the Christian Scriptures, and the Bible in general, clean or unclean, its dualism reflecting an important aspect of food's role in the life of human feeding. Descriptions of alimentary oppositions such as processed or unprocessed, simple or complex, are at the heart of anthropologist Claude Lévi-Strauss's influential *The Raw and the Cooked*, a book that analyzes the dualistic thinking of myths—focusing, in its title, on food: raw food is to nature (unprocessed) as cooked food is to culture (processed), in the most basic terms of Lévi-Strauss's structuralist analysis.[4] In the parable that identifies leaven as an image of the reign of God, Jesus subverts, we might even say that he "deconstructs," the dualism of biblical bread—a dualism he elsewhere subscribes to, as we have seen with the metaphorical yeast of the Pharisees and Sadducees. Biblical bread is understood as pure and unleavened or as leavened and impure, as either naturally fresh and raw or as cooked and corrupted by culture. Jesus challenges this clear distinction in his parable by finding divinity in the unclean, his kingdom in bread dough, God in the kitchen. So Jesus' baker, hiding a small amount of leaven in a huge quantity of flour, points to a sign of the divine, she announces an impending epiphany beyond her work space: this epiphany is visible—as well as, more suitably, tangible—in the batches of dough mixed, kneaded, and risen before her own.

When fleeing from slavery in Egypt, the Jews took along unleavened bread: they were escaping and in a great rush. Leavened bread takes time: it takes time for the small amount of leaven to spread and multiply through the floury mass, producing bubbles of carbon dioxide which, trapped within the dough, make it rise. Leavened bread requires connections: the baker must rely on a previous batch of dough to make her own. But dough inevitably does rise, revealing how God may take the apparently corrupt and contaminating, God may require the work of the seemingly unholy, to bring holiness into being. The transformative potential of leaven, small and suspect as it is, corresponds to the transformative power of the reign of God, taking place over time, taking place inevitably, taking place through the work of a woman, and, of all places, in a kitchen. Under her hands and in her work, God establishes connections with a beloved people, provides meaning for their existence, and promises them, in the divine presence, pleasure as sustaining and life-giving as bread.

Satiety from paucity and fullness from scarcity are leitmotifs in the lives of the holy women of Byzantium, saints who lived in or near this city during the early Middle Ages. Some of them survived as hermits in the desert (much like their better-known male counterparts, the desert fathers), their lives marked by austerities and renunciations. Over time, these women were organized in monastic communities and brought under ecclesiastical control: about 306, for example, the Council of Elvira obligated widows and virgins to make themselves recognizable through a certain way of dressing and by taking public vows.[5] Some of these Byzantine holy women were former prostitutes, others took religious vows as virgins or widows, and others still were married laywomen (though in the telling of their lives marriage is not usually depicted in a positive light). Like Catherine of Genoa, who will appear later in this chapter, and unlike most of the other protagonists of this book (chapter 5 is another exception), the holy women of Byzantium did not compose their own stories. Rather, their lives have been handed down to us through hagiographic narratives (from the Greek *hagios*, saint, and *graphos*, writing). These are saints' lives, aimed at teaching the reader how to follow the moral imperative implicit in the life of each saint. The authors of these Byzantine hagiographies, written in Greek, were usually males, and their stories, exemplary as they made their protagonists to be, tell of courageous women who, in their desire for God, rarely conformed to the social and biological expectations of their culture.

Among the protagonists of the volume *Holy Women of Byzantium*, for example, a collection of ten such hagiographies edited by Byzantine specialist Alice-Mary Talbot, one finds: a couple of transvestite nuns, Mary/Marinos and Matrona of Perge, who disguised themselves as monks; the former prostitute Mary of Egypt, who so enjoyed her trade that she required no payment in exchange for sexual favors; victims of domestic violence such as Thomaïs of Lesbos, a lower-class woman, and Theodora of Arta, an empress; and the dragon-slayer Elisabeth the Wonderworker.[6] Given the preponderance of male saints in this period and the dearth of writings about women, these are precious testimonies about women in the East and provide a vital historical link between the early Christian women we learn about from the Scriptures, the martyrs of the first three centuries of the Christian age (we will meet Perpetua and Agatha later on), and the relatively abundant writings by both cloistered and lay women during the later Middle Ages. Since these holy women's stories are thickly layered with didactic purposes, the information we can derive from them—about domestic households, about the spiritual life of laywomen and nuns, about daily monastic routines—needs to be taken with more than the proverbial grain of salt. Reading about these saints, nevertheless, gives us a taste of the historical continuities and disruptions between the spirituality of the centuries immediately after the life of Christ, that of the later medieval epoch, and—why not?—our own, as well.

Foods of various types are served up frequently to the reader of the lives of Byzantine saints. For the desert hermits among them, finding sufficient dietary sustenance and safe shelter was often a consuming part of the daily routine. In the desert, especially, the questions asked, like the foods eaten, are both basic and essential. Small wonder that in this barren land fasting should be exalted and culinary delight debased. In the *Life of Blessed Syncletica* (fifth century), we hear this Desert Amma (Mother), quote Scripture, saying that, "*a soul, when satisfied, scorns honey*" (Prov. 27:7). She says this because the sweetest of the earth's gifts is nothing compared to the spiritual fullness that comes from contemplating the divine. The biblical quotation is followed by the Amma's own words of wisdom: "Do not fill up with bread and you will not crave wine."[7] Even bread, a plain, subsistence food, can be a source of luxury and excess—leading to what is, in the dry desert, a double indulgence: wine slakes physical thirst, deceptively satisfying us with something other than God, even as it brings on the intoxicating pleasure that makes us forget God altogether.

Syncletica chose early on a life of virginity and austerity, to which, according to the pious legend that has handed down her name, she was faithful till death; she is one of only three women whose wisdom is included in the various collections entitled *The Sayings of the Desert Fathers* (the other two women remembered there are Sarah and Theodora). But the desert of early Christianity was also the home of several repentant harlots. Their past lives speak of the human body as needy flesh and of the reality, as well as the undeniable strength, of sexual desire in human experience. Still the holy harlots' lives, as they unfold in the desert and are transformed by it, embody the recognition that, in the words of Benedicta Ward, "such desire has a true and central role in human life as desire for God."[8] As necessary as God is the physical nourishment represented in the holy harlots' lives. Saint Mary of Egypt, described as a repentant prostitute from Alexandria, is probably the best known among the desert women of early Christianity (other popular holy harlots are Pelagia and Thaïs). Likely Mary's story is a collation of several different women's lives, for it brings together disparate elements found in a variety of sources.[9] The food featured in her life—the earliest version of which dates from the sixth century—is scant yet miraculously lasting, as necessary for Mary's subsistence as salvation itself and, like salvation, a gift of God available for the asking. In this earliest version, Mary lives for eighteen years on a jar of water and a basket of legumes. "One day, pierced to the heart with fear of God," she explains, "I went down to holy Siloam and filled this vessel with water; taking also this basket of soaked pulses, I left the holy city by night, commending myself to God, who led me here. And behold, I have been here for eighteen years," she continues, "and by the grace of God the water has not failed nor has the basket of pulses run short to this day."[10]

In another, much longer version of Mary's story, dating from about a century later, attributed to the theologian and writer Sophronios (c. 560–638), and popular in medieval Christianity, when Mary prepares to leave for the desert, she is given three copper coins with which she buys three loaves of bread. She tells the monk Zosimas that she ate half a loaf on the first day, washing it down with water from the Jordan, and the remaining two and a half loaves "little by little dried up and became hard as rock. In this way," Mary recounts, "I survived for years eating those loaves in small portions."[11] Like the waters of the river Jordan (signifying baptism) and the lion that appears when Mary dies to help with her burial (indicating the Prince of Peace), Mary's three loaves of bread are symbolic: they are three like the Trinity, bread like the Eucharist, miraculously abundant like the loaves multiplied by Jesus, and long-lasting like all gifts of the spirit.

Mary's consumption of hard bread was a necessity and a miraculous feeding, but also a practical, effective way to stretch her meager provisions: at least as late as at the time of early modern Europe, the poor used to eat hard bread, so that less of it would be consumed and it would last longer. Mary was in the desert seventeen years, and after the hard loaves were gone, she "yearned for meat and fish that abound in Egypt" and "longed to drink wine, which was constantly in my thoughts," she says, because, "I used to drink a lot of wine when I was living in the world." But in her present home she "did not have even water to drink," so she fed herself instead "with wild plants and whatever else can be found in the desert."[12] Desert hermits displayed a clear preference for eating what nature made available to them in its vegetation, but, far from being unprocessed and meaningless because natural and raw, these "wild plants and whatever else can be found in the desert," as Mary calls her food, are highly symbolic and, therefore, culturally, if not physically, "cooked" (in Lévi-Strauss's sense). Mary's plants, as described in her biography, are processed because they are gathered and consumed in a culture that saw in the hermit's gathering and consumption of desert foods a sign of her detachment from this world, but also evidence of her knowledge of this same world and of how to survive in it against all odds (not all plants were edible: a Syrian hermit had to learn from a goat how to avoid the poisonous greens and roots that had been making him sick).[13] Hunger need not be feared, though, because in the absence of bread, Mary says, "I feed and cover myself with the word of God." When Zosimas returns with "a small basket of dried figs, dates, and a small portion of lentils soaked in water," asking Mary to "fulfill an old man's wish" by accepting the food he brought her, all she takes are "three lentil beans"—then crosses back the Jordan by walking on its waters.[14] That is the last time Zosimas sees Mary alive.

Bread is the main dish of Matrona of Perge's daily life, as it is for Mary of Egypt, providing both physical and spiritual nourishment. Living between the fifth and the sixth centuries, Matrona was married to an abusive husband, from whom she fled; she wore a monk's habit and lived for three years in a male monastery, later becoming the abbess of a female convent. Since she lived in monasteries and not in the desert, Matrona had access to blessed bread: known as *eulogia* bread (because it is blessed) and as *antidoron* (because it is a substitute for the real gift, or, in Greek, *doron*, that is the Eucharist), blessed bread is more common in the Greek than in the Roman Catholic rite.

In her biography, probably dating from the late sixth century, Matrona first receives blessed bread from Bassianos, the holy founder of the monastery she had entered in male disguise. Upon discovering her true sex, Bassianos sends her off on a journey to a female monastery, giving her, at her request, nothing except "his worthy and holy prayers and a bit of bread as a blessing." She asked him for this because "she knew, she knew with certainty and was convinced that, with these latter as shipmates and traveling companions, all would proceed according to her desire and to her profit; by God's grace, this came to pass." But that is not all. As a protective shipmate, bread proves the holiness of Bassianos, as well as being evidence of Matrona's own holiness: she is able to stay away from it, to avoid ingesting it. "For she made the whole voyage with ease and calm, and consumed but very little of the blessed bread, a most remarkable fact and sure proof of her faith," the story narrates. Once she arrives at the female monastery, Matrona shares the bread given her by Bassianos but also receives bread from her new community. We are told that, "she gave them some of her bread, and received some from them." When Matrona leaves the convent for Jerusalem in order to escape her abusive husband, who because of her fame of sanctity had discovered her whereabouts, she takes "nothing with her save the hair-shirt she wore, a staff in her hand, and a bit of the blessed bread given her by the most holy Bassianos" (30–32). As it protected her during her earlier voyage, so this bread will take care of her now.

Bread alone extinguishes hunger, but not thirst. That is why Amma

Syncletica recommended not to fill up on bread, that we may not get thirsty and desire wine. God has other plans for Matrona, however. Her thirst, which she seeks to alleviate with "blossomy, tender greens," is fully quenched by God's miraculous indication, to her, of where to dig in order to make a well; around this water-filled well, she finds every day "tender, leafy greens." And, "coming, then, every day after her morning prayers and picking and washing the greens, she would let the water run off and then stop it again when it was clean; and eating the greens and drinking from the water, at the customary hour of repast after the evening psalmody, she glorified God for all His gifts to her." God provides food and drink: "Thus did that place supply her ever after, as if by way of tribute, with the amplest daily nourishment" (36). But the devil comes to tempt Matrona just as she is content with washing and eating her greens (he will do the same with Angela of Foligno several centuries later, as we will see in chapter 6, tempting her while she washes lettuce). The devil incites Matrona to seek a more comfortable life, and though the holy woman responds, "I have greens. I have water. Christ my Master provides for me in abundance. I am satisfied with these things and seek nothing else," the devil does not let up until angels come to Matrona's aid.

Blessed bread, icon of divine connection and supernatural meaning, keeps circulating throughout Matrona's biography, forming an alimentary thread that ties the saint's personal life to the life of her elders, after whom she models her vocation, and to the lives of those who, in turn, follow her and imitate her example. When, after her travels, Matrona, with a group of female followers, returns to Bassianos in Constantinople, he gives them, as a sign of blessing on their new community, three girdles, three cloaks, and three pieces of blessed bread, *eulogia*—and he is in ecstasy when he orders these things to be brought. Within a short time, Bassianos has two more opportunities to offer the women his blessed bread (46–48). Matrona's fame spread quickly—it is miraculous that her husband should lose track of her—and even the empress Verina goes to visit her. Matrona gives the empress "pieces of blessed bread that had been soaked with wine"—an action that the empress found surprising and beneficial both because Matrona, though poor, asked for nothing in return of such a great lady, and also because bread was at that time regarded as too humble a gift for a ruler, yet Matrona was not "ashamed to give such pieces of blessed bread to an empress" (48–49). The humility of bread is evoked as well in the life of Saint Theodora (ninth century), whose holiness is confirmed by the fact that, once in the monastery, "she performed by herself almost all the work of the convent: grinding grain, making bread with her own hands, and cooking, work which she had never done before" (184)—truly a woman in God's kitchen.

Matrona is eventually given a piece of property in Constantinople, where she is housed with her sisters. Blessed bread at the feast of Saint Lawrence is the last thing a young woman named Athanasia receives before conceiving the desire to join Matrona's monastery. When she joins, Athanasia does not bring along, as was customary for noble and wealthy women, fragrant wine, white bread, and fish, but rather she adapts to the monastic diet of greens prepared without oil, and dried figs. Athanasia remains three years in the convent, after which she must return to her husband; but she has reason to repudiate him when he is found stealing and implores the deacon Markellos "to send her some of the blessed bread of which the sisters partook." This he promises to do after ascertaining Athanasia's ability to withstand the hardships of monastic life—hardships identified by Markellos as dietetic ones: "You cannot bear such a way of life, for you are delicate and accustomed to divers dishes prepared with oil" (the use of oil for cooking was at that time a distinguishing factor between the lay and the monastic life). But, as her servants testify, since her first encounter with Matrona, Athanasia had not "partaken of her usual food, but of that which was light and plain" (57). Diet is what used to identify her as an aristocrat, and diet is what now proves the sincerity and predicts the success of her monastic vocation.

Significantly, Athanasia's gift to the sisters is a deal with a local bakery, since, "she arranged that the blessed Matrona should be supplied with a few loaves every day, for the sustenance of the sisters"; in remembrance of Matrona's first three years in the convent under a male identity, these sisters continued to don a male monastic habit. "The blessed Matrona, now able to provide her sisters with loaves, thanked God all the more" (57–58). The circulation of bread, blessed or about to be blessed, makes palpable and edible the spiritual and bodily connections that bind together the members of Christ's body. Bread, in this story, is not consumed but rather given, exchanged—its meaning clearly oversteps dietetic need to involve mystical connection and the pleasure of divine service. Bread is the ultimate gift: gift of bodily sustenance, gift of spiritual growth, gift of sacrifice, gift of plenty.

As staff of life and Eucharistic wafer, bread is the most symbolic of

Christian foods. "Give us this day our daily bread," Christians continue to be taught to pray (Matt. 6:11; Luke 11:3), mindful as well that they "shall not live on bread alone, but on every word that proceeds out of the mouth of God" (Deut. 8:3; Matt. 4:4; Luke 4:4). Bread is what Jesus breaks and serves at the Last Supper, it is what he identifies as his body, what his followers are invited to keep sharing in his memory (Matt. 26:26; Mark 14:22; Luke 22:19). It is in the breaking of bread, in the way he serves and shares food at the table, that the disciples first met on the road to Emmaus recognize Jesus resurrected from the dead and returned among his friends (Luke 24:30–35). Indeed, in the theologically dense sixth chapter of John's Gospel, Jesus repeatedly identifies himself with bread—bread that is both metonymy, i.e., part for the whole, and kenosis, namely divinity emptied out into humanity: "it is not Moses who has given you the bread out of heaven, but it is My Father who gives you the true bread out of heaven" (John 6:32); "the bread of God is that which comes down out of heaven, and gives life to the world" (John 6:33); "I am the bread of life" (John 6:35, 48); "I am the bread that came down out of heaven" (John 6:41, 50, 51, 58). Less symbolically, more practically, when Jesus returns to his friends after the resurrection, he cooks breakfast for them, who had been fishing all night, and serves them grilled bread (*bruschetta*, really), as well as fish (John 21:9–13).

Holy women are in good company when they offer themselves in sacrifice as food (like the English mystic Margery Kempe), serve loaves and fishes (like the Franciscan Angela of Foligno), prefer wine to water (Mary of Egypt but also American-born Elizabeth Ann Seton), or sit down for a meal with their friends (as they have all done). Whether at table or in the kitchen, whether cooking or eating, they are in the company of their beloved who, like them, ate and drank, cooked and served.

Bread appears in the texts of every holy woman I have read, whether as a Eucharistic figure for Jesus Christ, and thus as the Christian's necessary spiritual nourishment, or as a more mundane food—often the last substance, together with water, they gave up when fasting. It may be difficult for us to imagine just how crucial bread was in the diet of traditional European societies: Homer defined human beings as "bread eaters," and the practice of making and eating bread, in the Mediterranean world, defined civilization, indicated humanity itself: Pythagoras (sixth century BCE) described the world as having begun in bread; Augustine (354–430) developed in a sermon a detailed analogy between the act of making bread and the process of becoming a Christian—"This bread retells your history. . . . You were cooked in the oven of the Holy Ghost and became the true bread of God"—while Peter Chrysologus (fifth century) compared the conception, growth, Passion and death of Jesus Christ himself to the planting of wheat and to the kneading and baking of bread.[15]

Several mystics describe their fasting on bread and water—among them, Elisabeth of Schönau and Margaret Ebner. More metaphorically, Hildegard of Bingen, in the twelfth century, used the image of bread in order to illuminate human action. Just like, for Hildegard, "bread is baked so that people may be nourished by it and be able to live," so also in her view the human will controls the soul's works like a baker her bread: the will "starts by kneading [the work] and when it is firm adds the yeast and pounds it severely; and, thus preparing the work in contemplation as if it were bread, it bakes it in perfection by the full action of its ardor, and so makes a greater food for humans in the work they do than in the bread they eat." So essential is this bread to human survival that "a person stops eating from time to time, but the work of his will goes on in him till his soul leaves his body."[16] For Hildegard's contemporary Elisabeth of Schönau, bread is Eucharist and recognition: Jesus appears to her sitting down, he blesses and breaks the bread before disappearing, much like he did at Emmaus.[17] A century later, Angela of Foligno gives all of her bread to the poor and, in exchange, receives the Eucharist in a leper's scab.[18] Marguerite Porete regards bread as a gift of the earth, a gift that the "simple souls" in the title of her book would not hesitate to give away, should others need it more than they.[19] For Margaret Ebner, on the other hand, bread is both deprivation, as in the "bread and water" of fasting days, and a desirable dish: she has to prevent herself from taking more than her share; these two attributes of desirability and penance come together when she says, "I desired to honor Him by having to eat bread and water until my death. That would be an inner joy for me."[20] With a metaphor related to Hildegard's, it is to a good and clean will that fourteenth-century mystic Bridget of Sweden compares the bread God shows her in a vision: like bread, a good and clean will comforts, strengthens, and cleanses.[21] Teresa of Avila, at the time of the Counter-Reformation, claims that "the questions of sin and self-knowledge are the bread which we must eat" on the road to prayer and spiritual growth—it is a necessary bread but also a metaphorical bread that, like Margaret Ebner's more literal one, must be consumed in moderation.[22] In nineteenth-century America, for

Elizabeth Ann Seton bread is regular sustenance (she remembers "slips of bread" and "crusts of bread" eaten in Italy for breakfast or dinner) and spiritual fare: the "Bread of Angels."[23] And a few decades later in France, for Thérèse of Lisieux bread also moves from being the ultimate example of physical nourishment—in the convent, she breaks and feeds bread to a nun too aged to help herself, and in this she recognizes a priestly role—to starring in the liturgical procedures of her childhood, her sister's blessings of bread: these actions, although more playful, are just as profoundly transformative of baked matter as they are of the human soul.[24]

The holy women of Byzantium did not write their own lives. Though many women in the following centuries did tell their stories, the genre of holy women's biographies or hagiographies—*vitae*, i.e., lives, in the Latin term commonly used to describe them—continued to enjoy great popularity for many centuries. Of some holy women we have both biographical and autobiographical information. For others, the accounts of friends and collaborators have to suffice—and the authenticity of these accounts, their closeness to the life and teachings of their protagonists, must be established case by case. A prominent holy woman who never wrote but who is believed to have been faithfully represented in the texts associated with her is Caterina Fieschi Adorno (1446/7–1510), known to English speakers as Saint Catherine of Genoa: a married, childless noblewoman who dedicated her life, after a conversion in 1473, to the care of the sick poor. The titles associated with Catherine—*Purgation and Purgatory* and *The Spiritual Dialogue* being the most important—are the work of her friends, collaborators, and disciples who wrote down what she said and taught. Foremost among these was Ettore Vernazza, a wealthy businessman who became Catherine's devoted disciple during the plague of 1493, while she tended to hospital patients and contracted the disease.

Better known for her fasting, her penitential ways, and her administrative rather than her culinary skills, Catherine in *Purgation and Purgatory* describes bread as an image of God and a figure of hope. "Let us imagine," she says, "that in the whole world there was but one bread / and that it could satisfy the hunger of all. / Just to look at it would be to nourish oneself."[25] With its crusty shell and its soft, crumby middle, bread embodies in this mystic's view the only adequate way of figuring the human desire for unity with the divine. Human beings in good health need and desire bread; being human entails a need and a desire for God. Humans consume bread, and unite with God: without this consumption, without this union,

Catherine preaches, we are left hungry, incomplete, filled with the emptiness of longing. "Such is the hell of the hungry," she describes, "who, the closer they come to this bread, / the more they are aware that they do not as yet have it. / Their yearning for that bread increases, / because that is their joy." Food, and particularly bread, is for Catherine a fitting comparison for the joy of unity with God to which every human being aspires: bread is the hope of the souls in Purgatory, and bread, absent in Hell, is the despair of the damned. For without this bread, God is missing and death eternal.

In *The Spiritual Dialogue*, a discussion between body and soul, bread is a process rather than a product, an activity more than an object of desire, need, or consumption. Catherine's humanity, allegorized as human frailty, "realized that the Spirit wanted it to work with human misery as if it were kneading bread, and even, if need be, to taste it a bit."[26] The image is as conspicuous as it is obscure. Tasting misery, experiencing it physically with one's senses, is necessary for compassion, for empathy—and that is possibly the significance of the second part of the Spirit's suggestion. One must taste misery in one's mouth in order to comprehend it and therefore desire to relieve it in others. (More literally, the Spirit might also have been encouraging Catherine to ingest what she found repugnant: she is known, along with several other mystics, for ingesting filth; more on this abject practice in chapter 9.)

Contemporary spiritual writer Kathleen Norris writes: "I find bread baking to be a hands-on experience of transformation, and during quiet times when dough is rising, I often sit and write, aiming for transformations of my own."[27] Making bread with others, for writer and pastor Holly Whitcomb, is a way of learning how to manage the stress in our lives (compared to the heat of the oven) and how to handle sticky situations (by greasing pans); it is an opportunity to reflect on whether we are as dependable as flour, a time to think of what, like loaves, we shape, and what, in turn, has shaped us.[28] Norris's analogy between waiting for the dough to rise and waiting for literary inspiration is not too hard to understand; Whitcomb's comparisons are also clearly presented. But Catherine's reflections are subtler. She does not as explicitly state how making bread is similar to working with human misery, nor what the connection can be between kneading dough and consoling the desperate, relieving the suffering. Perhaps, Catherine's images suggest, it is the quality of patience, the act of endurance, the need for perseverance that bind kneading to compassion for others' needs. Bread dough is difficult at first to knead, its different ingredients must be brought together—as in the unity of will that human frailty desires and does not achieve—in order for a unified mass to form. The mass is at first sticky, hard to manage, but as the baker incorporates enough flour the dough becomes more obedient, elastic, and even pleasurable to work with. At this point a consistent application of physical strength becomes important, in order to develop the gluten which, along with yeast, allows the dough to rise.

Perhaps tending to the sick and desperate, like kneading bread dough, is a process in which the human being is an active vehicle for the manifestation of a divine intervention. Perhaps making bread, like ministering to the afflicted, involves providing the hands and strength that allow something the human being does not control—the rising of the dough, the consolation of the afflicted—but for which human intervention is necessary, like that of the Gospel baker hiding her leaven in the three measures of flour. By mixing flour, water, and yeast (and, usually, salt), then kneading it long enough, the dough will rise; the next step is to shape and bake sustaining loaves. Going to the needy, as Catherine did (she spent much of her life in the Pammatone hospital of Genoa, as administrator, nurse, and spiritual adviser), and staying with them, praying with them, caring for their wounds, may lead their spirits to rise like dough, lifting them from despair. In both cases, it is not the human being who effects the change: as in the parable recounted by Matthew and Luke, it is the yeast that, in time, leavens all the flour. Also, in both cases, however, there is a woman: by hiding the leaven in the flour, she works physically and sacramentally hard enough to allow a divine transformation, a kitchen miracle, to take place.

Central as bread is to dietetic and social needs, it is not on bread alone that Christians can survive. In her chapter "Kenosis and Subversion: On the Repression of 'Vulnerability' in Christian Feminist Writing," Sarah Coakley notes that silent contemplation, because of the spiritual and psychological vulnerability it entails, is deeply transformative and empowering: "this rather special form of 'vulnerability' is not an invitation to be battered; nor is its silence a silen*cing*. (If anything, it builds one in the courage to give prophetic voice)," claims Coakley—who is an Episcopalian pastor as well as a respected theologian. Contemplation is a grace-filled activity that makes space for God, and though the self-knowledge it brings can be painful, contemplation and the vulnerability it demands do not in themselves produce pain—much less meaninglessness or destruction—for "this special 'self-emptying' is not a negation of self, but the place of the self's transformation and expansion into God."[29]

Though she mentions women mystics only in her footnotes, it is clear that the contemplative prayer Coakley is describing is of the same type that Teresa of Avila teaches in her *Interior Castle* and that Angela of Foligno, Julian of Norwich, and other holy women practice when they experience their visions and union with the divine. In fact, Coakley's recurrent expression "waiting on the divine" is reminiscent of what Simone Weil has termed "l'attente de Dieu," "waiting on (or for) God." As Weil puts it, "waiting patiently in expectation is the foundation of the spiritual life." Human beings cannot actively seek out God, rather they can at best predispose themselves to receive God by waiting with expectancy and by practicing attention—a suspension, detachment, and emptiness of thought. The link between attention, kenosis, and bread is clear to Simone Weil: "We must become nothing, we must go down to the vegetative state; it is then that God becomes bread."[30]

God becomes bread. In the spirituality of the desert and of Byzantium, as in the theology of kenosis, the meagerness of the earth's gifts, and the paltry measure of human ability, are matched only by the abundance of God's grace. For Simone Weil, "our situation is just like that of little children who cry that they are hungry and who receive bread."[31] So also in the stories of many women during the first millennium of Christianity bread signifies physical need as well as the quasi elimination of that need. Bread in the desert means physical and spiritual hunger and its paradoxical satiation only found in one's self-gift to the divine. Bread is a connection to God through a disconnection from the body, but it is also an object of circulation that ties the monastic to her superiors and to her followers, under the sign of humility; it is thus also a link in the mystical chain of being, in the body of Christ. Bread, hardened and scanty, is the obverse of pleasure in eating, surely, but it also binds the uncommonly holy saint to the numerous poor whose bread was also, by necessity and not by miracle, hardened and scanty.

As we read these stories, the relationship of bread to food seems analogous to the way that the life of Jesus is related to the omnipotence of God: diminished, ruined, kenotic—the bare minimum. In the desert, aided by the consumption of hard and insufficient bread, women and men strive to become holy, to become divine, by imitating the self-emptying that defines the God-man. It is a process that, in its mimetic force, implies difference between the human and the divine, and it is a process without end because there is no fullness of signification to arrest it, no one single image of God that the saint can succeed in resembling. The kenotic God is an ever-moving God, an ever-shrinking God: by definition, the God of kenosis cannot be represented as presence, as full meaning. God as bread: If the crucified Christ is what remains when God is stripped of all attributes of power, might, omnipotence, then perhaps bread—also unstoppable, full of multiple meanings, also impossible to represent in a single way—is in this like God: bread is what's left when food is stripped of culinary grandeur, nutritional completeness, satisfying fullness. And yet, like God, it is enough, it is all we need, it is the All we need.

2

How to Make Cheese and How to Eat Love

Hildegard of Bingen with Hadewijch

*I*T IS DIFFICULT TO SPEND much time in the kitchen without finding something miraculous in the rising of bread and the curdling of cheese. In the prescientific age of our past, and even today to nonscientific minds such as mine, an aura of mystery envelops bread that puffs up, cheese that thickens—a mystery frequently understood in history to be akin to the bodily secrets of growth and generation and to the reproductive body of women: a body that also puffs up even as, within it, bodily fluids thicken into a child. It is true that, practically speaking, bread and cheese are labor-intensive and time-consuming, and their domestic production had to be carried out by those who, like women, spent much of their time at or near the home and thus remained available to the waiting and periodic work that the making of these two foods requires. But more compellingly, bread and cheese are connected with the female sex in intimate, bodily ways. Pregnancy is sometimes likened in European folklore to the process of baking bread, the womb being an oven that cooks its contents until properly done and ready to come out: "A good oven bakes good bread," says a Romanian proverb about the similarities between a mother and her child, but "Neither lovemaking nor baking always succeed," a German proverb warns—children and bread cannot be counted on as the assured end-product of sex and kitchen work.[1]

Resembling the rising and swelling sun, bread, in the words of an anthropologist, "'impregnated' in the fiery oven that stands for the uterus and vagina, heat and light," was central to the life of traditional peasant societies of northern Italy: bread was a symbol of fertility and childbirth, of the regeneration of life, of the principle of reproduction, of the connection between the animal, vegetable, and mineral kingdoms; bread was "a reproductive and sexual image that is daily ingested, assimilated and digested."[2] In English, the word "bread" has been used to refer to the female genitals: Chaucer's Wife of Bath says that "we wives are called barley bread."[3] Encased within the mysteries of nature and the supernatural, the connection between the female body and bread is rich in literal, metaphorical, and symbolic meanings: not only are wombs like ovens, but bread itself is like a child and like the sun, its significance deriving from the meaning of life itself. Bread is a connection between worlds: between the world of humans and the world of plants, between this world and the next. Bread points to the pleasure and the fulfillment of generation and regeneration.

Bread and cheese are well-known, traditional table companions. They are also joined together by analogous symbolic uses. Famed gastronome Jean Anthelme Brillat-Savarin (1755–1826), author of *The Physiology of Taste* (1826), insisted, Frenchman that he was, that "a dinner which ends without cheese is like a beautiful woman with only one eye."[4] Cheese is feminine because it is made of milk, an exquisitely female product that is excreted by female mammals for the feeding of their own offspring—or, occasionally, the offspring of other females unable or unwilling to lactate. Its long alimentary history and central role as source of proteins and general nutrition throughout the West, as well as its proximity to sexuality and the female body, have led to rich metaphorical uses of cheese in popular culture: a Spanish proverb claims that "Cheese without a rind is like a maiden without shame," "cheese and cheese" in England refers to two women kissing or else on horseback together, medieval German monks were called "cheese-hunters," and Anglo-Irish expressions include "a nice piece of cheese" or "a tasty piece of cheddar" for a good-looking woman. In American slang from a few decades back, "checking the cheese" referred to watching young women go by and "cheese" is also a word for

an attractive young woman, maybe because "cheesecakes" were photographs showing, in a provocative pose, the legs and figures of seminude
or nude young women. In Italian, as well, the word *caciotta*—a semisoft
cheese—can be used as a metaphor for the female sex.[5] And though
"cheesy" is a popular adjective among young people today, it is a negative
one, because "this society doesn't have endearments like milky, cheesy or
buttery," notes feminist writer Rosalind Coward, and "indeed," she continues, "the connection between women and milk is used by men as the
insult of 'cows and sows.' Perhaps there has been a repression here, an
attempt to avoid making explicit the incestuous reference behind food
endearments."[6]

Lactation is not the only connection between cheese and women.
Cheese is, in a sense, feminine because curdling is like conception: like the
rising and the baking of bread, so also the curdling of cheese has been
likened to the reproductive process, to the making of human beings. In
contemporary English, we speak of intense, negative looks as looks that
"could curdle milk," but in the biblical Book of Job the metaphorical
potential of curdling milk is used for a more productive simile: the unfor-
tunate protagonist perceives his own creation as a process of making
cheese, rhetorically asking God, the master Cheese Maker, "Didst thou
not pour me out like milk and curdle me like cheese?" (Job 10:10). Conception is in Job's view a life-giving curdling of milk, and this image will
inspire holy women writers in centuries to come.

Thus God makes cheese again—sheep's milk cheese—in *The Passion of
Saints Perpetua and Felicitas*, a third-century document in which the martyr Perpetua (who died around 203, in her early twenties) tells of visions
she had while in a prison in her native Carthage, shortly before being
killed in a Roman arena. Much of this story is anonymous, but Perpetua
herself is believed to have written eight of the twenty-one short chapters,
as a prison diary. In her first visionary dream, Perpetua goes up to a garden where a tall, white-haired man, surrounded by thousands of people
dressed in white, is milking sheep. "And he called me," remembers Perpetua, "and gave me a morsel of the cheese which he was milking and I
received it in my joined hands, and ate; and all they that stood around said:
'Amen.' And at the sound of the word I woke, still eating something
sweet."[7] In this account, the acts of milking and of making cheese are fused
into a single moment: the main translation offers for the Latin word
"*caseum*" the English "milk," in order to make the passage easier to read;

but "*caseum*" unequivocally means cheese and not milk. Mysteriously, the milk that has just been obtained from the sheep, for this divine shepherd, instantly becomes cheese to be handed out in a morsel to his beloved, who cups her hands (it must have been a fresh, dripping cheese). Not just any morsel, furthermore, but rather a sacred one—eucharistic, maybe, or baptismal: Christians in Carthage consecrated and distributed milk and cheese along with wine and bread, and the newly baptized, for their First Communion, drank honeyed milk—symbolic of the flavors of heaven (some have also seen the influence of the Montanist heresy in Perpetua's *Passion* because the Montanists consumed bread and cheese for their Eucharist).[8] Perpetua, in the sweetness lingering in her mouth, remembers the sweetness of her First Communion; in God the shepherd she finds cheese to be a physical and spiritual nourishment; and in the sheep being milked, it is hard not to see an identification with Perpetua's own situation: on the day preceding this dream, Perpetua succeeded in having her newborn baby brought to her, and she "suckled him, for he was already faint for want of food."[9] Having fed milk to the one who depended on her for survival, Perpetua is given a more adult version of milk—cheese—so that she too will live beyond her earthly demise.

Few people make cheese at home today. Though cheese appears in several cookbooks inspired by the medieval period published in recent years, it is always as a ready-made ingredient rather than the central object of a recipe—including in the fascinating volume *Foods of Health, Foods of Joy: Recipes from Saint Hildegard's Kitchen*. Famed medieval visionary Hildegard of Bingen (1098–1179)—also a physician, musician, and artist, hailed in recent years as an illustrious forerunner of today's feminists—repeatedly turns to cheese making in her discussions of the human body, sexuality, and reproduction.

Known as the "Sybil of the Rhine," Hildegard was a Benedictine religious from a German aristocratic family, dedicated at birth to the religious life (she was the tenth child and therefore described by some of her biographers as a tithe for the church). At an early age, Hildegard was sent to be educated and eventually live with the prominent anchoress Jutta of Sponheim. At Jutta's death, thirty-eight-year-old Hildegard took her place as abbess at the head of the convent of Saint Disibod. It wasn't, however, until the age of forty-two that Hildegard began writing down the extraordinary experiences she had been having since childhood. She obtained the support of Bernard of Clairvaux and apostolic license for her writings. Hildegard founded her own convent in Rupertsberg when she was fifty-two, and fifteen years later founded another community in Eibingen, just across the Rhine. She continued to write for the rest of her long life, though her education had been informal and she required the aid of a secretary.

Between 1151 and 1158, Hildegard wrote much about food, ingredients, and cooking in her scientific books, particularly the book *Physica* and the companion, unfinished volume *Cause et cure*; these works, significantly and unlike some of her other writings, do not make a claim to divine inspiration. In *Cause et cure*, the processes of cooking are repeatedly compared to the workings of human reproduction. Cheese making is found by Hildegard to be a particularly useful analogy in describing conception, and she writes that, "at first, the semen inside the woman is milky. Then it coagulates, and afterwards it becomes flesh, just as milk first curdles and then becomes cheese." But if a woman has intercourse with a man shortly after she has conceived by another, her semen "becomes polluted as from a fetid wind, just as milk would become tainted if somebody added another liquid when the milk was about to curdle." The cheese making analogy is still valid after birth, for just "as curdled milk must constantly be added to cheese pressed into a vessel until it is done, so too food and drink must constantly be administered to infants and children until they have completed their growth."[10]

In Hildegard's book of visionary theology known as the *Scivias*—written before her scientific treatises and more closely related than *Cause et cure* in tone and content to the writings of the other holy women in God's kitchen—cookery and cheese making continue to be invoked as precious analogies, with a scope more ambitious than in the scientific treatises. The title *Scivias* is a contraction of the phrase *Scito vias Domini*, meaning, "know the ways of the Lord." Completed around 1151–1152, after ten years of work, this volume gained much popularity because of its approval by the Cistercian pope Eugenius III.

The *Scivias* is divided into three books dedicated to creation, redemption, and sanctification; each book is made up of six, seven, and thirteen visions respectively. The visions are described in detail and are all accompanied by elaborate explications. Hildegard repeatedly has recourse in the *Scivias* to images of cooking, eating, and food in general. Book 1, in particular, because of its emphasis on the connections between the macrocosm that is the world and the human body as its microcosm, uses examples drawn from the world of food preparation and ingestion. These examples are reflections of God's creation and are useful to Hildegard in order to teach about the proper place and function of, for instance, sexuality and reproduction.

In the second vision of this first book, focused on creation and the fall and on the proper use of sexuality between men and women, Hildegard turns to the process of cheese making to illustrate her argument against having sexual relations with relatives—both blood relatives and in-laws. It is God who speaks through Hildegard's voice and states that, "Milk that is cooked once or twice has not yet lost its flavor, but by the time it is coagulated and cooked the seventh or eighth time, it loses its qualities and does not have a pleasant taste except in case of necessity." In the same way as milk should not be cooked more than once or twice, people should not have sexual intercourse with those to whom they are related, whether within marriage or outside of it: "let no human being join in such a coupling, which the Church by its Doctors, who established it in great responsibility and honor, has forbidden."[11] With the possible exception of egg pasta in tomato-and-meat sauce, reheating a dish rarely improves its flavor, and in Italian the expression "*minestra riscaldata*," "reheated soup," is used to describe something, or someone, that may be presented as new but is in fact old, overused, outdated—in politics as in business and personal relationships: "rehashed," also echoing a frugal culinary technique, is a close equivalent. The same is true of milk, in Hildegard's view, for its taste does not benefit from repeated cooking much like human beings should not have sex, and potentially replicate themselves, with those related to them. The natural law against incest, expressed in the flavors of cooked food, confirms, for Hildegard, the justice of divine law formulated by church doctors.

In her fourth vision of this same first book of the *Scivias*—a vision devoted to the relationship between body and soul and explaining, among other things, the infusion of the soul into the embryo's body—Hildegard saw "*on the earth people carrying milk in earthen vessels and making cheese from it*; these are the people in the world, both men and women, who have in their bodies human seed, from which the various races of people are procreated." Hildegard then goes on to explain the significance of these people:

> One part is thick, and from it strong cheeses are made; for that strong semen, which is usefully and well matured and tempered, produces energetic peo-

ple, to whom brilliant spiritual and bodily gifts are given by their great and noble ancestors, making them flourish in prudence, discretion and usefulness in their works before God and Man, and the Devil finds no place in them. *And one part is thin, and from it weak cheeses are curdled*; for this semen, imperfectly matured and tempered in a weak season, produces weak people, who are for the most part foolish, languid and useless in their work in the sight of God and the world, not actively seeking God. But also *one part is mixed with corruption, and from it bitter cheeses are formed*; for that semen is basely emitted in weakness and confusion and mixed uselessly, and it produces misshapen people, who often have bitterness, adversity and oppression of heart and are thus unable to raise their minds to higher things.[12]

The three types of cheese Hildegard mentions correspond to three different types of people—the strong, the weak, and the misshapen—whose bodily and spiritual makeup, their gifts and their inabilities, are directly related to the quality of the semen that engenders them. Strong people (*"strenuos homines,"* in the original Latin) come from strong semen just as strong cheeses (*"fortes casei"*) come from thick milk; similarly, thin milk makes weak cheeses (*"debiles casei"*) like weak semen makes weak human beings (*"teneros homines"*); and milk that has gone off, milk "mixed with corruption" (*"tabe permixta"*) makes bitter cheeses (*"amari casei"*), much like misshapen people (*"informes homines"*) are made by semen that is mixed and impure. It is human beings in general, according to Hildegard, and not women alone, who are made in the same way that food is made. What is left unclear, though, is whether milk alone—the man's semen—is sufficient for the making of cheese. Generally, Hildegard subscribes to the Aristotelian one-seed theory of reproduction, according to which only the male provides the seed of new life during intercourse—his active sperm forming the child within the passive female substance, menstrual blood: "her blood has no semen because it is weak and thin," Hildegard says of woman in her *Cause et cure*. Later in the same book, however, Hildegard resorts to the Hippocratic-Galenic two-seed theory—claiming that conception needs two elements, two seeds: the man's and the woman's. In this, too, Hildegard employs food metaphors: though woman and man both produce semen, hers "is sparse and scanty compared to man's foam, like a piece of bread compared to a whole loaf."[13] The difference between a whole loaf and a piece of bread, though, is a quantitative rather than a qualitative one, indirectly claiming for woman, through memorable images of food, a more active role in human conception.

The creation of human beings through the acts of sexual intercourse and reproduction is comparable for Hildegard to the production of cheese through different varieties of milk. Both reproduction and cheese making are related, furthermore, to God's own creation of human beings. God is a doctor, yes, but God, for Hildegard, is also a cook, *the* cook. God is our celestial chef: a critic has noted, about *Cause et cure*, that, "at creation God uses cookery to show how it is done: matter becomes something other and more when God touches it, just like food."[14] The image of God as both doctor and, more originally, cook is dear to Hildegard. Its effect is the disruption of the very hierarchy between these two professions—one, that of doctor, distinctly masculine and the other, of cook, hierarchically lower, typically feminine. These two categories, Hildegard implies throughout both her visionary and her scientific work, cannot be neatly separated, because "for Hildegard, the human body is like a kitchen"[15]—the human body, we might further specify, is God's kitchen. Cooking and creating, feeding and healing become one for Hildegard, much as they do, as we will see in later chapters, in the writings of other holy women such as Cecilia Ferrazzi and Elizabeth Ann Seton. Conception and pregnancy are reminiscent of cooking techniques, and the meaning of bread as well as the meaning of cheese both point to the female physiological processes as conspicuously analogous to foods.

The writing of these kitchen and bedroom instances in holy women's religious texts, then, is something we might read as an intriguing representation, even a construction, perhaps, of a woman's path to the divine through the activities of her body—not in spite of them. These activities may consist in cooking and serving food at a table, as well as in feeding with one's own body. In the first vision of book 2 of the *Scivias*, for instance—a book dedicated to sacramental redemption—God's creation of humanity is related both to maternal nourishment and to the use of milk in cooking, since God, in creating the earth, "poured fresh warmth into it, for the earth is the fleshly material of humans, and nourished it with moisture, as a mother gives milk to her children." God is in this passage like a nursing mother who feeds her children into existence out of the juice of her own body: *"nutriens eum suco suo sicut mater lactat filios suos."*[16]

God is a lactating mother, God is milk, and God is food. Reflecting on the foodness of divinity as well as of our body illuminates for Hildegard divine rulings—such as the prohibition of marriage among relatives—as undesirable and ineffectual as an excessive reheating of milk when making cheese. A reflection on the ways our body is like food and indeed resembles milk, can also clarify for some writers and readers the rules of language. Because of her 1975 essay "The Laugh of the Medusa," French-Algerian writer and theorist Hélène Cixous is famous in literary circles for having equated the metaphorically white ink with which women write their *écriture feminine*, their women's writing, with a mother's milk. This connection, for Cixous, gives women writers a privileged relationship with the voice: "a woman is never far from 'mother,'" Cixous states, for "there is always within her at least a little of that good mother's milk. She writes in white ink."[17] As romantic as this image is, and potentially essentialistic—that is, freezing women in all their differences into one essence, the essence of Woman—it is expressed with the awareness, and the implicit warning, that white ink can be invisible, particularly when it is used on white paper. Women's historical exclusion from the scene of writing has to do with this milky connection to the voice, an embodiment that is incompatible with the fact that the history of writing is the history of the separation between the body and the word—and thus between voice and writing. Mother's milk, then, though a positive force, is ironically connected with the silence of the infant (*in-fans*, the one who does not speak), and Cixous's compelling, if a bit obscure, figuration of women's writing embodies both a hope for the future—when maternity may no longer imply silence, when the mother's white milk, and her daughter's recollection of it, will be heard and understood—and the awareness that silencing has already happened, it has already been perpetrated. For the former hope to be realized, and for the latter silence to be broken, the white milk of infancy will have to become a speaking, writing milk, an inky milk, even.

The metaphors linking milk and ink, infancy and voice, mother and writing are redolent with the metaphorical flavors of food in history and in culture. Breastfeeding a child, for Hildegard, is a bodily remembrance of God's creation of the world: like a mother (*"sicut mater"*), God nursed the children She created, for the nourishment Hildegard describes as divine breastfeeding is an essential part of the creation of humans by God. On a smaller scale, the womb is an oven where metaphorical bread is baked, and it is also the place of curdling and coagulation, the place where liquids turn solid, where milk, sperm, and blood come together to produce a human being made of flesh and bones. Conception was itself conceived of in the prescientific age as a process of food preparation analogous to, and as mysterious as, the curdling of milk that initiates the process of cheese making. Curdling milk represented a mystery to the premodern mind, an almost alchemical transformation that turned an ephemeral and perishable product, milk, into something solid and long lasting, cheese. Milk, furthermore, was considered a distillation of blood, and Jesus was loved by the faithful as a mother in the medieval period, because the blood issuing from the savior's side was the equivalent of a mother's milk flowing from her breast or into her pregnant womb. In Hildegard's words, "the woman's blood is drawn up towards her breasts, and what was to become blood from food and drink now is turned into milk to nourish the child growing in the mother's womb."[18] Margaret Ebner, to cite just one example, writes that she "recalled the sweet drink [St. John the Apostle] drank and sucked from the sweet breast of Christ."[19] So Jesus repeats in history what God the Creator had done at the historical beginning: feeding newborn children and giving them life with the milk of the divine body.

Hildegard's description of copulation and conception as a cheese making of sorts sets up an analogy between making children and making food: sexual contact results in a coagulation of milk-like fluids, just as cheese is produced through the coagulation of milk. Hildegard's description involves an image of food preparation, rather than of food consumption. But if making human beings is much like making food, then humans must share meaningful traits with food itself. Their common origin indicates a common function. And the essential attribute of food is its edibility: if it cannot be eaten, it is not a food. In the fifth vision of book 2 of her *Scivias*—a vision devoted to the three orders of the church and the mystical body—Hildegard describes in what ways particular groups of human beings—monks, clerics, and laypeople—are like food:

> Because they who are vowed monks are like grain, which is the strong, dry food of humans; so this people of Mine is bitter and harsh to the taste of the world. And the clerics are like fruits, sweet to the taste, and show themselves sweet to people by the usefulness of their office. And the common laypeople are like meat, but meat comes partly from chaste birds; thus those who live in the world according to the flesh have children, but among them are found followers of chastity, such as widows and the continent, who fly to heavenly desires by their appetite for virtue.[20]

In Hildegard's symbolic elaboration, human beings make up, in the variety of their gifts and of their flavors, some of the nutritional staples savored by humans themselves: grains ("*granum*"), fruits ("*poma*"), meat ("*caro*"). Be they strong and dry, sweet to the taste, living according to the flesh, or flying to heavenly desires, all play a role in the hierarchy of the church, "*Ecclesia*"—who appears as a woman in her glory at the beginning of this vision. Though taste has traditionally been among the most reviled of the five senses—along with smell and touch—Hildegard (like other women mystics, as we shall see) does not hesitate to use it as a means of ascertaining people's role in life and place in the world. In theology as in science, in music as in art, Hildegard sought harmony. Each of the foods with which human groups are associated finds its proper place in a balanced diet, and similarly also each group of human beings has its assigned seat in the world that is God's kitchen.

If humans are grains, fruits, meat, if humans are made in the way that cheese is made, then can humans, like cheese, be eaten—figuratively, if not physically? Many metaphors and idiomatic expressions answer this question affirmatively. "*Bello da mangiare*," beautiful enough to eat, is a phrase Italians are fond of repeating—particularly of babies and young children; despite its cannibalistic undertones, this is a familiar and commonly expressed sentiment. The love and passion inspired by the beauty of one's own child, the intense attraction of a baby's large eyes, or the shape of the mouth of a loved one, can leave us speechless. This experience borders on the ineffable and requires excessive, paradoxical language. Passion, erotic and poetic as well as mystical, can have transformative effects on language, pushing it to its limits, demanding that it express that which language is ordinarily considered incapable of conveying.

Food metaphors can be helpful in the representation of a love object considered to be beyond representation itself. American poet Anne Sexton, in one of her most touching poems, "Little Girl, My String Bean, My Lovely Woman" (1966), describes her preadolescent daughter as "little girl / my string bean," an edible plant, a legume she wishes she had seen growing in her womb: "if I could have seen through my magical transparent belly, / there would have been such a ripening within." Likewise, another American poet, Sharon Olds, in her poem "Eggs" (1987), speaks of her ten-year-old daughter's growing dislike for eggs, relating it to the little girl's impending transformation: the arrival of her first period. For Olds, the girl's first menstruation is "the bright, crimson dot appears / like the sign on a fertilized yolk," and her daughter's ovaries are egg baskets: "She has carried / all her eggs in the two baskets," from which "soon they'll be slipping down gently, / sliding."[21] In both poems, a beloved daughter is delicious but unspeakable, almost edible yet barely representable with words, however poetic.

Mystics complain about the ineffability of their experience and then go on speaking and writing; they claim that what they saw and did cannot be described and then go on to tell of it for pages and pages of prose or poetry. This is at least in part thanks to their linguistic fearlessness, their willingness to push language to and beyond its limits—like the best of poets. Eating God under the species of the Eucharist is a regular practice for many Christians. For poets as for mystics, metaphorically eating one another is an act of love, of passionate, fearless, needy love. This is alluded to in Anne Sexton's string bean poem and explicitly affirmed in the work of Hadewijch of Antwerp (or of Brabant), an early thirteenth-century Flemish visionary and poet.

Hadewijch is known for her poems of intimate and often erotic love of God: in the connections enacted by her mystical union she discovers the meaning of her quest and the pleasure that is her reward. Unlike Hildegard, we know next to nothing about Hadewijch's external life: she lived in or near Antwerp, in the Netherlands, and she was a beguine—that is, she belonged to a medieval spiritual movement of laywomen devoted to the care of the poor and sick and to a life of celibacy, prayer, and manual work. Her poems and letters, written in her vernacular, Middle Dutch, speak of love (imaged as a lady) as eating: "She impels us to long desiringly for her / And to taste her without knowing her being."[22] Whereas Hildegard imagines the body as food in order to explain how human beings are conceived (like cheese) and how they fit within the categories of this world (grain, meat, fruit), Hadewijch imagines the body as food in order to better express a passion so intense that it borders on silence. In both Hildegard and Hadewijch the representation of human beings as food—specific foods for Hildegard, a generic object of consumption for Hadewijch—is necessary for communicating, according to the divine will, the knowledge each visionary has received concerning humanity's role and duties, purposes and desires. For Hadewijch, it is a consuming union with the other that leads to knowledge, and mutual knowledge, in turn, provides the path to union—knowledge to be had only through eating each other: "The heart of each devours the other's heart, / One soul assaults the other and invades it completely." Indeed, "love's most intimate union," Hadewijch continues, "is through eating, tasting, and seeing interiorly." In this we may resemble Christ, for "He eats us; we think we eat him, / And we do eat him, of this we can be certain."[23] The identification of tasting with loving, of loving as eating and eating as loving, is a recurring theme in Hadewijch's works. Human beings are like God and like food in that they, like God and like food, can be consumed by, and consumers of, love; and they, like God and like food, can be tasted. While for Hildegard human conception is similar to the making of cheese—with all its pitfalls—and the variety of human beings is analogous to the variety of specific foods—grain, meat, fruit—in Hadewijch's love poetry humans are edible because passion makes them so.

That lovers are eaters, that the expression of passion is a way of devouring the beloved, that the soul in love is hungry, famished, even . . . these physical, spiritual, textual connections, striking as they are if we pause to think about their literal meaning, occur not only throughout Hadewijch's works, but also in the language of idioms, love poetry, religious mysticism, amorous passion (sexual passion, spiritual passion, parental passion). Mothers can say to their baby, "I could just eat you up" (I have certainly said this over and over again), and lovers might whisper similar words to their beloved. And if one's loved one is Christ, and if he gives himself to eat in the Eucharist, then it can only be expected that this image of ingesting the beloved should be a dominant one in the writings of medieval holy women—who fast, feast, and revel in the erotic imagination of their bridegroom. Uniting with God is a fundamental aspect of the mystical journey, and here on earth this union—a complex union, one in which the body and the spirit are inextricably intertwined—is well and often expressed by invoking eating as lovemaking, and the kitchen as a privileged space for that encounter, the kitchen as a sensual chamber.

For Hildegard, a systematic thinker and writer who expressed herself in the language and the genres of the cultural aristocracy, the identification of human beings as food explains God's rules, illuminates divine will and divine order: like cheese we are made, like cheese we are of varying quality; like wheat, meat, and fruit, our place in the menu that is this world changes; and variable like food, like menus, like the world, are the different ways in which humans can love and give praise to the divine. Hadewijch, that passionate soul, used the language she and those around her spoke in their everyday life in order to share with her reader, through the most intimate of words, the workings of her desire and the encounters with her lover. Hildegard explained the rules, but Hadewijch repeatedly broke them. Eating, tasting, and sexual intimacy, for this visionary poet, describe her direct contact with the divine, the very happenings of her densely meaningful and intensely pleasurable meetings with her lover. And it is the abundance of God's banquet, the delights of the divine feast that this mystic, in the kitchen or at the table, experiences, enjoys, and communicates with words of love and words of food.

3

How to Taste Sugar and Spice

THE FLAVORS OF ELISABETH OF SCHÖNAU

PIRITUALITY AND SWEETNESS have throughout history made excellent tablemates. Frequently attended by women—women who were cooking, eating, praying, writing—the flavorful table of spiritual writings is loaded with dishes that taste, to employ a stereotype, feminine: light, creamy, and, especially, sweet. We can sit at that table and taste that sweetness by reading about the late-nineteenth-century French saint Thérèse Martin, the Little Flower of Lisieux. Thérèse is such a sweet young woman, and though her stories may well be the climax of sugary sanctity, the connection they epitomize has a very long past—and a bittersweet one at that. Learning to taste it, if not to enjoy it, requires careful readings, an eye for detail, and a strong stomach: the mixture of sweetness and gender, of honey, sugar, and sainthood, is not the main course of holy women's stories, but rather, like dessert, it is an afterthought, a delightful tidbit often hidden within the folds of writings more interested in the main dish of deprivation as a path to sanctity.

And still an object as mundane as daily food and an activity as transcendent as the mystic's quest can come together to best reveal the flavor of each. Indeed, one way to avoid the dilemma between bodily needs and desire on one side and spiritual preoccupations on the other is to focus on a food that is not *really* a food because it is not necessary, a food that is not *only* a food because it is laden with so much metaphorical significance that its caloric content—however high—comes a distant second to its symbolic weight. I am speaking of those items we alternately call sweets (if we refer to the taste sensation they evoke), desserts (when we describe their position in our menus and in our culture), or treats (recognizing their interpersonal nature as objects of exchange).

If regular, daily food appears now and then in the writings of holy women, the metaphor of sweetness, in contrast, so saturates these writings as to be easily overlooked. All the holy women I know speak at some point or another, and usually throughout, of the divine sweetness that touches their taste buds and flavors their lives. Maybe this is because, as women, they experienced God as a sensuous bridegroom. And maybe this is also because, as women, they felt especially enriched, intellectually and spiritually, by the sense of taste—a sense, unlike the more objective sight and hearing, traditionally considered "feminine," especially when used emblematically or metaphorically.[1]

In the words of Hadewijch of Antwerp: "This is a criterion of Love, that the name of the Beloved is found sweet. Saint Bernard speaks of this: 'Jesus is honey in the mouth.' To speak of the Beloved is exceedingly sweet; it awakens Love immeasurably, and it lends ardor to works." Her Beloved is Jesus and her love divine. Elsewhere, Hadewijch remarks, "What is sweetest in Love is her tempestuousness."[2] Medieval German nun Margaret Ebner notes the persistence of love's sweetness, reminding her reader that, "When I drank from the chalice I perceived great sweetness, which I tasted for three days."[3] Angela of Foligno, who lived near Assisi between the middle of the thirteenth and the early fourteenth century, tells us in the very first part of her *Memorial* that she "began to taste something of the divine sweetness." Later, when the Holy Spirit speaks to her for the first time, she "felt a sweetness, an ineffable divine sweetness"; and the divine sweetness, granted by a sweet God to his sweet beloved (twice God calls Angela "my daughter, you are sweeter to me than I am to you"), is the ineffable essence of the consolation God provides for Angela when they are not together.[4] The late-medieval English anchorite Julian of Norwich says that when we come to God we will be "sweetly tasting him."[5] Her near contemporary and compatriot Margery Kempe describes "the sweetness that she felt in the conversation of our Lord" and she so "could not bear the sweetness and grace that God wrought in her soul" that she almost falls off the ass she was riding into Jerusalem.[6] Catherine of Genoa, in fifteenth-century Italy, invokes the soul's "sweet God," who "infused such sweetness into her heart that she was almost over-whelmed."[7] A century later, mystic and reformer Teresa of Avila, in the very passage that inspired Bernini's controversial masterpiece in Rome—a statue depicting the Spanish nun in the throes of ecstasy—describes being pierced by the arrow of God's love as "so sweet a pain that no delight in the whole world can be more pleasing," and that "the sweetness caused by this intense pain is so extreme that one cannot possibly wish it to cease."[8] Even that most sensible of saints, the American Elizabeth Ann Seton, speaks of "tast[ing] the sweetness of his presence" when we "feed on the Bread of Angels."[9]

The scriptural antecedents to these mystical exclamations are familiar. Most poetically, the psalmist wrote of God's love, "How sweet are your words to my taste, sweeter than honey to my mouth" (Ps. 119:103), and "the judgments of the Lord are true and righteous altogether. More to be desired are they than gold, yea, than much fine gold; sweeter also than honey and the honeycomb" (Ps. 19:9–10). The promised land was the land of milk and honey (a phrase that recurs some forty times in the Bible), the "antidesert" was the land—to put it more prosaically—where water would flow so abundantly that milk-producing livestock would not lack for fodder nor bees for the flowers that would allow them to make honey. God's people would thus abound in the milk that was such an important part of their diet in the years of wandering and in the honey that, in a culture that did not yet know sugar, represented the pleasures of life—the pleasures of life on earth as well as the pleasures of the love of God.[10] God's words and judgments are "sweeter than honey." This sweet sensation represents not only the consolations of love but also the goodness and wisdom of language, so that sweetness and speech are again linked in Proverbs—where we are told, "Pleasing words are a honeycomb, sweet to the taste and healthful to the body" (Prov. 16:24).

The language of the beloved's sweetness is not unique to holy women, and certainly such figures of speech so pervade the vocabulary of lovers' discourse as to be almost invisible, even insipid. Love is sweet, inebriating, satisfying, love dispels all other hungers and thirsts. We speak of honeymoons and call our loved ones "sugar," "honey," "sweetheart" (originally a sugar cake shaped like a heart), "sweetie pie," "honey bun(ch)." Sweetness is linked with love (we give chocolates to those we desire), with reward (how many times have we heard or, alas, said, "eat your vegetables and you can have dessert"?), with need at our beginnings (mother's milk), and celebratory birthday and wedding cakes as our paths unfold. Kids' medications taste like bubble-gum and not like macaroni and cheese—admittedly also a children's favorite—because it is a spoonful of sugar that makes the medicine go down, as Mary Poppins teaches.

But of course, despite the purity, chemical and metaphorical, of sugar's whiteness, there is a dark side to sweets, a side touched by guilt and self-image, by loss and disease, as well as by gender, class, race, and exploitation. If obesity is tied in no small measure to the empty calories of the sweets in our lives—and particularly in the United States in the lives of the poor—the historical growth of refined sugar consumption is in turn indissolubly tied, for example, to the industrial revolution, the rise of capitalism in Europe, the colonization of America, and the slave trade in Caribbean countries.[11] The taste for sweetness, like most sweets, is sticky, it leaves a mark: our sweet tooth, no matter how much we brush it, cannot be wiped clean of the social, public power our taste buds exercise.

Women mystics draw time and again from metaphors of sweetness in order to tell of their encounters with their Lover—his body, his words, his actions, as well as the writer's sensations, her passion, her grace. But some writers more than others find sweetness an indispensable ingredient in understanding their spiritual life and in composing their stories. The German nun Elisabeth of Schönau (1129–1165), mystic and visionary, repeatedly borrows words from the most delicious shelves of the pantry when she would otherwise be at a loss to describe divine love. Though less known today than other medieval visionaries, such as her contemporary Hildegard of Bingen (with whom she corresponded and whom she visited), Elisabeth—who was, like Hildegard, a Benedictine nun from childhood until her death—was among the most famous women of her time and very widely read. The large number of manuscripts of her works that still survive provides ample evidence of this. One of the reasons for Elisabeth's decline in popularity over the centuries could be her lack of uniqueness, subversion, originality: Elisabeth is "a mystic of supreme objectivity," she may seem unrelated to spiritual movements of our present day because, unlike women such as Julian of Norwich (prophetess of God as our Mother) or Marguerite Porete (unswerving in her heretical beliefs), she is "profoundly ecclesial," bound to the language and rituals of the church of her time.[12]

Like many other holy women, Elisabeth of Schönau wrote both letters and systematic accounts of her spiritual and visionary experiences—more autobiographical than Hildegard's, Anne Clark notes, but also rooted in "the very strong communal dimensions of her piety."[13] From the time of his arrival at Schönau, Elisabeth's brother Ekbert worked actively as her scribe and editor—transcribing, encouraging, questioning, and collecting his sister's visionary and epistolary production. Close collaborative relationships between visionary women and their confessor, who often worked as a secretary, editor, or scribe, were not uncommon in the Middle Ages: Hildegard of Bingen had a lifelong friend and secretary, Volmar; Margaret Ebner corresponded at length with Henry of Nördlingen, who encouraged her to write her *Revelations*; Angela of Foligno relied on the transcriptions and translations of her Franciscan relative Brother A.; Catherine of Siena's close relationship with Raymond of Capua is perhaps the best known case of this collaboration. Thanks to the work of her brother, Elisabeth's works are preserved, like Hildegard's, in Latin. Though Ekbert claims that his sister never learned the language of culture, and that her knowledge of Latin was a gift of God, this might have been said in order to confirm the divine origin of her experiences. As Clark explains, "Given the obviously apologetic motives in Ekbert's comments, and given the various references within the text that suggest Elisabeth's Latin skills and the unusualness of German speech, we should be wary of accepting Ekbert's words at face value."[14]

A memorable one, among Elisabeth's letters, contains a direct reprimand to a priest and a warning in favor of temperance: "And I turn to you, Father H., and admonish you above everything else to abstain from wine, since your soul suffers a great danger from this. Know for certain that one who is always drunk is always oblivious to God's presence."[15]

While Elisabeth's references to the real food in her life are memories of alimentary rejection—wearied by temptation, she recalls in her *First Book of Visions*, "I could only take but the slightest food and drink, and I became weak and my whole body wasted away" (45), and on another occasion, also exhausted by the fight against the tempter, at lunch, she writes, "I hardly touched my food because of a severe distress" (49)—in vision and hope food nourishes Elisabeth with strength and with pleasure. Elisabeth's positive references to food are figural, expressed through metaphor or similitude, or else they are the object of revelation: the liquid in her mouth is like honey, the fish and honey she sees near Jesus belong to one of her visions; the bitter, sweet, and sour flavors she refers to are the material aspects of spiritual graces; even the spicy cinnamon and balsam are a projection into the future of the flavor to be savored by herself and by her friend and fellow nun.

The love of God is sweet to Elisabeth, who tastes it intensely in the frequent visions that she begins having and recording in 1152, eleven years after she entered the convent. A sickness afflicting her for several days, for example, forbids her from eating and drinking; still in the *First Book of Visions*, "Seven days before the Annunciation of our Lady, I became sick and fell upon my bed, languishing throughout my body in such a way that I was able to take almost no refreshment into my body." This paralyzing, self-starving illness is finally relieved by the sweetness of God's love—a love liquefied in the form of that oldest of sweeteners, honey: "On that day, around Nones, I began to have a liquid in my mouth like a comb of honey, and I was as refreshed by its sweetness as if I had taken sufficient food, and I was strengthened throughout my body and emitted a copious sweat, and I remained like that until the following day" (69). Honey acts as nourishment for Elisabeth's soul and for Elisabeth's speech, through her mouth: honey is a food that is not simply, not only a food, it is a food whose effects are figural as much as physical, scriptural as well as personal. Honey refreshes and strengthens her like food but also more than food, for its symbolic weight overpowers its caloric import: she is refreshed "as if" she had eaten sufficiently, implying that the honey-like liquid is not, at least on a certain level, sufficient fare.

After feeling refreshed and strengthened by honey, Elisabeth mysteriously sweats and remains still. Then, she experiences pain followed by a vision of Jesus with thousands of saints: the sweetness of honey preludes the sweetness of Jesus' presence—as physical as honey, but also as figural. Honey again bring her close to Jesus during an Easter morning vision in the same *First Book of Visions*, when Elisabeth sees him eating with his disciples after the resurrection: she saw "how he ate with them," and that "on the table there was a dish holding fish and another containing a honeycomb" (76). Though the honey is the addition of Elisabeth's spiritual sweet tooth, the fish refers to the last chapters of the gospels of John and Luke. In Luke, Jesus asks for food ("Have you anything here to eat?") and takes and eats, as a sign of the physicality of his return, the piece of broiled fish he is served (Luke 24:41–43). In John's account, which takes place at the lakeside rather than in a house, we see Jesus who cooks and serves, and not only eats, maternally inviting his friends, who had been working all night, to "Come, have breakfast" (John 21:12). Jesus had grilled bread and fish for them at the beach before they even brought in what they had just caught, so that, "When they got out on land, they saw a charcoal fire there, with fish lying on it, and bread" (John 21:9). Jesus cooks, serves, and eats bread and fish, but honey—which in the gospels is eaten by John the Baptist as an accompaniment to locusts—is something that Elisabeth gives to Jesus, too, as a condiment for fish (maybe because of that same association between Jesus and honey that led Hildegard to write, in a letter to Bernard of Clairvaux, that the father "sent the Word with sweet fruitfulness into the womb of the Virgin, from which He soaked up flesh, just as honey is surrounded by the honeycomb.")[16]

Be it scriptural or visionary, divine sweetness is not a single sensation touching on a lonely taste bud. Divine sweetness stretches out to a variety of flavors: not all of God's sweetness tastes like honey, for divine flavor is far more complex and nuanced. In the New Testament book of Revelation, bitterness accompanies the sweet flavor of God's words: "So I went to the angel and told him to give me the little scroll; and he said to me, 'Take it and eat; it will be bitter to your stomach, but sweet as honey in your mouth.' And I took the little scroll from the hand of the angel and ate it; it was sweet as honey in my mouth, but when I had eaten it my stomach was made bitter" (Rev. 10:9–10). The mixture of bitter and sweet seasons the spirituality of many mystics—Gemma Galgani and Thérèse of Lisieux are two examples of this paradoxical blend. Elisabeth's variation on this mixture is the sweet and sour taste of God's judgments, as she explains in her *Third Book of Visions*: "Therefore, that kind Father chastises His children by mixing the sweetness of mercy—by which He consoles the soul—with sour justice—which avenges the insolence of the flesh."[17] Merciful and just is our paternal God, sweet and sour, and the analogy Elisabeth goes on to employ to better describe the divine ways is a culinary one: "This is just like an oxymel, which is a mixture of honey and vinegar, that one drinks so that the core of sin, if it is already in the soul, is dissipated, or if it is not, will not be allowed to arise" (153–54). Still used today in herbal medicine, oxymel ("*oxymelle*," in Elisabeth's Latin, "*quod est mixtura mellis et asceti*") was recommended by Hippocrates, in the fifth and fourth centuries BCE, as an effective antidote against a variety of complaints of both the digestive and the respiratory tracts. For Elisabeth, oxymel is like God because just as the flavor of this medicinal drink is a combination of two tastes, the sweetness of honey and the acidity of vinegar, so also God's discipline is double: certainly God is merciful, and in this we learn of divine sweetness. But God is also fair and administers a justice that, to our fallen nature, tastes sour. This sourness is accepted by our soul thanks to the mercy that accompanies it, much like our body, in consuming the healing oxymel, tolerates the acidity of vinegar because it craves the sweetness of honey.

In a different text, by focusing instead on the sophisticated sweetness of a spice such as cinnamon, Elisabeth of Schönau displays a medieval (because spice-centered) approach to food and flavor. It is in her conclusion to a letter to the Abbess of Dietkirchen that Elisabeth describes the reward awaiting her fellow virgin and nun: the physical sweetness of God the bridegroom, described as imparting a variety of spiced flavors to the vision, "He will lead you into the upper room of His tent," Elisabeth tells the abbess, "you will eat with Him and He with you. There you will always rejoice with the angels. There will be cinnamon and balsam and the sweetest aroma" (245). God's love, this time, is sweet and spicy like cinnamon and balsam ("*cynamomum et balsamum*": no longer commonly used, balsam is the oily part of the resin of the balsam tree, employed during medieval times both in medicine and as a spice). God's love is tasted in the upper room, "*cenaculum*" in the original Latin, i.e., in the location of the last supper (what English speakers know as Leonardo da Vinci's "Last Supper," for example, is known in Italian with a cognate word, "Cenacolo").[18]

Elisabeth's brother and secretary Ekbert, however, objected to this letter with its largely unexplained sensual description of cinnamon and balsam—though Elisabeth's kitchen metaphors ended up having a lasting impact on Ekbert's own language, for in his eulogizing narrative about Elisabeth's death he writes, using his sister's food images, of "her honeyed mouth" and describes Elisabeth as "the sweetness of my soul" and "the delightful spice of all my labors" (255). So as to satisfy Ekbert, Elisabeth returns more at length to her image of cinnamon in the next letter to the Abbess, where she develops, through the voice of an angel, the allegorical significance of her spicy images:

> So after this, on Easter Vigil, when he [the angel] appeared to me and I asked him about this, he looked cheerfully at me and said, "Cinnamon has a naturally pleasing sweetness that delights the taste. At the same time, it also has a sharp strength that inflames the palate of the one who tastes it and that becomes more piquant and aromatic the more one chews it. Such is the Lord our God to us who always wait to see His desirable face. To us He is sweet beyond all things that can be tasted; nothing among other desirable

things can be compared to His sweetness. It touches us with ineffable strength and penetrates us most intimately. It ignites and continually enflames us to love Him. And the more we feast on the taste of His sweetness, the more piquant and appetizing He is for us and the course of our desire for Him will have no end." (246)

Rivaling today's best food writers, Elisabeth carefully describes the effects of cinnamon on the palate: it is sweet and delightful ("*habet gratam dulcedinem*"), sharp and strong ("*habet acutam fortitudinem*"), increasingly flavorful the more one chews it ("*quo magis masticatur tantomagis sapidum et odoriferum est*"). Such must have been the effects of Christ's appetizing presence on Elisabeth's soul and palate, a presence that, like cinnamon, is aromatic and penetrating, a presence that, rather than dissipating over time, becomes more flavorful, more desirable, more effective the longer she dwells within it.

The meaning of cinnamon (and, in the earlier passage, of balsam) is not exhausted by the richness of its aroma, for spices represented more than sweetness and added flavor in the medieval period. At the time when Elisabeth was writing, balsam was so rare as to be almost unobtainable, and cinnamon, though somewhat less scarce, was nevertheless very expensive. Still, among the upper classes, the quantities of spices used are astounding to the modern, post-seventeenth-century palate: it was not unusual for a dish serving twelve people to call for a half pound of spices![19] While they were not used to disguise the flavor of rotting meats nor as a preservative (though both of these claims were common assumptions for a long time, food scholars no longer believe them, as spices were expensive and thus used only by the rich—those who could certainly afford fresh meat), spices were believed to aid in the process of digestion, medically regarded at that time to be a sort of "cooking" that took place in the stomach: the "heat" of spices (a temperature-based metaphor still in use today) was believed to radiate from the digestive tract, allowing food to be absorbed faster and better. For this reason spices were not only used in cooking but also eaten at the end of the meal or before going to bed, often in the form of a confection. Thus for example, Thomas Aquinas allowed for the consumption of candy during Lent because, eaten in the form of sugar-coated spices, or comfits, they were taken not as nourishment—and therefore food—much less as a treat, but as an aid to digestion, a form of medicine. Confectionery, seen today as the very opposite of healthful eating ironically began as a pharmaceutical practice.[20] The high cost of spices made them unattainable for the poor, whereas for the rich, they were a much sought-after object of desire and a status symbol that was the privilege of few.

And this, in addition to their being a signifier of pleasure, is how spices function in Elisabeth's writings, where they indicate the healing presence of the divine, God's pleasurable love, and Elisabeth's position of honor in her noble bridegroom's chamber. The experience is a personal one, but its message is not reserved to Elisabeth alone, for her testimony, in Clark's words, "is offered to the world as consolation, as witness to the power of divine intervention in the course of troubling human history" (24). Though not a kitchen, in the dining room Elisabeth summons up in her letter and further described thanks to Ekbert's prodding, privileged brides of God such as Elisabeth and the addressee of her letter (the Abbess of Dietkirchen) are to share in the gustatory pleasures of the One. Christ will provide them with the flavor of his sweetness, enduring and, like cinnamon, even intensifying the more they physically partake of him, chew him, share in his body. But also, Christ will bestow on them the health and salvation of his spiced persona, through whom the healthfulness of cinnamon and balsam transforms the cater into a saved soul, a beloved of God. And in his prodigality of sweetness and spices, God will make them rich and noble as only God—besides spices—can demonstrate wealth and nobility; he will feed them sweets as only God—besides sugar—allows those who love him to feast on sweetness; he will grant them pleasure as only God—besides cinnamon—can encourage those who taste him to experience enduring flavor and endless desire.

Novelist Joyce Carol Oates's hypothesis that "Civilization is the multiplicity of strategies, dazzling as precious gems inlaid in a golden crown, to obscure from human beings the sound of, the terrible meaning of, their jaws grinding" resonates with the subtle, partial truth of an absurdity.[21] The Eucharist, I was taught, should not be chewed—because it is not common food, because the body of Christ that the wafer has become should not be subjected to the noisy grinding of human teeth. Practices have changed, and chewing the host is no longer discouraged: if the Eucharist is indeed a meal, why deny its foodness? Taking it in the hands and putting it into one's own mouth, chewing it like all food needs to be chewed, getting the jaws and the taste buds working in order to taste and enjoy the wheaten flavor of God made bread: these are actions and gifts for all Christians. Not having been successfully taught to ignore the fact that the Eucharist is food—it is admittedly difficult to recognize Communion wafers as bread—my children's first reaction to the unconsecrated hosts they consumed at the numerous rehearsals for their First Communion is that they tasted stale. Mystics had no such impression about the host's flavor and no qualms about swishing it around their mouths in order to better enjoy it. And this is good because "an eaten world is an intelligible world, a world in which body and spirit are united," a South African philosopher has written, and, more specifically, "herbs and spice do for your dishes what grace does for your action—they give them zest and an inner meaning. The graceless life is life which has lost its savor."[22] Eating the Eucharist is a way of uniting body and soul, of bringing closer to the communicant—in certain moments even making intelligible, perhaps—the mystery of God made man, of God made bread. Good manners should quiet down our grinding jaws, but there is little reason to obscure the fact that, in eating, jaws move and to varying degrees make noise. It is true that by fasting many holy men and women completely silenced their jaws. But holy men and women—and Elisabeth of Schönau is among them—also strained, in the silence of the desert, of the convent, of their kitchen, and sometimes, as in Elisabeth's case, of a dining room, to hear the more subtle noises of God's gifts to their mouths: gifts of words and gifts of flavor, gifts that loosened their tongue in order to speak and gifts that flavored their taste buds with sweetness to be relished and shared.

4

How to Bite with Grace into Forbidden Fruits

Apples, Sweets, and Margaret Ebner

S LOWLY EXPRESSING hard-to-find words, or quickly moving in
recitation of a rosary, lips are good to pray with. Lips are also good
for kissing, though, and for easing food into our mouth. The part-
ing lips of holy women are a prelude to prayer, to loving intimacy, as well
as to eating and drinking. Lips speak—literally, with words, and
metaphorically, by kissing and eating—of the history and the vocabulary
shared by sex and food: two physical necessities for living beings but, for
humans, much more than that. The first problematic food to be linked
with spiritual pursuits, the apple—to start at the beginning—is both
naughty and nice: despite its current associations with vitamins, fiber, and
general healthfulness, not to mention doctors kept away and teachers kept
at bay, the apple is the forbidden fruit picked and eaten at the inception of
human sin—indeed, its unlawful picking and eating *was* the inception of
human sin. The first recorded activity humans did with each other in the
Judeo-Christian tradition was eating the forbidden fruit of Eden growing
on the Tree of Knowledge, as the biblical book of Genesis recounts.
Whether it was an apple or, more likely, an apricot or a pomegranate that,
in Eden, started the juicy connection between sweets and the female sex

might remain a botanical mystery. Less mysterious is the popular assumption that, since the object of exchange was a forbidden fruit offered to a naked man by a naked woman (not to mention the crucial intervention of a phallic-looking snake), the partaking of its succulent flesh must have referred to something more, something other, than simply eating fruit. Theologians may tell us that Adam and Eve's sin was a sin of pride, wanting to be like God in the ability to know good and evil. But many readers of this passage have seen in the Fall the sins of gluttony and, especially, of lust.

Pride is the gravest among the seven deadly sins, gluttony and lust among the least severe. Pride has caused the Fall of human beings and of angels, and in Dante's *Inferno* the proud are found at the very bottom of Hell, frozen over by the flapping of Lucifer's enormous wings. The gluttonous and the lustful are closer to the top, undergoing milder punishments, evoking greater sympathy though still in Hell. Among the first artistic representations of the connection between the Fall and sexual, rather than gluttonous or proud, excess may well be Hans Baldung Grien's chiaroscuro woodcut *Fall of Man* (1511). Eve's left hand is offering Adam an apple, but Adam seems to want to harvest his own and of a different flesh: standing behind Eve, his right hand is picking twin apples off the tree while his left is fondling the left one of Eve's twin breasts. There is a snake, of course, but also a pair of rabbits—symbols of fertility.[1]

Grien's woodcut associates, through visual metaphors and symbols, the apple and the breast—from Adam's perspective: the pleasure of the round, smooth apple is akin to the pleasure he derives from Eve's breast. Visionary Hildegard of Bingen, four centuries before Grien, had also linked the flavor of the apple with the flavor of sexual sin, though from Eve's perspective; Eve, as Hildegard tells in the second vision of her *Scivias*, "conceived sin in the taste of the fruit": Eve's conception, both sinful and reproductive, is a consequence of eating the apple and of sexual contact, of eating the apple *as* sexual contact, and is brought on by the twin bodily pleasures of sex and the fruit.[2]

(Symbolically analogous to the apple is the banana: a luxury item in the United States in the 1870s, then imported as cheaply as possible beginning in the 1890s, its advertisers consistently addressed women as the primary consumers of this fruit. Currently the most popular fruit in the United States, bananas were promoted as a substitute for meat; their sweetness and creaminess combined with their cheapness and ease of preparation made them the ideal homey food for women and children, and this despite their most risqué aspects: associations with exotic cultures and, especially, their phallic shape and size. The assumption was that women and children crave sweets, while men need red meat. So in the late nineteenth and the early twentieth centuries, bananas became increasingly known as "women's food.")[3]

"Whatever the consequences of wanting and of eating it, the apple is always meant to tantalize, always Aphrodite's enigmatic offering," muses a contemporary writer: "Its arrival in a story portends that Love's strict lessons will soon be instructed. The apple belongs to Love's Teacher. Look at Her desk, littered with the gifts."[4] The fruit of Eden is the didactic symbol of sin and female temptation, of illicit desires and obstinate hungers—for another's body, but also for another's knowledge. This is as true of Eve and Adam as it is for those "tempted by the fruit of another" in rock 'n' roll lyrics as it is also for Snow White, whose demise is brought on by her inability to resist the offer of a shiny and juicy apple. In Latin, *malus* could mean both apple and evil, a homophony likely related to the apple's sullied reputation. Apples are tossed as tokens of love in stories from the classical tradition and employed as metaphors for women from ancient Greek and Roman times through the Renaissance and in the present day. Compared in literature and art to women's breasts and buttocks, or more chastely, to women's cheeks, the apple is a symbol of desire and passion, of beauty, sex, and fertility. Its double nature—sacred and profane, pure and tempting—makes the apple the botanical equivalent of woman, herself divided between Eve and Mary, original stain and immaculate conception, temptress and co-redeemer.

As emblems of the female condition, apples are ambivalent, notes Piero Camporesi, paraphrasing one of Sappho's fragments: "virgin and bitter they cling to the branch; when mature, they fall suddenly, do not last and rapidly decompose."[5] The physical appearance of apples has so often been associated with female body parts—cheeks, buttocks, and especially breasts—that in the Renaissance some claimed that the origin of the word for apples (*mala*) was found in breasts (*mammae*). Binding botany and breastfeeding, Anne Sexton's poem "Jesus Suckles" begins with the divine baby's words, "Mary, your great / white apples make me glad."[6] As Camporesi muses, "Linguistic relationships and subliminal associations are propagated by these analogies between the apples and breasts, and vice versa, the caressing and touching of nipples, and apples, based on sexual and vegetable fantasy, the color of the human skin and the skin of the fruit, swelling of flesh and the shape of the fruit itself."[7]

In contemporary idiomatic English as well, fruit is sometimes used as an image of women's breasts: "*apples, casabas, cantaloupes, grapefruits, lemons* (especially used of small breasts), *melons*, and *watermelons* (large breasts), as well as *cherries, raspberries*, and *strawberries* for nipples, all of which accentuate the *ripe, fresh, juicy* quality of desirable women (compare a *wrinkled old prune* 'a woman past her sexual prime.')"[8]

From a more literally nutritional perspective, fruit is the most common natural source of sugars, that most pleasurable of tastes. If it is true that the promotion of social relationships is "the role of sweets, as a root symbol for all that is 'naughty but nice' in the world of food," still it cannot be said about the past that "an apple a day may keep the doctor away but it does little to promote social relationships,"[9] because the association between fruit and healthfulness and the separation between fruit and sweet treats are relatively recent phenomena.

From a medical standpoint, fruits have been viewed as desirable yet dangerous at least as early as the second century, the time of the immensely influential Greek physician and philosopher Galen of Pergamum. Galen warned that fresh fruit risked upsetting the balance among the four humors of the human body described in the Hippocratic corpus: yellow bile (hot and dry); black bile (cold and dry); phlegm (cold and moist); blood (hot and moist). So, fruit could be helpful to patients whose humors were out of balance, but it would cause imbalances in those whose humors were already balanced. Other writers, for example, the English Robert Burton (1577–1640) and the Italian Bartolomeo Sacchi (1421–1481)—known to historians of gastronomy for his influence on the cooking arts of the European Renaissance, with the pseudonym "il Platina"—warn about the possible bad effects of eating fresh fruit: an excess of black bile, for example, manifesting itself in melancholy.[10] The popular Italian combination of pears and cheese (a popular dessert) and of melon with prosciutto (the favored summer antipasto) originates in the humorally dangerous nature of fruit: eaten by itself, fruit such as pears and melons would prove too moist or too cold for a proper balance of humors, but cheese and ham, regarded as dry and hot, were thought to warm or dry out, and thus balance, these otherwise unhealthy eats.

The abundance of fruit is a recurrent image in the Song of Songs.

Filled with seed and thus with the possibility of new life, fruit is coupled with the erotic practices so central to this beautiful book-poem of the Hebrew Scriptures, the shortest among the Wisdom Books, and attributed by tradition to King Solomon. Fruit and body are united by desire, pleasure, and reproduction as they once were in Eden. Now there is no death-dealing serpent to spoil the lovers' snack, but still the painful separation of lover and beloved hints at the human condition of lack, at the fundamental absence of the other to the self. The Song of Songs tells of a link between literal and metaphorical sweets, it sings of physical pleasure, but (tradition teaches) its meaning revolves around divine love—although the name of God is never mentioned. It is a favored biblical book for Christian spiritual writers, who regard its vivid sexual images as equally powerful signs of divine union. The Lover is God, and the Beloved has been interpreted at different times as the human soul, the people of Israel, the Church, and Mary the mother of Jesus.

Even the most famous of Christian commentaries on the Song of Songs, Abbot Bernard of Clairvaux's twelfth-century sermons bind this text from its very beginning with the act of eating and drinking. The first paragraph of Bernard's first sermon on the Song of Songs, "On the Title of the Book," is a series of instructions detailing the differences between people who are consecrated and people who are worldly, those who are spiritually advanced and those who, spiritually, are just beginners. These differences manifest themselves most openly in the kinds of foods each of the two groups may profitably consume:

> The instructions that I address to you, my brothers, will differ from those I should deliver to people in the world, at least the manner will be different. The preacher who desires to follow St Paul's method of teaching will give them milk to drink rather than solid food, and will serve a more nourishing diet to those who are spiritually enlightened . . . Be ready then to feed on bread rather than milk. Solomon has bread to give that is splendid and delicious, the bread of that book called "The Song of Songs." Let us bring it forth then if you please, and break it.[11]

Only the spiritually enlightened are able to consume this solid food, this bread "that is splendid and delicious," this dish that is the Song of Songs. And the Song of Songs, in addition to speaking of food, is itself a food in at least two ways: it is bread and it is fruit, Bernard says in the third paragraph, for the Song of Songs is the fruit of two other biblical books,

Proverbs and Ecclesiastes. To those who are not among the spiritually enlightened, and are therefore immature, milk—the food of infants, the food of those who have not yet grown and developed—will have to suffice. No bread for them, yet, and no Song of Songs.

Bread and milk are nourishment for adults and children respectively, but there is more to the Song of Songs, and even to the foods featured in it, than dietetic sustenance. In the fifth paragraph of Bernard's seventh sermon on the Song of Songs, "Intimacies of the Love of God," the author reminds us that,

> As food is sweet to the palate, so does a psalm delight the heart. But the soul that is sincere and wise will not fail to chew the psalm with the teeth as it were of the mind, because if he swallows it in a lump, without proper mastication, the palate will be cheated of the delicious flavor, sweeter even than honey that drips from the comb. Let us with the Apostles offer a honeycomb at the table of the Lord in the heavenly banquet. As honey flows from the comb so should devotion flow from the words.[12]

Bread and fruit nourish and give energy, and the Song of Songs is both bread and fruit and provides at once nourishment and energy. But this biblical poem gives more than sustenance and strength, for to the reader who is appropriately prepared for it the Song of Songs will give delight, and for the reader who chews properly the Song of Songs will supply pleasure comparable only to the sweetness of honey. Food and love in the Song of Songs are an inseparable combination of need and pleasure, sustenance and excess, both for the protagonists of the poem and for its readers—who, if properly instructed, have the opportunity to experience the pleasure of the lover and the beloved even if, and actually only if, they are spiritually advanced, celibate, consecrated men. A properly performed devotional reading, that is, provides the sweetness that in the text is experienced through sexual intimacy and depicted through fruits and treats for those who have made vows not to experience sexual pleasure.

"Refresh me with apples, for I am faint with love," sings the beloved as her lover's caresses entrance her (Cant. 2:5). Depicted as a token of love and as a metaphor for women, in the Song of Songs fruit is an image of the body: sweet and nourishing, sensually delightful. Apples were not known in Palestine at the time of the Songs of Songs, and recent interpretations favor apricots or quince as the fruit to which the beloved and her breath are compared, the fruit with which her lover surrounds her, the fruit under which the beloved was both seduced and conceived in this most erotic of all biblical books.

Sweet fruit is an image of women's physical beauty: the beloved's cheeks are like grains of pomegranate and, later, like the skin of pomegranates.[13] Recalling both the shape of female breasts and the fecundity of female wombs, pomegranates (literally, "seedy apples") have long been associated with woman's sex, her desire, and her fertility. In Renaissance paintings pomegranates are often symbolic of Mary's chastity. Pomegranates are also Persephone's (Proserpine's) distinctive fruit, signaling both the death of winter and the springtime renewal of life. Used to symbolize the church itself—which gathers the multitudes into its unity like a pomegranate its seeds[14]—breaking into a pomegranate is the symbolic equivalent of renouncing the unity of being and of dangerously choosing, instead, multiplicity itself. Evoking the rounded shape of pomegranates, the beloved's breasts are also described as clusters of dates (surely among the sweetest of fruits) and later as bunches of grapes (source of that most beloved and Mediterranean of inebriating drinks).

Many flavors, not limited to fruit, are suggested in this sensuous poem. All of them are sweet, some are especially nourishing, others downright intoxicating: pomegranates, figs, grapes, dates, apples, nuts, and raisin cakes, as well as honey, milk, wine, sweetness (maybe sugar), and intense, precious spices such as cinnamon and saffron.

Icon of loving bodies and of bodily desire in the Song of Songs, fruit remained an object of craving for Christian holy women as well, who sometimes chose to train themselves to give it up as an exercise in self-control and/or as a gift to their Beloved. Of Catherine of Genoa, it was written that God "made her moderate in her eating so that she stopped eating fruit (of which she was very fond) or meat or anything rich."[15] Teresa of Avila had a craving for melon during one illness (a craving miraculously satisfied by a half melon brought to the convent where she was staying) and for oranges during another (oranges that instead, this time, Teresa gave to the poor).[16]

Margaret (or Margaretha) Ebner's dealings with fruit, told in her own words, are worth exploring in greater depth, along with her treatment of food more generally. A Dominican nun who was born around 1291 and died in 1351, Margaret Ebner was the first person to be beatified by Pope John Paul II, in 1979 (her feast is celebrated on June 20). Margaret's intimate knowledge of God was frequently expressed through food. Like her fellow monastics, Margaret often gave up food in abstinence and fasting: the influence of Bernard of Clairvaux on Margaret Ebner has been noted by her editors, who claim that he was "the authority for her lack of desire for food."[17] But Bernard's representation of food, as we have seen, is more complex than a simple refusal, and so also Margaret savors food, with taste buds or with soul, well beyond its earthly flavor: she had learned her lessons from Bernard's commentaries on the Song of Songs, which she is believed to have read. Margaret Ebner's major written work is entitled the *Revelations* (*Offenbarungen*), composed in her native German and written down by herself, without the aid of a scribe, at the insistence of her spiritual director, the Dominican Henry of Nördlingen (Margaret's hope was that he would be the one to write of her experiences, since he was so familiar with them, but he refused and encouraged her to write instead). The *Revelations* were begun during Advent of the year 1344, cover the period from 1312 (when Margaret was afflicted by a mysterious illness) to 1348, and share several traits with both Hildegard of Bingen's and Elisabeth of Schönau's vision cycles. Representing the self as worthy of imitation, as exemplary of human grace, Margaret Ebner's book of *Revelations* is a kind of "autohagiography," for its author tells her own story as the story of a saint. Best known about Margaret, and most prominent in her *Revelations*, are both her debilitating illnesses—interpreted as *imitatio Christi*, a reproduction of Christ's own sufferings—and her binding Silences, uncontrollable Speakings (which usually meant repeating the name *Jesus Christus* unstoppably, until exhaustion prevailed), and loud Outcries (screaming with or without words). These were spiritual graces over which Margaret had no control, she frequently stated; they were a witness to God's continual touch and to Margaret's mystical authority.

Silences, Speakings, and Outcries are not the only graces Margaret receives. The Eucharist is certainly central to the spirituality of this mystic, who does not hesitate to treat the Eucharist as food and to write, "when I drank from the chalice I perceived great sweetness, which I tasted for three days."[18] Initially, her approach to regular food, as Margaret explains toward the beginning of her book, was a thoughtful and positive one, reasonable by today's standards and reminiscent as well of Francis of Assisi's advice to his own brothers (see chapter 6). "I also intended not to bother anyone about the food that I would eat or about what I needed or anything else. And truthfully I have done so ever since," Margaret admits, continuing: "Whatever was placed before me I enjoyed as much as I was

able. I was always careful to eat only what I needed so that I would have
no gnawing pangs of conscience about breaking off too much bread for
myself" (92). Simplicity and temperance, guided by appreciation for those
who cook for her and concern for those who share her meals, guide Margaret's behavior at table. Her care for other people's work and needs is
generously rewarded with supernatural flavors and absolute satiety. This
she explains a few pages later, after receiving the gift of joy and lightness:
"From that moment I never felt any desire for bodily food, no matter how
long I waited to eat." Filled with God, she can no longer be hungry. The
consumption of regular food has some negative side effects in terms of
spiritual gifts, however: "I have noticed too that, after eating, I never
received the grace to speak or to do other things which I had done previously." But though "all food except plain cloister fare seemed evil to me,"
and though "whenever I saw something tempting before me it also
occurred to me to go without it joyfully for the sake of my Beloved" (98),
this sacrifice of enjoyment and flavor is not ultimately accepted by God,
who makes Margaret's simple cloister fare suffice in satisfying the most
discriminating of tastes, the most refined of palates.

Thus, later in the *Revelations*, Margaret describes how in "the ordinary
fare of my convent I often perceive the best taste and the greatest sweetness so that I think nothing better could be found on earth. I wish that the
entire convent could perceive this." While her fellow nuns "complain that
the food is not good and point out a certain failing," Margaret says that
she "never found it so"—even admitting that she has "a special craving for
oil, because it suits me better and because I perceive more divine joy from
it than from anything else" (104). And "on the following Easter Sunday,"
Margaret recalls, "I had special great grace when I came to table where I
perceived such great sweetness and such delightful taste from the food
that the sister who was eating with me noticed it" (109). Margaret did
nothing to silence the noise of her grinding jaws! What expressions or,
more likely, what noises, was Margaret making for her table companion to
realize the "great sweetness" and the "delightful taste" she was experiencing? Was she moaning, crunching, sighing, sucking? This is a wonderfully
realistic image of a nun communing with God, a nun who, in meeting
God, forgets the rules of polite eating and makes audible noises at table—
even though immediately after describing her eating commotion she says:
"Silence suits me so well and I have such great grace and peace from it."
But this kind of noisy table pleasure must have been frequent if indeed, "of

all bodily food and drinks," Margaret says, "I take the greatest delight in water. It seems so sweet to me that I wonder why everyone does not prefer water to other drinks" (158).

Margaret's delight with food and drink was also experienced in the less tangible, quieter circumstances of visionary experience. In a November 1348 dream of this mystic we read of apples that are at once religious symbol and juicy flesh, apples that, as noble fruit that grew high on trees and thus far from the ground (unlike some other produce), were in the medieval period a sign of aristocracy—much like the spices preferred by Elisabeth of Schönau: "fruit made an impression, both because (and in so far as) it was expensive and difficult to come by, and also because according to the scientific co-ordinates of that culture it occupied a 'high' position in the hierarchy of the vegetable world. Culture, power, image and reality all intertwine inextricably."[19] In Margaret Ebner's visionary dream the apples indeed come from another world, distant in terms of flavor and meaning from the simple food of the convent refectory. The apples grow on a tall tree located in "a beautiful green place" near Purgatory—"a strange place" where she "found many sorts of deceased people whom [she] knew" asking her "to pray to God for them" (the visionary dream took place on All Souls' Day). Offered as they are by fellow nuns, the two contrasting apples convey without doubt nobility of shape, taste, and purpose. In Margaret's words,

> I came to a beautiful green place where there were tall trees from which beautiful apples were falling . . . two others, who were sisters of our monastery, came over to me. They gave me two of the apples. One of them was sour, the other sweet. They asked me to eat them. I took the apples and bit into them. Then I felt such great grace from the apples that I said, "No one on earth could eat both." They said, "If you do not like them give them back to us." Then I awoke still chewing, and the grace was so sweet and so strong that I could not speak a word and could not take in breath and was really without any of my bodily senses. (171)

These apples of Margaret's dream fall much like the one on Sir Isaac Newton's head: they lead to increased knowledge and understanding rather than to loss and fall as in the case of Adam and Eve's encounter with the same fruit—though in the case of Eden, too, increased knowledge upon the fruit's consumption had been promised (and the apocryphal book of Enoch has the archangel Raphael say that Adam and Eve "ate and came to know wisdom").[20] Margaret experiences what also the monks who entered earthly paradise in medieval legends must have seen and eaten when they said: "These are the apples of eternal health and youth, apples that beatify."[21] In Margaret's vision there are two apples rather than the scriptural single one of Eden—though even that single apple has been multiplied in the artistic and religious imagination, as we have seen in visual representations such as Eve's apple-like breasts in Hans Baldung Grien's woodcut. But in the dream the two apples are the gift of two sisters of her monastery—not the forbidden fruit of a male-identified deity. Margaret is encouraged to eat them rather than ordered not to taste of them. And in spite of the fact that only one of the apples is sweet while the other is sour (sweet like a Golden Delicious and tart like a Granny Smith, perhaps?), still both give grace. The grace comes from "the apples" not from just one of them, and Margaret's statement that nobody could eat both shows her own limitations, not the fruit's. For the pleasure these apples give outlasts the vision itself—Margaret still chews and tastes the sweetness after the end of her supernatural sleep—and causes a paralyzing ecstasy.

We can better understand this transfiguration of fruit and the incorporation within the apple of conflicting and even contradictory tastes by turning to an earlier passage of her *Revelations*, set in 1334–1335, where Margaret had explained well the connections between love, sweetness, and the quest for God—and a gourmet's choice to give up the lower, earthly foods if the better flavor of divine sweetness is to be fully enjoyed. Later in her convent life she is overtaken with a taste for the divine that seems to numb her earthly predilections. Margaret describes how she has lived "thirty years without drinking wine and without taking a bath," and "neither water nor soap have touched my head or body in these same thirty years." The ability to withstand this is obtained "by the help of God." Along with baths and wine, Margaret has "given up fish and meat." More pointedly for our context, although Margaret "took especially great delight in fruit," her delight was not to last: "Then it was revealed to me with great joy, 'I want you to give it [fruit] up for the sake of my love.' And I had the desire to give up all sweet things for the sake of the sweetness I received from God" (128).

This woman could see herself clearly enough—lack of baths notwithstanding: washing had to be sacrificed along with food and drink so as to better control, and ideally erase, the needs of the flesh—to understand the motives for her actions, the meaning of her sacrifice, the pleasures of monastic life: fruit is the most delightful food, yet not as sweet, not even nearly as sweet, as the love of God. Indeed, no food is in her eyes or in her mouth as flavorful as the presence of the One she desires, the only One she wants. But the sacrifices of Margaret's sense of taste do not go unnoticed, much less unrewarded, and God's sweetness does not fail her, letting itself be intensely enjoyed in the course of her visions. For "Whenever an Outcry was about to occur," Margaret recounts, "I would perceive a sweet taste in my mouth before." God comes to her taste buds before reaching her tongue and vocal chords, and this became a predictable pattern for her: "in the following week, I came to understand that when the Outcry strove to rise up from within my heart into my mouth, this would be preceded by a sweet taste in my mouth." Not only does the sweetness precede the mystical grace of the Outcry: it also accompanies it and then goes on to connect the Outcry to the Speaking and thus give it a more understandable—because verbal—meaning: "The sweetness lasted as long as the Outcry continued and then, after that, the same sweetness increased during the Speaking. Note: *'De ore prudentis procedit mel . . . ,'* and also *'Favus distillans, etc.'"* (152).

The sensation of divine honeyed sweetness is a flavor for which Margaret provides scriptural references in the Latin quotations of her last sentence—loosely referring to the Song of Songs: "Your lips distil nectar, my bride, honey and milk are under your tongue" (Cant. 4:11). One flavor explains the other, and the Song of Songs becomes central to the self-understanding of the mystic both for its focus on the love of bride and bridegroom and for its emphasis on the sweet and intoxicating flavors of this love. Sweet flavors punctuate Margaret's entire mystical path, flavors perceived through the senses rather than through the imagination: it is "a sweet taste in my mouth," she repeats twice, that comes to her before an Outcry. Originating in the senses, it is also through the senses that this pleasure thins out and comes to an end: "And I did not drink from Wednesday until Sunday, and during these five days I felt all the time as if there were sweet sugar in my mouth accompanied by pleasurable sweetness in my heart. And when I took liquid on Sunday the sweetness decreased" (160). God's is a specific sweetness: it is the sweetness of sugar, now, and not simply a metaphorical pleasure so spiritual as to have no earthly equivalent. Sweetness in the heart accompanies a better-known sugary sweetness in the mouth, diluted and eventually dissolved by the intake of material liquid, her Sunday drink.

Sweet is the frequent flavor of Margaret's visions, and liquid is their texture. On the last page of the *Revelations*, Margaret describes the dream of a bishop who offers her "a very clear drink in a glass"—after offering others a "murky drink from a chalice." Margaret notes:

> My heart and my soul were filled completely with grace so sweet that I cannot write about it. And I began with my usual Speaking, in the powerful sweet grace which had been given me from the drink and which I had received from the presence of the bishop and the servant. My Lord knows well that I have ever felt an increase in the sweet joy attending the grace which I had received from eating and drinking. Especially when I said my *Pater Noster* and came to the petition about my lord St. John, then I perceived with the sweetest grace that it had been he who had given me the drink. (172)

This visionary dream is related immediately after the dream of the two apples. The sweetness of grace, enjoyed through eating and drinking, is ineffable yet commands speaking—and Speaking is how Margaret's graces are shared with others, making her unable to go to Mass in times of great grace because it is impossible for her to keep quiet. The sweetest grace proceeds from the drink, yet not without the presence of bishop and servant; and though the drink comes from the bishop, nevertheless, Margaret realizes, it is to her "lord St. John" that she owes it.

Saint John, earlier in her book, had, as Margaret wrote, "drank and sucked" a "sweet drink" from "the sweet breast of Christ" (125)—a maternal Christ, who, like God in Hildegard's book, feeds his children with his own body. Is Saint John then sharing with Margaret Christ's milk, which once filled his mouth and is now poured into hers? If that is true, then Margaret and Jesus share more than sweetness: they share milk and a mother's ability to feed with it, and with herself. In one of the better-known episodes of Margaret's *Revelations*, when God tells Margaret "If you do not suckle me, then I will draw away from you and you will take no delight in me," the nun dutifully takes the statue of the Christ child lying in the manger and "placed it against my naked heart with great delight and sweetness" (132). This delight and sweetness are not purely spiritual, though: as she pressed the statue of the Child "against my naked heart as strongly as I could," she "felt the movements of His mouth on my naked heart" (134). Jesus is suckling Margaret much like she, via the intermediary of Saint John, will suckle him. There are two maternal beings busy with nursing, and each maternal being has two breasts—round like apples and, like apples, sweet and nourishing beyond mere survival. Meaning, like the apples Margaret will later taste in the dream cited above, is double: there are always two meanings, which, again like the apples, are different, of opposite flavor, even, yet equally filled with grace. Hunger and fullness are one in vision and in practice. Fasting and feasting, for all their difference, imply no noticeable contradiction. In the words of this nun, who is an example, in some of her writings, of the inedia that was such an important part of medieval holy women's piety, I also read the delights of a gourmet, the sensitive taste buds of a sommelier, the sweet tooth of a lover so satisfyingly nourished by her beloved—with milk, with fruit, with sweetness, with grace—as to need little more sustenance and pleasure than what he, already, abundantly gives her.

Abundance in produce is a gift of the summer. Before the advent of freezers and supermarkets, the most effective and delicious way to savor nature's bounty in the off season was to preserve fresh fruit by jarring it in sugar. This method, still practiced today in preserves, jams, and conserves, is effectively used as the source of important spiritual metaphors in a seventeenth-century spiritual classic. Fruits are mortification when unripe, consolations when ripe—sweetened or preserved, respectively, by the sugar that is devotion; soft fruits such as cherries, apricots, and strawberries, are our hearts, preserved by the sugar and honey that is the body of Christ; fruits are our virtues, preserved in the sugar of divine love; fruit is our chastity, preserved, whether undamaged or bruised, by the sugar and honey of a very strong devotion; fruits are married people—acid and harsh like husbands and quinces, soft and frail like wives, cherries, and apricots. I wish it had been a holy woman to have so well described in one book all five of these sweet metaphors, but it was, instead, a man—though a man very popular with women: Francis of Sales (1567–1622), bishop of Geneva, who founded the Order of the Visitation with his friend Madame Jeanne de Chantal.[22] His *Introduction to the Devout Life* (1609), from which the above metaphors are drawn, was addressed to a fictive woman, Philothea—meaning "lover of God." Francis's repeated references to preserving fruit in sugar and honey, as well as his comparisons of dances with pumpkins and mushrooms ("the best of which, according to doctors, are good for nothing"), of human beings with children eager for candies, of spiritual graces with sugar plums, and of God with a nursing mother "who honeys her breasts to entice her child," make him a fitting and helpful companion to the women in God's kitchen.[23] Francis de Sales was no fan of excessive fasting, however, for "to weaken our body exposes us to temptation as much as to pamper it," and "in general it is better to over-strengthen than over-weaken our body; we can always curb it when necessary, we cannot always restore it when we want to."[24]

Not all the women in God's kitchen were always so reasonable, but although their emphasis on fasting from regular food and feasting on the Eucharist has been an important and, in recent years, amply studied aspect of their spirituality, their focus on the meaning of the noneucharistic food they did eat, or imagined eating, also deserves some consideration. In the miraculous bread that was their physical sustenance, dried up and rock hard in the desert or blessed by a priest in the monastery, the holy women of Byzantium might have read humility and its supernatural rewards: the binding of distant bodies, the significance of the apparently meaningless, the pleasure to be had in God's gifts. Hildegard's cheesy metaphors alleviate the distance between body and food, and between the shortcomings of each— their common thickness, weakness, bitterness—through the ability body and food share to be perfected and made whole in Christ. Another distance, that between woman and God, between human bride and divine bridegroom, can be shortened through the intercession of food: the flavor of spices is for Elisabeth of Schönau the sample of an experience so rich, sweet, and lasting that only cinnamon can effectively prelude it in this life. And Margaret Ebner's apples, like Eve's, like the bride's of the Song of Songs, like Snow White's, certainly signify beyond their crispy, juicy flesh. These apples, like the bread of the holy women of Byzantium, bind material food and immaterial nourishment, spiritual closeness and geographical distance. They point, like Hildegard's cheese, to meanings across and below the veil of appearances—their shiny peel, their variable tastes. Like Elisabeth's cinnamon, these apples are flavored with divinity, with eternity. As much as Margaret's inedia, and more than her renunciation of the delights of fresh fruit, the apples in her vision establish her worth and her ability to speak and be heard, to mediate between God and humanity, to share the good news and to eat of the very fruit once forbidden—and to eat it while writing at a table located, of all places, in God's kitchen.

5

How to Confect Convent Treats

Sweet Traditions and
the Martyrdom of Saint Agatha

G OD IS SWEET: divine words, in the Psalms, are to the tongue
"sweeter than honey" (Ps. 119:103); divine visions, for medieval
mystics such as Elisabeth of Schönau and Margaret Ebner, drip
honey, cinnamon, and sugar on the holy woman's taste buds; divine love,
in the Song of Songs, fills the beloved's mouth with a sweet fruit. Woman
is sweet: as a girl she is made of sugar and spice, and as she grows into
adulthood sweetness flavors her childlike innocence (she is a cupcake, a
sweetheart), or, instead, links her temptingly to the pleasures of sweets
(she is a cheesecake or, worse, a tart). No wonder that the institution
where God and women come together, the convent, is a place traditionally associated with sweets: both Elisabeth and Margaret resided in convents when they had their sweet interactions with the sweetest of lovers.
But this bond is more than metaphorical; it is historical and it is gastronomical. "Nunneries in the old days were veritable storehouses of the
most delectable tidbits," notes food writer Brillat-Savarin.[1]

Scholars have attributed to the cooking of convents and monasteries
the invention of gastronomy: just as the large numbers of people eating
every day at the same time and in the same place led to organized ways of
preparing and distributing food, for example, so also the desire to break

the monotony of daily feeding during the special yet frequent times of fasting, abstinence, and religious holidays led to creative ways of preparing the foods that were allowed, available, or encouraged. The religious obligation to abstain or fast on the one hand, and the needs and desires of the inhabitants of individual convents on the other, did not always make good tablemates—particularly in the many cloisters where the residents came from noble and/or wealthy families: these people's rich habits of taste and eating continued to be expressed and indeed to grow and develop in the food practices of their convent.

The frugal eating regulations laid down by founding saints of western monasticism such as Pacomium (c. 290–c. 347), Cassianum (360–c. 430), and especially Benedict (480–547), certainly shaped the rules and customs of monastic eating, but they did not always limit nor precisely define the food practices connected with each cloister. Different orders, and even different communities, had varying views of what their obligations of fasting and abstinence would or should put on their plates: barnacle geese, for instance, could be consumed during Lent according to some because they were believed to reproduce without sex "and therefore might be expected to nourish without exciting inappropriate lusts."[2]

Significantly, women's religious communities in southern Italy between the seventeenth and the nineteenth centuries ate larger and more luxurious quantities of food not only than men's religious communities but than most people in general—their food closely resembling the food of these women's aristocratic and/or wealthy families of origin. Small wonder that the financial situation of each community was among the dominant factors in deciding what, when, and how much would be eaten there.[3] And most likely Benedict could not foresee the popularity of convent-made sweets, prepared at first as gifts to confessors and other ecclesiastics and as treats for the nuns themselves, and later as a profitable business of many women's cloisters—sweets that would leave a lasting trace in the long convent shopping lists of costly ingredients such as sugar, honey, eggs, almonds, cinnamon, raisins, nutmeg, cloves, and more.

In the words of Italian food historians Alberto Capatti and Massimo Montanari, "the most fascinating aspect of studying culinary history is the discovery of how ordinary people, with their physical effort and imagination, sought to transform the pangs of hunger and the anxieties of poverty into potential moments of pleasure."[4] In this transformation, consecrated people—living in communities of varying incomes and committed to the dietetic vagaries of the liturgical year—faced unique challenges and enjoyed particular privileges. For many celibate nuns in the history of Italy the allegorical pleasures of the Song of Songs—a poem that praises fruit and sweets as well as other sensual delights—can be tasted in convent-made confections and pastries, pleasurable to make and to eat, capable of breaking the monotony of daily feeding and the work of food preparation. Even in convents where the diet was not poor, the effort and imagination required to make these complicated sweets had a transforming power: of creativity, of connection, of physical and psychological survival. Those sweet delicacies that have been a traditional source of pride and income for Italian nuns can thus be understood to belong in the genealogical line of the fruits and sweets of the Song of Songs: they represent desire earthly and divine, they embody a delight in the spirit expressed through delicious bliss mixed, baked, served, and tasted.

The complexity of the ties between religious celibacy and the pleasurable sensuality of sweets is well illustrated by the legendary medieval origin, in the Sicilian convent of the Martorana in Palermo, of the *frutta di Martorana*—the most famous among the sweet delicacies produced by Italian convents. *Frutta di Martorana* consists of marzipan realistically shaped like fruits:

> It is said that once their mother superior, Sister Gertrude, wishing to celebrate the pastoral visit of the bishop, instructed the nuns to mold the paste into apples, peaches, pears, and oranges, which were then hung on the trees growing in the cloister garden. Strolling in the cloister before dinner with the mother superior, the bishop marveled to see so many different trees bearing fruit all in the same season. Still greater was his surprise when, at the dinner table, he bit into a bright red apple and discovered that it was made of almond paste.[5]

This story evokes the sensuality of a man entering a convent of consecrated virgins, specifically, their highly symbolic enclosed garden; it points to the fertility of trees bearing fruit among, and thanks to the care of, sterile virgins; it reminds us of the forbidden nature of the apple of Eden—as well as of women's, even cloistered, virginal women's, creative ability to give surprising physical pleasure to the few men able to enter their enclosure. That the origin of this delicacy should be found in Sicily is no coincidence, since it is through this island that the Arabs introduced cane sugar to

Europe in the thirteenth century—an introduction that in turn encouraged the increased use of almonds as sweeteners and thickeners.

From a different perspective, one that reads in convent sweets the absence of pleasure rather than an increased play with it, anthropologist Sidney Mintz surmises that marzipan, white and immaculate as its ingredients (almonds must be skinned before being ground into a paste), is an icon of purity and health produced in pure places—nunneries and monasteries—by pure individuals—virginal, enclosed brides of God.[6] Though that may have been the case in the Portuguese convents Mintz is discussing, in Sicily as well as the rest of Italy convent sweets were a more complicated affair: the marzipan's whiteness might have connoted purity, but its sweetness was more ambivalent—and in Italian convents, anyway, marzipan was rarely left white, for elaborate shapes and colors were an integral part of the confections of which it was the star ingredient.

In sixteenth-century Venice, cloistered nuns would send to their relations presents of sweets, and, comments a 1596 source, "this accounts for half the food which the convent is squandering, because the nuns are continually making biscuits, cakes, doughnuts and pastries in great quantities. And to this end, at certain times of the year, several *quarteroli* of flour are doled out to the nuns, with the result that they consume five hundred *stara* of grain a year, two hundred *stara* more than they should reasonably expect to use." Commenting on this source, historian Mary Laven notes that "such frenzies of cake making, which strained the resources of the convent, were commonly reported in the records of contemporary visitations," and refers to such frenzies as signs of "the unequal degree of compulsion in demonstrations of generosity between nuns and their families."[7] In practical terms, the gifts of food prepared by the enclosed nuns allowed them to preserve their connection with a world from which they were shut out; the time, energy, and money needed to keep this bond by baking must have seemed a small price to pay. The complicated ways in which this association of convents and sweets appears in history and literature suggests that it was not an unambiguous cohabitation, not simply a way for convents to support themselves or for nuns to keep busy.

Not only in Venice was there a strong historical and cultural connection between women's convents and good food—and, particularly, elaborate and time-consuming, caloric, sweet and spiced, and thus rare and expensive treats. A series of eighteenth-century watercolors details the specialties of convents in Bologna—a city still known for its excellent food, and because of it often called "Bologna la Grassa," Bologna the fat one. These convent delicacies include quince preserves, rose water cookies, marzipan *mortadella*, sponge cakes, fruitcakes, donuts, and more. The French Dominican missionary Jean Baptiste Labat (1664–1738), traveling to Bologna in 1706, wrote about the trade in quince and quince products that was flourishing in that city. This fruit was at its best when made into a jam, and the nuns, he notes, "compete with and try to surpass each other in this sweet manufacture, and in the making of all sorts of fruit products, in the preparation of which they spare neither musk nor amber." Their sweet work did not stop at quince jam: "They also make some excellent fruit waters; and when I was invited to say Mass or to participate in it at their convent, or to visit them, they never failed, according to the hour, to present me with some refreshments."[8]

Just a few decades later, another man of the cloth, Giovanni Meli (1740–1815)—a Sicilian intellectual who wrote in dialect and donned an abbot's garb without having actually taken vows—wrote around 1790 an ode entitled "Li cosi duci di li batii," or "The sweet things of convents," an ode that describes the various specialties of the convents of Palermo. The stanza dedicated to the *frutta di Martorana* well expresses the strong sentiments this confection elicited of its devotees:

> The Martorana, this Eden, paradise on earth,
> I wish to praise with verse, with viol and horn.
> Blessed the man these sisters deem of worth,
> For here the fruits of marzipan are born.
> How sweet the chestnut, sweet the carob bean,
> The plum, the apricot, the quince so round:
> For such as these three Jesuits were seen
> To brawl and fight and roll upon the ground.[9]

The *frutta di Martorana* is now produced, since the pastry boom of the sixties, by pastry chefs throughout the city and the island (and imitated throughout the world), and, though still rather pricey, it is available year-round: one can easily order it over the Internet, for example. Originally, however, these delicious confections were developed by the nuns residing in the twelfth-century Monastero della Martorana, and were available only around All Souls' Day: children used to receive *frutta di Martorana* (some still do) as a present from their loved dead ones on November 2, All Souls' Day. The ingredients of *frutta di Martorana* are sugar, ground almonds, and egg whites; the shaped marzipan is then dried, painted with food coloring, and shined with gum Arabic. Besides the famous *frutta di Martorana*, many monasteries in Sicily have sweet specialties for which they were renowned and sought out: ricotta cakes known as *cassate* at the monastery of Valverde (Palermo), *cannoli* at the monastery of Saint Catherine (Palermo), *bocconcini*, or sweet morsels, at the Abbey of the Holy Rosary in Palma Montechiaro (Agrigento) and at the Benedictine monastery of Saint Michael in Mazara del Vallo (Trapani), and more.[10] But many of these centuries-old culinary traditions are dying with the old nuns, since the young ones—and there are fewer and fewer of them—are not attracted to pastry making and prefer those socially committed activities so needed in a large and busy city such as Palermo. These days, only the Benedictine nuns in Palermo's Piazza Venezia still support themselves by producing and selling their intricate and extremely sweet delicacies.[11]

It is hard not to ask oneself why the nuns produced so many of these sweets and for so long. For a passionate reader, moreover, it is even harder not to "read" this sweet-making practice as if it were a story—seeking to discern, that is, the connections it makes, the meanings it shares, and the pleasure it gives. The aesthetic enjoyment of pastry making involves sight, touch, and taste; it brings the fun of playing with food, the satisfaction of difficult work well done, and the pleasure of producing by hand elaborate and much-admired pastries and confections. The sweets represent for the nuns a connection to history as well as to the world outside. Given that these sweets have little nutritional value and an even smaller official place in the notoriously simple monastic diet, most basically their meaning is economical (because starting with the second half of the nineteenth century, pastries and confections were not only used as gifts, but were also sold to help the finances of the convents) and also psychological (cooking must have been for the nuns, as it is for so many cooks, a vent for creativity). Beyond all this, and encompassing it, there is a sense of excess in this practice, underlined by the conflict between the self-mortifications of convents on the one hand and the proximity, the identification, even, between sweetness and physical pleasure. The enjoyment of sweetness, and the Song of Songs confirms this, borders with sexual enjoyment: both invite a relationship with pleasure even as convent life questions its excess, possibly its very presence, and therefore its legitimacy. And the bond of nuns with sweets gives us pause much like the Song of Songs makes us wonder. Can religion, and particularly the ascetic Christianity of cloistered nuns and holy women, comfortably coexist with the pleasurable sensations of sweetness—and of the bodily love this sweetness evokes?

In the tragic account of former Italian nun Enrichetta Caracciolo's 1864 memoirs, *Misteri del chiostro napoletano* (The mysteries of the Neapolitan cloister), this devotion to pastry baking is believed to be a symptom as well as a cause of an obsession that was impossible for cloistered nuns to avoid. Caracciolo describes in her book the preparation of sweets as the "main occupation of the convent, its quintessence." After detailing the various specialties of Neapolitan convents, Caracciolo explains how each nun was given, shortly before Easter, one day to bake (though the activity usually took much longer than that), and how this practice was so important that, surprisingly, "more than one white-haired old nun told me that she had never participated in the liturgy of the Holy Week, since during those times she never had a free moment to enter the choir and look into the church." This unavailability for church due to the demands of sweets production lead, during the holiest period of the Christian calendar, to the desertion of the chapel and the anger of preachers. And in her usual polemical tone, Caracciolo notes bitterly, that, "in the distribution of sweets the relatives get the worst part. And do you want to know why? On the advice of priests"—who control the nuns through their spiritual direction, made more powerful by the women's physical distance from their families, and who control the sweets by pocketing them for their own consumption.[12]

Forced to become a nun by her parents in order to preserve the family's finances (a common practice in Italy and other Catholic countries for many centuries) and freed from the cloister only after, and in part thanks to, the arrival in Naples of Garibaldi and his troops (1860), Caracciolo's autobiographical story is full of biting resentment and acerbic flourishes. Like all literary works (and, to a different extent, most written texts), it is not meant to be taken literally in terms of historical accuracy. But her narrative, however embittered, however cynical, reveals much about convents, and it dares to deal with uncomfortable topics that no other book of that time touches in such a direct manner. In its anger at the condition of nuns and at the abuses of the priests involved in their care, Caracciolo's book reveals the complications, hinted at in other texts as well, of a practice—convent pastry making—whose meanings exceed the economic demands of the convent much like its products exceed the demands of nutrition. This practice, furthermore, could be as symptomatic of the nuns' predicament then as the excessive consumption of sweets today points to problems that, be they interpreted as sociological, psychological, existential, or spiritual, profoundly connect our bodies and souls to the demands of the Other within us and around us.

The bonds between convent women and complicated sweets must be numerous and diverse. Rational explanations will not exhaust the reality of a practice embodying a metaphor, a physical realization of the connection between celibacy, women, and sweets. Some of these delicious, elaborately produced foods make overstated symbolic statements—the sweet-and-sour contrasts between bodily desire and celibate duty, between the practices of spirituality and the obligations of domesticity. Some are so over-the-top as to become playful, humorous, even—such as the marzipan *mortadella* favored by the eighteenth-century Bolognese nuns mentioned above. Others draw inspiration from erogenous body parts: the pistachio-flavored pastries called *fedde* linguistically refer to and physically resemble buttocks; their most popular version is called *fedde del cancelliere*, or "chancellor's buttocks." In their original version, however, *fedde* outlined the image of female genitals: marzipan clamshells filled with oozing custard and jam. Still other confections, even as they are suggestive of erogenous body parts, seem self-forgetful of the eroticism coupled with violence that once shaped their origin. *Le minne di virgini* or *minne di Sant'Agata*, literally the "breasts of virgins" or "breasts of Saint Agatha," for instance, are edible icons of sexual sadomasochism; their sugar glaze highlights rather than cover the perversion they evoke. Believed to originate in the city of Palermo, at the Monastery of the Virgins—hence their name, *minne di virgini*, meaning "breasts of virgins"— the production of these small round cakes, glazed with white icing, spread southeast to the city of Catania, where a nipple-like cherry was added to their top and where their name was changed to *minne* (breasts) or *minnuzzi* (little breasts) *di Sant'Agata*, referring to the city's patron saint, a martyred young Christian named Agatha.

The breasts of Saint Agatha present too appetizing a shape for literature to ignore them, and thus make a sensuous appearance in an Italian twentieth-century bestseller set in nineteenth-century Sicily. "Why ever didn't the Holy Office forbid these cakes when it had the chance?" we might exclaim along with Don Fabrizio, the protagonist of the Sicilian novel *The Leopard* (1950), by Giuseppe Tomasi di Lampedusa. During an important party scene, when he realizes that his social class is doomed, Don Fabrizio (admirably played by Burt Lancaster in the 1963 Visconti movie adaptation) held in his plate "shameless 'virgins' cakes' shaped like breasts." At that moment Don Fabrizio, the narrator amusedly notes, "looked like a profane caricature of St. Agatha"—the martyr often depicted holding a platter with her breasts on it—and reflects: "St. Agatha's sliced-off breasts sold by convents, devoured at dances! Well, well!"[13]

As is the case with most traditional dishes, we do not know exactly when these pastries were invented. In summoning the name of Saint Agatha and the shape of her breasts, however, they take the eater back to the early centuries of Christianity, the age of the martyrs. These sweets connect that period, and one of its protagonists, to today—through centuries of cooking and baking the *minne*, centuries of remembering a dead young woman through prayer and through eating. Agatha's is a story about Christian celibacy, the rejection of paganism and marriage, and the embrace of martyrdom. The salacious elements of this narrative become the sweet and spicy ingredients of its transformation into food: the sexual arousal, feeding ability, and amputation of women's breasts, body parts that, like sweets themselves, balance between the childhood of those they feed and the pleasure of the adults titillated by them. The cakes thus become a pastry reproduction of the breast of this third-century Sicilian martyr, mutilated by the sword of the Roman governor of Sicily, Quintian (probably not his real name), during the persecutions of Christians under the emperor Decius—who was intent on uniting the empire under a common, mandatory, solidarity-building practice of sacrificing to the Roman gods. Many complied with or evaded his edicts, but a few resisted unto death. For female martyrs, resistance to paganism often involved faithfulness to virginity and refusal of marriage. Having rejected Quintian's marriage proposal, Agatha chooses death as a Christian virgin over life as a pagan wife—a death preceded by mammary amputation. Although the young woman's breast is miraculously healed by Saint Peter himself, who visits her at night and heals her without touching her, Agatha dies a martyr because the next day Quintian has her killed on burning coals.[14]

With its colorful mix of virginal young woman and lecherous older man, sexual passion and passionate religiosity, tortured martyrdom and eternal salvation, Agatha's story—a hagiographical narrative loaded with moral imperatives—we could read as the pernicious message that, for a woman, death is preferable to sexual defilement (a message claimed and reclaimed, for example, in the more recent story of Saint Maria Goretti, 1890–1902, who chose death over rape), and that dying young is heroic and glamorous, not to mention salvific. Agatha's legend can also be read as a barely disguised form of pornography—particularly if we glance at its sexy pictorial representations, dwelling on Agatha's bare torso and anguished facial expression as well as on the torturers' pleasure in her naked pain. More positively, however, Agatha's story contains the ultimate rejection of the patriarchal code that oppresses the vulnerable by objectifying and making dispensable women who choose celibacy, who reject a life of marriage and reproduction. Agatha and other young women martyrs of old, theologian Elizabeth Johnson tells us, "chose to define themselves in relation to God rather than husband," they "seized the opportunity to be protagonists in their own history," and "in that moment they meant something dear for the hope and self-understanding of their fellow Christians."[15] As such, Agatha's is a narrative of wholeness in spite of mutilation and of the persistence of the two—a gendered, female sexuality and identity that is double like its breasts and its lips—against the unifying desire of her torturer.[16] Agatha, in other words, does not submit to the pagan demand for uniformity, she insists on preserving her difference and the complexity of her sexual-yet-celibate identity. Thus, for example, Agatha's other breast refuses to be forgotten, even if it has to return in the eroticized depiction of her martyrdom: while in the Latin and Greek texts that recount her story only one breast is cut off, the paintings depicting the martyr in her glory display both breasts on a platter held by the saint herself. In many of the more gruesome depictions, those representing the martyrdom itself—the most famous of these is probably Sebastiano del Piombo's at the Pitti Palace in Florence (1520)—both breasts have been, or are about to be, mutilated.

The oldest documents telling of Agatha's martyrdom are found in Greek and Latin manuscripts: the earliest Greek ones date from the sixth century, the earliest Latin ones from the eighth. In these manuscripts, Agatha's reaction to the mutilation of her breast ("Then, raging, Quintian ordered that one of her breasts be tortured and then slowly torn out completely"), identifies it as the origin of the torturer's first food, Quintian's own mother's milk: "Impious, cruel, and inhuman tyrant, are you not ashamed of amputating from a woman what you yourself sucked in your own mother? But I have other intact breasts ["another breast," in the

Greek version] in the depths of my soul, with which I nourish all my senses, and since childhood I have consecrated them to Christ the Lord." Indeed the breast that Quintian had torn out grows back thanks to the intervention of Saint Peter: "Can you not see that, in exchange for the breast that you have torn out of me, another one has grown back through the power of my Lord Jesus Christ?"[17] In spite of her insistence on remaining celibate, Agatha identifies her breasted self as the active subject of motherhood rather than the passive object of sexual desire, and she herself alludes to a multiplication of breasts through divine intervention. Thus, the transformation of her story into a sweet dish was inspired by Agatha herself, the ingredients provided by her body, their visual and gustatory effects unimaginably more playful and delicious than visions of a mutilated torso may suggest.

Looking at the pictures of Saint Agatha in her glory, the iconography favored by holy cards and popular representations (we should remember that, and speculate why, Agatha is always identified with her temporary loss of breast rather than with her more permanent death on the coals), one is led to wonder whether it is also the platter's fault: Were the bakers and pastry chefs inspired by the fact that Agatha's breasts are usually displayed on what looks an awful lot like a cake stand? The most beautiful and best known of these images is Francisco de Zurbarán's "Saint Agatha," completed in 1633. In a peculiar mix of food, eroticism, and piety, breast-shaped sweets and breads are inspired by Agatha's mutilated breasts—or, in their original version, by the nuns' own, the residents of the Monastery of the Virgins, who give the convent its name through their sacrifice of sexual pleasure—and still today are routinely offered up to saint Agatha on her feast day, February 5, in Sicily and elsewhere. Their composition varies according to the cook, but the best consist of a glazed sponge cake topped by a cherry or an almond, filled with candied squash or pastry cream—the latter considered by many to be the only appropriate filling because, naturally, breasts should be filled with cream. All varieties of this sweet, regardless of the occasional differences, are light-colored half-spheres topped by a darker small round.

The two round body parts sitting on a platter visually connect the breasts of Saint Agatha, of flesh or cake, with the eyes of Saint Lucy: another Sicilian virgin martyr, another Sicilian sweet dish. Lucy died in the fourth century, a victim of Diocletian's persecution of Christians.

When Lucy visits Agatha's tomb to pray for a healing miracle, the saint tells her not only that she will be healed, but also that she will become the patroness of the Sicilian city of Siracusa—a position for which, Lucy assumes, celibacy is a requirement. Her jilted boyfriend does not take it well and turns her in to the authorities. But God makes Lucy's body so heavy that it is impossible for her tormentors to take her to a brothel in order to pierce her virginity, nor does she succumb to the fire in which the authorities try to burn her—though she is eventually killed by a sword driven into her belly by the consul Pascasius himself.[18] Lucy is usually represented carrying her two eyes on a platter, like Agatha her two breasts (a beautiful painting of this is by Palma the Younger, 1544–1628). Some legends say that her eyes were plucked out during her martyrdom, others that she herself plucked them out of their orbits so that their beauty would not prevent her from remaining celibate and marrying Christ. Eyes and breasts, two of each, both round, sexy, sweet, and easy to reproduce in the kitchen. The *uocci* (eyes) or *uccialeddi* (little eyes) are in fact also cookies, popular in southern Italy but especially in Lucy's native Sicily and the city she protects, Siracusa.[19]

Breast-shaped sweets in honor of a saint whose own breasts were mutilated as a prelude to rape and murder . . . eye-shaped sweets representing the plucked-out eyes of a devotee of the breastless woman. . . . Though I may well have crossed the line between what tastes good and good taste itself, the identification between women and food, particularly in the context of spiritual writings, does not end here, with what are after all, outside of Sicily, relatively obscure pastry items associated with the feast days of particular saints. As I hope to have made clear, these sweets are not some strange curios, novelty items worthy only of Ripley's *Believe It or Not*, but rather they embody in a particularly dramatic, spectacular way a connection very much alive in the Christian tradition and beyond: a connection between the pleasure of the female body, the pleasure it takes and the pleasure it gives, and the pleasure of sweets, and especially a connection between the meanings of the two. These complicated meanings include, but are not limited to, flavorful mixtures of religious asceticism and aesthetic delight, physical privation and supernatural grace, and pleasure that comes at a cost. Like the three loaves of bread which for years feed Mary of Egypt, like the cheese described in Hildegard of Bingen's *Scivias*, though more spectacularly—almost scandalously, one might say—the cakes bearing the name "breasts of Saint Agatha" display that significant and not always appetizing bond between food and the human body. This bond, made of flesh and made of language, derives from common shapes and shared functions, common pleasures and shared meanings. This bond confects sweets and stories that are equally capable of giving life or of destroying it, of constructing meaning or of slicing it away, of giving pleasure and of plucking it out.

6

How to Sift Flour, Wash Lettuce, and Serve Bread and Fish

LESSONS FROM ANGELA OF FOLIGNO

*H*ILDEGARD OF BINGEN, Elisabeth of Schönau, and Margaret Ebner were all cloistered nuns—Benedictines the first two, a Dominican the third. Francis of Assisi's spiritual partner Clare of Assisi (1193–1253), also a nun, was the first woman who wrote her own rule and had it approved by the pope. Clare's was an extremely austere rule, founded on poverty, labor, and the common life; its objective was to encourage intimacy with God. Thus, except for "the weak and the sick," none of those who are "healthy and strong," among Clare's nuns, "should eat anything other than Lenten fare, either on ferial days or feast days." On the contrary, says Clare, "we must fast every day except Sundays and the Nativity of the Lord, on which days we may have two meals"—indeed, "we who are well and strong always eat Lenten fare." But Clare was a wise leader, and knew well that "*our flesh is not bronze nor is our strength that of stone* (Job 6:12)." Thus, she "begs" her "dearly beloved sisters" to "refrain wisely and prudently from an indiscreet and impossible austerity in fasting," and to offer God a "*sacrifice* always *seasoned with salt* (Lev. 2:13)."[1] Francis likewise insists on fasting on Fridays and during Advent and Lent in his rule, but his brothers are not cloistered like Clare's followers, and so he tells them: "whenever necessity would come upon them, all the brothers, wherever they may be, may eat all foods which people can eat," and "they may eat and drink whatever their hosts have offered."[2]

The Franciscan movement did much to encourage the development of women's spirituality both within and outside the convent: Angela of Foligno, to whom this chapter is dedicated, was a widowed Franciscan Tertiary, never a nun. Following the reforms Francis brought on, women in large numbers decided to devote themselves to the love of Christ while remaining in the world, either as beguines (in northern Europe, and particularly the Low Countries—Hadewijch of Antwerp, encountered in chapter 2, was a beguine), or, in southern Europe, as Tertiaries (Franciscan, like Angela, or Dominican, like Catherine of Siena).[3] Especially starting in the second half of the thirteenth century, more and more lay female visionaries and ecstatics gained visibility and, in some cases, fame by practicing an intense asceticism and prayer life, and performing works of charity for the needy. Their experience of God was privileged and unmediated, their insistence on God's love unrelenting, their claims derived from nothing less than divine authorization. Authority was a problematic issue for holy women, who did not possess theological degrees and could not receive the sacrament of holy orders. What authority they did have was derived from revelation and visions; these were encouraged by ascetic practices, embodied spirituality, and the excesses of love: madness, ecstasy, desire, annihilation, often expressed in erotic or apophatic language. Surely there were male mystics, including some that used the affective language characteristic of their female counterparts (Meister Echkhart and Bernard of Clairvaux are often mentioned as examples), but men experienced visions less often than women did, and they did not use them as the basis for their authority as often or as profoundly as women did—as women, perhaps, had to. "Given all the other restrictions on women, along with the expectations of the time, it is not at all surprising that women might be more open than men to visionary experiences in the first place, make more of them when they occurred, and use them as the basis for their authority as teachers of theology and spirituality," writes scholar of mysticism Grace Jantzen. "Provided that they and others believed their visions to come from God, no stronger justification for their teaching role could possibly be required. Conversely, without such divine validation, who would bother to listen to a woman?"[4]

And many did indeed bother to listen to Angela of Foligno, dubbed in later centuries "*magistra theologorum*," (female) master of theologians. Her *Memorial* is a book notable for its reticence concerning practical details and physical matters, focusing instead on the soul's movement toward God in vision, prayer, good works, and the Eucharist: eucharistic hunger is an overwhelming presence in Angela's life. But why does this book say practically nothing about Angela's past and precious little about her present, yet dwells, while exploring her spirituality, not only on the Eucharist (Angela's great love) but also, to a lesser extent, on the sifting of flour, the serving of fish, the flavor of meat, the mixing of wine, the washing of lettuce? Why does it mention these foods at all?

Angela's writings tell us close to nothing about her life circumstances, and although conjectures abound, not much is known with certainty about her doings. She lived in Foligno, near Assisi, where she was probably born around 1248 and died in 1309—the only sure date in this woman's life. Angela refers in her writings to a sinful past, and although some scholars believe that this was a sexual sin, we in fact do not know why its memory was so painful to her. In her mid to late thirties, while she was still living with her family, Angela experienced a conversion to penance, and the desire grew within her to undertake a spiritual journey. Around the time of the death of her mother, her husband, and an unspecified number of children (a death she notoriously prayed for) Angela underwent a spiritual crisis. Probably around 1291 she made her profession in the Franciscan Third Order, gave away all her belongings, and lived with a female companion (Masazuola is what one important manuscript calls her), likely also her serving woman. During a pilgrimage to nearby Assisi, Angela was overtaken with divine passion and fell to the ground shrieking about God's love—a scandalous behavior that convinced her confessor and relative, known as Brother A., to order her never to go back to Assisi.

This same event, however, attracted Brother A.'s attention and motivated him to become Angela's spiritual adviser and scribe. For six years the two dialogued. Unable to write, Angela dictated her experiences in her Umbrian vernacular to Brother A., who wrote everything down in a hasty Latin (or, alternately, took notes that he later expanded). He then read and reread his manuscript to Angela so as to confirm its accuracy.[5] The text became known as Angela of Foligno's *Memorial*, and it recounts Angela's story from the time before her conversion until 1296. The story is divided in twenty short steps plus seven supplementary, longer ones; each step corresponds to a degree of self-transformation in and through God.

Angela had many followers, and her teachings inspired a series of texts, known as the *Instructions*, usually appended to the *Memorial*. Although they tell of Angela's life and work, these—with possibly two exceptions—were neither written nor dictated by her. She died on January 4, 1309, and was buried in Foligno.

Food is mixture; it is a place of convergence, for the mystic, between self and other, between humanity and divinity. Food for many mystic writers establishes a connection of the earthly with the divine, of corporeality with spirituality, of the mundane with the supernatural. This bond is in every sense a mixture, a "mesclun"—the Provençal term for a mix of lettuces (*misticanza*, in Italian): Angela's is a "mystical mesclun," to invoke her lettuce-washing episode. For just as eating involves mixing food in one's mouth (food that then gets mixed up with our body as it gives us energy or extra pounds), just as cooking involves mixing ingredients and techniques, so also reflecting on food may indeed allow, encourage, even, the mixture of critical speculation with a sympathetic experience of the mystic's path to the divine. The importance of mixing is particularly evident in, and materially supported by, late medieval cuisine, for nine recipes out of ten during this time period begin with the invitation to "chop" or "grind."[6] But food can at the same time also function as distinction and difference: separating—skin and bones from meat, peel and seeds from fruit, shells and stems from legumes, and so on—is a necessary initial step in many recipes. The physical process of separation in cooking has a social equivalent, for in the Middle Ages, "These distinctions through food, whereby the upper classes were meant to eat more 'refined' foods, leaving coarser foodstuffs to the lower classes, were commonplace."[7]

It is precisely on distinction that Angela's scribe dwells, in a metaphor located toward the beginning of the *Memorial*, a metaphor through which Brother A. explains, in a self-deprecating way, his secretarial role. Angela, he writes, "began to reveal her divine secrets to me, and I wrote these down. In truth, I wrote them, but I had so little grasp of their meaning that I thought of myself as a sieve or sifter which does not retain the precious and refined flour but only the most coarse."[8] The scribe is a cooking instrument and Angela's words are food. Her best words are the best flour, white flour, refined flour—nutritionally inferior, science today claims, yet traditionally preferred by Europeans as a distinctive marker of status and abundance: the refined nature of the flour mirrored the distinguished social position of its eaters. But the best flour, and with it Angela's most important words, goes right through the sieve; the coarser flour, including the bran, stays behind in the sieve, to make bread for the poor and fodder for animals—as well as the book produced by Angela and her scribe. The scribe is a sieve; Angela's words are grains of flour. Angela confirms this identification between writing and food a few lines down the page, when she notes that the scribe's words "were dry and without any savor" (137). Words, then, are indeed to be eaten, they are the grains of flour with which bread is made—regular bread as well as eucharistic bread. Conversely, in the Eucharist food is word, the Word. Ironically, however, the scribe is the means through which the best flour, the best words, are lost to us: he retains bran and whole-meal flour and lets go of the flour that is "precious and refined." Through this metaphor, then, the scribe is not only protesting his incompetence—one of his favorite topics—but he is also establishing the spiritual value of Angela's words through their association with the bread of life—and this association remains despite his incompetence, despite his loss, despite his inability to capture what is most valuable. His intervention, even within a rhetoric of humility, and in spite of the loss he causes, is a necessary step in the transition from nature to culture, from the raw to the cooked, from unprocessed grains to the flour that makes bread—from oral to written language, from the fleeting exchange of an experience to its enduring record. The transformation from spoken word to written paper is the step that will make Angela's words, and journey, immortal even as it breaks them asunder and only retains the worst.

With bread, and especially with the bread of life, comes wine. In contemporary America, wine is an odd and contradictory commodity: it is true that wine is associated with the dangers of alcohol abuse (accidents and other, slower deteriorations of physical and mental health) and that a certain puritanical ethic links wine consumption with spiritual perdition. But on the other hand wine, and particularly red wine, according to widely publicized medical studies carried out in the 1980s, protects from coronary heart disease. In the European past, wine had different connotations. By the late Middle Ages, for example, wine was seen in Italy as a nutritional necessity and no longer the symbol of aristocracy or the privilege of a few. But in the Christian West wine was much more than social symbol or nutritional essential. It is because of its Mediterranean origins and identity that Christianity "easily incorporated the products which constituted the material and ideological basis of that civilization as nutritional symbols and tools of worship: bread and wine became—following considerable controversy—quintessentially sacréd foods as symbols of the miracle of the Eucharist."[9] To the social, nutritional, and religious meanings of wine, we must add historically variable gender limitations. In the Greco-Roman world, for example, women were not allowed to drink wine, and for women temperance in drinking was considered essential to sexual temperance. Adultery and the drinking of wine were connected for the Romans, since both introduced in the guilty woman an alien life principle.[10] These strict classical laws concerning wine and women left a mark in the medieval period, when women's consumption of wine, though allowed, was regarded with suspicion, and injunctions to temperance, particularly for women, were the rule.

Immediately following the episode with the lettuce and a devil (to which I return below), an episode that caused a four-week-long crisis she characterized as a "period of sadness and trial," Angela receives a divine message that is both drinking advice and an effective spiritual counsel, one that itself realizes, at the psychological level, the very tempering it recommends in the consumption of wine:

> Shortly after this period of sadness and trial—only a little while after—I heard the following, and it was a source of great joy for me: "It is good that the wine be tempered with water." These words immediately dissipated my sadness and drove it away. All this was told to me on a Friday, beginning before None and continuing until after the meal. Until that day I had been in the state of the aforesaid sadness for more than four weeks. Then, that very day, I experienced the joy of which I have already spoken, but it was not strong enough to lift my sadness away completely; it only tempered it. (172–73)

The mixing Angela desires in flour, which instead gets separated by a scribe unable to perform correctly an operation Angela herself is incapable of (writing, and writing without excessive sifting) can instead be carried out with the literal and metaphorical consumption of wine: tempering is good, tempering heals sadness and in so doing increases in Angela faith and hope—virtues incompatible with, and healing of, grief and sorrow.

Angela's text shares with its reader a personal account of how bread and wine, foods once emblematic of the Mediterranean diet, became instead the foods connoting one specific medieval Mediterranean religion: Christianity. And even as bread and wine unite Christians, they also separate them from the non-Christians—Jews and Muslims—with whom they shared these markers of Mediterranean identity. Physical mixing is indeed central to Angela's considerations about the tempering of wine: because medieval wine was strong, even harsh, it was usually diluted with water to make it less dense and acidic; hence the Italian word *mescere*, meaning both "to mix" and "to pour." (Conversely, water was mixed with wine for reasons of hygiene: people were suspicious of water, seen as a carrier of germs and disease, and wine acted as an antiseptic of sorts.)[11] For Angela—and here is an effect of the mixing of food rather than of the distinction food enacts—wine tempered with water, under the advice of none other than God, leads to the dissipation of sadness, to the dilution of grief. Wine tempered with water is the invitation to temper sorrow with the joy of God, and to overcome difficulty and temptation through a conscious acceptance of divine grace.

One of the temptations at the root of Angela's month-long sadness occurred while she washed lettuce, presumably in her kitchen—the place of homemaking, of bodily sustenance, the place where the family identity is cooked up, served, processed, and reshaped. This episode is located in the fourth supplementary step of Angela's *Memorial*. This is also the step in which: (1) Angela is immersed in an intense three-day-long connection with God, so that she must ask God's permission "to depart from prayer in order to eat"; (2) Angela makes her poignant cry "This world is pregnant with God!"; (3) God announces to Angela that "he loves [her] more than any woman in the valley of Spoleto"; (4) at table, God takes away Angela's sins directly, without the normally needed intermediary of a priest in confession (169–72). It is, then, a step in which the female aspects of her spiritual quest are highlighted: eating and food preparation are described as connections between homemaking and mystical wandering, pregnancy is evoked as the connection between God and the world, being a woman binds Angela to God as lover and spouse, and the very womanhood that prevents Angela from becoming a priest encourages her unmediated connection with the divinity—at table, no less. Angela washes her lettuce on the same day that she asks God to "take away all [her] sins" and grant her absolution "when it came time to eat" (172). On the same day, then, food acts twice as a mediator between heaven and earth, between Angela's ordinary life and her mystical movement toward the divine. But finally, here is the story of Angela's lettuce washing:

On the very same day, while I was washing lettuce, I heard these words meant to trick me: "How can you consider yourself worthy to wash lettuce?" Clearly aware of the deception, I retorted not only with indignation but also with sadness, because these words made me doubt what I had previously heard, and I said "I am only worthy that God send me immediately to hell, and I am likewise only worthy to collect manure." (172)

Angela's dramatic answer shut the devil up—how could he respond? The ultimate self-disparagement that concludes the encounter, Angela's "I am only worthy that God send me immediately to hell, and I am likewise only worthy to collect manure," admits no reply and gives this woman the last word. Her response, swift and powerful, leaves the devil speechless. Angela's dramatic reply may be less related to the self-hatred it superficially conveys, than to the rhetorical self-deprecation so characteristic of women mystics—who often claim ignorance, stupidity, female inferiority, and then proceed to sophisticated analyzes of their divine encounters. But still, this is not an easy passage: what does this story really mean? It is not clear for example what the devil is saying: his question, "How can you consider yourself worthy to wash lettuce?" reads in the original Latin as, "*Quomodo es digna quod tu laves lactucas?*" A more literal translation would be "Are you worthy to wash lettuce?"[12] This question could be interpreted literally, as if Angela were *not even* worthy to wash lettuce, or it could also mean, ironically, is washing lettuce *the best* you can do? Is that all you are good for? The latter interpretation makes more "food sense": the devil's taunt would then imply that Angela belongs in the kitchen, doing menial chores, rather than in the grace of God's presence, where her spiritual journey should take her.

Like Martha in Luke's Gospel (who is gently chided by Jesus for working so hard instead of choosing, like her sister Mary, the better part—listening to the word of God) Angela is washing the lettuce herself, and it is here that the demon tries to get to her: Is washing lettuce too much or too little for her, who strives to be God's lover, God's spouse? Is the kitchen a place too lowly or too lofty for her, a would-be holy woman? Angela is not prodigal with the details of her daily life: Why does she include this one? What did she make of the experience and its retelling in the story of her love affair with God? Is it a purposeful depiction of her domestic abilities, an unwitting window into a life she prefers to keep private, an unself-conscious detail no different from the others in her tale? And, finally, those who seek in Angela a spiritual teacher are bound to wonder with her whether daily and prosaic activities such as the preparation of food are an occasion for sin (by taking us away from the presence of God), or the opportunity to demonstrate our spiritual strength in the face of evil. Is the quotidian transfigured into the sacred, or is holiness debased by contact with the ordinary? Do Luke's narrative of Martha and Mary and Angela's lettuce anecdote stage the conflict between headwork and housework, or do their stories work instead to dispel this opposition, represented in Angela's book as nothing less than a diabolical temptation?

Like the Italian *lattuga*, the word "lettuce" comes from the Latin "lactuca," meaning milky, a name due to the white look of its sap (evident in wilder varieties, not in the shrink-wrapped icebergs at the supermarket). Its milky sap traditionally linked lettuce to female sexuality in the Mediterranean region: Alciati's *Emblemata* (1546), for example, calls lettuce *amuletum Veneris*, Venus's amulet. Described by ancient humoral medicine as cold and soporific and as, alternately, aphrodisiac or "anaphrodisiac"—its opposite, that is—lettuce was regarded as a calming food. Because of this and because it was cold and wet and therefore a feminine food, lettuce was used to stimulate maternal milk production. Interestingly, today we still perceive salads to be feminine, along with quiche and dainty dishes. Renaissance culinary treatises indicate that in medieval and early modern Europe lettuce was eaten simply with vinegar and oil, much as it is today.[13] Salad, furthermore, commonly defined its eaters as Italian. Literary expatriate Giacomo Castelvetro (1546–1616), for one, associated the consumption of fruits and vegetables with the inhabitants of the Boot, and a 1569 text also claims, more tartly, that, "Salad food, according to those who live beyond the Alps, are almost exclusive to greedy Italians, who have appropriated the food of those base animals that eat raw greens."[14] It is perhaps to create some distance from the animals' way of eating greens that Castelvetro is very fastidious about what makes a good salad: "to make a good salad the proper way, you should put the oil in first of all, stir it into the salad, then add the vinegar and stir again. And if you do not enjoy this, complain to me." But he devotes even more effort to detailing how to *wash* salad properly: "it is important to know how to wash your herbs, and then how to season them."[15]

As straightforward as lettuce was and is to prepare—a simple process of washing and seasoning—Angela and the devil dwell on this step, perhaps as significant as the food item itself: Angela is washing the lettuce at the time of her temptation, much like Matrona of Perge was rinsing her greens (see chapter 1). Lettuce was and is synonymous with simplicity, purity, cleanliness: it was and is eaten plain, it must therefore be pure, unspotted, unwilted, and above all clean, uncontaminated by dirt or culinary technique. The act of washing lettuce, of purifying the gastronomically pure, reaffirms Angela's wholeness in the face of the dirty devils; it restates her holiness, her simplicity and cleanliness. She is what she eats and what she prepares; she identifies with the foods she comes in contact with. And that her food metaphors should center on preparation rather than ingestion is tied not so much to her improbable anorexia, I would claim, but more importantly to her role as one-time wife and mother first, and of caregiver of herself, still.[16] This confirms my impression that images of food preparation tend to be more important for holy women who did in fact prepare food on a regular basis for themselves and their family.

But Angela's family is dead. She is no longer cooking for them. Her husband, mother, and children have all died following the infamous prayer for which she is known even among nonspecialists (126). Angela is then cooking for herself and maybe for her companion Masazuola—or maybe for others yet. We do not know, and Angela is not telling—she is stingy with worldly details, though overwhelmingly generous in sharing the findings of her mystical path. And it is in the context of her spiritual story that the lettuce-washing episode appears as an instance of her relationship to God, which mixes her past as wife, mother, and daughter with her present as widowed, childless, and orphaned; a relationship that tempers her love of God in heaven with the demonic encounters in the kitchen; a relationship that sifts out of her contempt for food as an attachment to this world, her appreciation for the process of food preparation as a movement toward another space and another time.

Before leaving lettuce behind, let us turn to a story also featuring a religious woman, lettuce, and a devil, a story that appears in the first of Gregory the Great's *Dialogues* (594 CE):

> Once upon a time there was a greedy nun who came across a large and succulent lettuce in the monastery garden. She could not be bothered to say grace or to pause and bless the plant before seizing and eating it, with the result that she swallowed a small devil who happened to be sitting on one of the lettuce's leaves at the time. When she was finally cured of the fit which followed, the little devil came out of her mouth and addressed the exorcist in an aggrieved tone: "Why blame me? What have *I* done? I was sitting on this leaf, and *she* came along and swallowed me up."[17]

This lettuce story, like Angela's, in a way, "contains a lesson about greed, haste, and ingratitude, about cleanliness, and also about the possibility that all might not be well, even if our lettuces look fresh and green."[18] The episode also warns against the sin of gluttony as well as against ignorance about the vegetable world—since this careless nun should have known better than to ingest a food, lettuce, known for its connections with sexuality (as aphrodisiac or anaphrodisiac, no matter). The nun is punished for not remembering this crucial botanical detail.[19] In our context, the story might also reinforce the connections between food and otherworldliness, and particularly the hagiographic predilection of devils for lettuce. The purity and cleanliness of lettuce, doubled in Angela's book by her act of washing it, serve as a foil for the devil's rottenness and as an instrument, even, of divine grace.

Angela's passage ultimately asks a question that informs much feminist theology as well as feminist theory and criticism. In the secular terms of theory: Can women's experiences of embodiment—pregnancy and childbirth come to mind (how could I forget?), but, more modestly, less biologically, daily activities such as lettuce washing, food preparation, housekeeping—express the continuity between body and language, between the physical world and our symbolic constructions? Turning to the theological: Can housework, for example, have a meaning beyond female enslavement or bourgeois privilege, can it become part of a spiritual discipline? Or, must we believe that washing lettuce entangles us beyond repair to patriarchal oppression and to the limitations of drudgery work?

Feminist theologians are an optimistic bunch, but they too must ask whether the mundane can indeed be transfigured into something holy, or whether preoccupation with the ordinary—cooking and eating, say—debases holiness: again, the different roles of Martha and Mary come to mind. If this sounds like a predictable dilemma in a religion, like Catholicism, that encourages fasting and vaunts a long and respectable tradition of distrust toward the body and its pleasures, a tradition in which holy women are, sadly, more famous for their unfulfilled hunger than for their culinary and literary talents, these slim pickings ought to be accompanied by heartier fares—fares to be found at the kitchen table. In the writings of holy women, food—the preparation, the distribution, and the consumption of daily food, and not just the Eucharist—is often engaged as a salvific, life-enhancing support through which the authors emphasize and embrace the continuity, rather than the contradiction, between body and language, the physical and the spiritual, the personal and the political, the self and the other. These are what I like to call their cooking lessons.

Though an effective weapon against intruding devils and an expressive means to assert her worthiness, lettuce alone does not suffice for Angela's sustenance, and other life-giving foods are called upon in the course of her journey. Food is in Angela of Foligno's *Memorial* a privileged place for a dialogue with God and with spiritual beings. In the form of flour, it is an apt metaphor for the collaborative practice of living and writing one's life: all authors write for others, but this particular author could not have written without the physical help of a particular other, Brother A., described as we have seen as an imperfect yet vital sieve. Food marks the ethical moment, the moment of the encounter with the other and of becoming oneself through that encounter—even as human others are made divine by their mystical connection with God. We have read of this encounter in the lettuce-washing episode, and we read of it again, though with different ingredients, in Angela's distribution, along with her companion, of food to the sick and needy at a local hospital. This may be the most evident and relevant example in Angela's book of the ethical character of food practices, and of the connections they realize both physically and spiritually. I quote from the third supplementary step of the *Memorial*, a meditation on the identity of Christ's legitimate children:

> On Maundy Thursday, I suggested to my companion that we go out to find Christ: "Let's go," I told her, "to the hospital and perhaps we will be able to find Christ there among the poor, the suffering, and the afflicted." We brought with us all the head veils that we could carry, for we had nothing else. We told Giliola, the servant at the hospital, to sell them and from the sale to buy some food for those in the hospital to eat. And . . . she went ahead and sold our small head veils and from the sale bought some fish. We had also brought with us all the bread which had been given to us to live on. (163)

Angela and her companion bring food to hospital patients: bread from home and fish purchased through the sale of their head veils—figures of body and of femininity, yes, and symbols of the submission of women to men (women must cover their head while praying or prophesying as a sign of this submission, 1 Corinthians 11:5–6). But also, quite simply, these head veils represented all their possessions, for the two "had nothing else."

The gesture of stripping for Christ is an exquisitely Franciscan one, and early on in her journey Angela, like Francis, had taken off her clothes in order to follow, naked, the naked and crucified Christ. Stripping is chosen within a context of self-giving, where its figural value (the clothes stand in for the self) doubles up with the mystic's imitation of Christ to form a total sacrifice that divinizes even as it annihilates. Could this be yet another way—we have encountered one in the first chapter—to relive the paradox of kenosis, an image of Christ's own self-emptying (Phil. 2:5–8)? Indeed, "the greatness of the great Christian saints lies in their readiness to be questioned, judged, stripped naked and left speechless by that which lies at the centre of their faith."[20] Greatness lies in nothingness, and divinization in the eradication of the self. This questioning, judging, nakedness, and speechlessness are ways of imitating Christ and, more specifically, Christ's passion, in kenosis: a self-emptying that alone allows the mystic to get close to and even become one with God.

Angela's initial stripping is partially, metonymically repeated in this later hospital episode, where the only clothes she has left—her head veils—are given away and exchanged for food for "the poor, the suffering, and the afflicted." Out of little or nothing, out of herself, Angela too, like Christ once did, multiplies loaves and fishes to feed the hungry. And the experience is sweet. Angela uses the example of her hospital visit to show to her interlocutor, her scribe, that the flavor of eating from Christ's plate and drinking from his cup, for herself and her companion, is a sweet and not a sour one: "*non asperum sed dulce erat.*" Brother A. argues that their experience was sour, but Angela does not hesitate to contradict him and prove him wrong: "Christ's faithful one related a story to me through which she tried to show me that it was not sour but sweet" (162).[21] So she tells him the story of her and Masazuola's trip to the hospital, following which Angela's gift of ordinary food is rewarded with the consumption of a surrogate Eucharist.

And after we had distributed all that we had, we washed the feet of the women and the hands of the men, and especially those of one of the lepers which were festering and in an advanced stage of decomposition. Then we drank the very water with which we had washed him. And the drink was so sweet that, all the way home, we tasted its sweetness and it was as if we had received Holy Communion. As a small scale of the leper's sore was stuck in my throat, I tried to swallow it. My conscience would not let me spit it out, just as if I had received Holy Communion. I really did not want to spit it out but simply to detach it from my throat. (163)

Conquering one's disgust and showing love for one's neighbor despite his repulsive body is a recurrent aspect of the mystical quest that is difficult for our modern sensibilities to appreciate: Angela drinks the water used to wash a leper's sores, Catherine of Siena swallows the pus oozing out of a woman's tumor, Margaret Mary Alacoque ingests the vomit of a sick fellow nun . . . all this is hard to take. Psychoanalyst Julia Kristeva explains these actions with the concept of abjection and the abject, and I return to this in chapter 9. But how can we possibly find personal meaning, be it ethical or spiritual, in repulsion itself, and share in the pleasure experienced by the mystics who did perform these extreme acts of connection to the other?

The story of Francis of Assisi's kiss to the leper might be of help here. In this episode, accepting the other, making the other feel loved and welcome, is more directly expressed, more understandable than Angela's or Catherine's filth-drinking stories: we can imagine that the leper, outcast because disgusting and contagious, appreciates a physical contact usually denied him, and certainly the act of touching and caring for the untouchables is in itself redeeming for both oneself and the other. It is redeeming and it is rewarding.[22] Many have been moved by Mother Teresa's mission among the dying pariahs, as untouchable to many of their compatriots as Angela's bowl of dirty water is to us. In recognition of her sacrifice, Christ gives himself to Angela directly, without intermediaries, precisely in that bowl of dirty water, in its most disgusting particle—human flesh before and not only after transubstantiation. Christ communicates himself to a woman who would ordinarily need the collaboration of a priest in order to receive the sacrament of Communion. Christ tastes sweet, in this abject piece of flesh, and it is thanks to this "intense sweetness" that his beloved, like the bride of the Song of Songs, recognizes him. Once again Christ shows his preference for Angela (he had already declared more than once his love, greater for her than for any other woman in her region, 171–72), and she is rewarded with a food that is not really a food—but rather scab, and also Eucharist—for her gift of herself, and of all her possessions, materialized in loaves and fishes.

"Tell me what you eat and I will tell you who you are," Brillat-Savarin famously said.[23] So, what do Angela's food choices—the food she eats as well as the food she imagines, prepares, and distributes—tell us about who she was? How does her writing about food help her reader understand this woman's identification with Jesus through suffering and union in the

Trinity, her very transformation into Christ—not to mention her experience of darkness, of the abyss, and her simultaneous emphasis on God's love? Angela's relational treatment of food witnesses her understanding of self as founded in human and divine relationships. The eucharistic bread Angela eats, physically resembling the meat or flesh it has become at consecration—the flesh of God, no less—involves her in the mystical body of Christ. Her distribution of fish and loaves to the sick enacts the same participation through a sharing of food that, although it does not involve consumption, leads to it eventually—the eucharistic scab of the leper Angela ingests: another meat, another flesh. Her washing of lettuce results in a participation of the daily into the divine, of the natural into the supernatural, and in a battle between good and evil where food—a cold, wet, feminine food—is the weapon of choice.

In these episodes, each and every one of Angela's complex food expressions, however ordinary, can potentially turn into a transubstantiation of sorts. In the words of French scholar Louis Marin, "One might say that every culinary sign is Eucharistic in some sense and to some extent; or, to pursue this vein of thought one step further, one might say that all cookery involves a theological, ideological, political, and economic operation by the means of which a nonsignified edible food stuff is transformed into a sign-body that is eaten."[24] This is what occurs in the episode of the lettuce and the devil: washing lettuce, with all its more generic connotations of purity and sexuality, is in Angela's experience a homemaking act, an episode of daily routine, which in being dictated to her scribe—a scribe who is to Angela's words as a sieve, a defective sieve, is to flour—becomes charged with supernatural significance: diabolic temptation, first of all (be it pride or self-deprecation), but also resistance to that temptation, upturning of its significance, and reaffirmation of her spiritually privileged position. It is hard to miss Angela's evangelical transformation of the loaves and fishes she brings to the hospital into a eucharistic sign—an example of God's direct empowerment of the woman mystic. The lettuce-washing story is perhaps less dramatic, though no less eucharistic. Cookery, of which food washing is a preliminary step, reaches into the realms of theology, ideology, politics, and economics. And so does the washing of lettuce, a homemaking and, because it is done in God's kitchen, a mystical practice through which Angela transforms foodstuff into sign, inert object into living body, vegetable matter into the stuff of theology.

7

How to Skin Stockfish and Chop Stew

MARGERY KEMPE'S SACRIFICES

*T*HE WOMEN IN GOD'S KITCHEN are, by and large, amateur cooks. Mary of Egypt made do with purchased loaves and desert herbs, while Matrona savored the greens she herself had so thoroughly washed. Also in the East, Athanasia, endowed with more money than cooking skills, showed her love for Matrona's convent by arranging for bread to be delivered there by the local bakery; Theodora, on the other hand, fully participated in monastic life by grinding wheat, baking bread, and cooking food. Hildegard writes in detail in her scientific treatises about how to prepare food and cook it, but given the hierarchical structure of medieval German convents, it is doubtful that she—an educated noblewoman—actually did any of the kitchen work. The same holds true for Elisabeth of Schönau and Margaret Ebner: the devil would be unlikely to surprise them while they were washing lettuce—as he did instead with Angela of Foligno, a relatively uneducated laywoman, as well as a wife and mother. But, in seventeenth-century Mexico, Sor Juana, one of the most educated people in her continent, spent much time in the kitchen, boiling and frying in butter and sugar, as a way of learning; at around the same time in Italy, Cecilia Ferrazzi made lasagna in order to show God's work;

and a few decades later in the United States and on her Italian journey, Elizabeth Seton cooked so as to sustain and heal the ones she loved. As a daily part of homemaking, cooking participates in the creation and, especially, the preservation of the self and of the community one belongs to. "The activities of homemaking," writes a political theorist, "give material support to the identity of those whose home it is."[1] Rather than being statically fixed, this home-based identity is always in process, always subject to change and growth, because it is located in history and because it is developed in relation to others—themselves changing and growing beings. This is the fluid identity of those holy women who did not hesitate to trade places with their old selves, to abandon their former lives, in order to explore new worlds; it is the malleable identity of those women whose sense of who they were was transformed by the transformation of their lives in the kitchen and in God.

Cooking practices intersect at various points in history with the spiritual practices of holy women. Saint Agatha was the object rather than the subject of cooking, herself a dessert and not a pastry chef (she was also the object, and not the subject, of writing). Angela of Foligno cooked and served; and the protagonist of this chapter, the medieval English mystic Margery Kempe, in addition to cooking for her family, was also a professional in the food and drink business—before God called her to a different path. If Angela's texts are generously seasoned with food references, more abundant yet is the table set by Margery, who speaks of food consistently and with too much gusto for anyone to count her among the holy anorexics. Margery Kempe was a troublesome and eccentric English woman, whom my former teacher Valerie Lagorio so appropriately called a "noisy contemplative."[2] Born around 1373, Margery married local businessman John Kempe in 1393, quickly became pregnant, and had fourteen children with him over the course of twenty years of marriage. We do not know how many of them survived to adulthood: Margery does not write about them other than briefly mentioning a son and very generally referring to them in some of her prayers. Neither do we know much of Margery's own childhood and youth: she does tell in her book that she never learned how to read—unusual for a middle-class girl of her time—and that she committed an unknown sin, which was to haunt her for the rest of her life. As to her marriage, it seems to have been a happy one.

After the physical, emotional, and spiritual difficulties experienced following the birth of her first child, Margery went into the food and drink business: first brewing, then grain milling. Both businesses eventually failed, and this is when, following a series of compelling visions, Margery turned to loving Christ as her primary occupation. She was about thirty-five years old. Love of Christ involved asceticism and, particularly, chastity, and Margery attempted for several years to talk her husband into celibacy. She finally succeeded at the age of forty, once she proposed to pay John's debts in exchange: Margery's father's death had left her an inheritance, and her husband's business was bad. At this time Margery started her spiritual and geographical travels, to Lincoln, Canterbury, Norwich (where she sought spiritual guidance from Dame Julian, the mystic of the hazelnut), then Rome and Jerusalem as well as to Santiago de Compostela in Spain. But Margery was no travel writer, and while ecstatic experiences of God and generally less positive experiences with locals and fellow travelers figure prominently, Margery had little to say about the places she visited. It was her spiritual journey that mattered most. When she finally returned to Lynn in the 1420s, Margery nursed her sick husband for several years until his death in 1431. During this time, she hired at least two different scribes to record her life story in writing, and this process of putting down on paper her experiences was a troubled and complicated one, as the proem of the book makes clear. Unlike Angela's scribe, who translated into Latin what Angela said in Italian, Margery's dictations were taken directly in her vernacular Middle English. Margery's later trip to Norway and Germany provides the content of the second part of her book. Upon her return, she completed the dictation of her autobiography, which ends rather abruptly and anticlimactically with her coming home.

Margery is mentioned in a 1438 town record, though of her life after that date we know nothing. Her book was not discovered until 1934, when the scholar Hope Emily Allen, while examining a manuscript at a private Lancashire library, found that it was the massive autobiography of a middle-class English woman—indeed, the first autobiography in the English language: *The Book of Margery Kempe*.

Three idiosyncrasies may be said to characterize Margery Kempe. First: Her transgressive, polemical decision to dress in white, despite the ridicule that a forty-year-old mother of fourteen dressing like a girlish virgin aroused; although she was a wife and a mother, the white costume signals her honorary, spiritual virginity, and that she must not be approached sexually (dress was often an important trait in women's holiness: several centuries later, Gemma Galgani also drew much attention to herself by donning day after day a black outfit that looked much like a religious habit, even though she was not—though she wanted to be—a nun). Second: Margery's irrepressible outbursts of loud and public sobbing, weeping and crying at the sheer thought of divine love. Third: Margery's repeated, almost obsessive references to food and drink even at the height of her spiritual experiences. Indeed I would make the same claim about food in Margery's *Book* as a critic makes about her tears, namely that "Margery's affective mourning exerts a unifying effect that is twofold, binding together both the *Book* itself and, at times, the women represented in it."[3] Food and drink, too, unify the various parts of the book, as well as connecting the women represented in it: Margery and Mary of Nazareth, as well as the female friends met in her travels.

The first important appearance of food in Margery's autobiography marks the desire to prepare food for herself and to eat it as a clear sign of health. With the traumatic birth of her first child, Margery underwent a difficult period: physical illness gave way, after a failed confession involving the unnamed sin of her youth (which no amount of fasting on bread and water, as the very first paragraph of the book recounts, could erase), to mental disturbance—so serious as to cause her to be "tied up and forcibly restrained day and night" for eight months in order to halt her violently self-destructive behavior.[4] The vision of a loving Christ brought her back to happiness and calm. Margery's first act as a healthy person, immediately after the calming vision of Christ, is to request the keys to the buttery, i.e., the pantry:

> And presently the creature grew as calm in her wits and her reason as she ever was before, and asked her husband, as soon as he came to her, if she could have the keys of the buttery to get her food and drink as she had done before . . . her husband, who always had tenderness and compassion for her, ordered that they should give her the keys. And she took food and drink as her bodily strength would allow her, and she once again recognized her friends and her household. (43)

As a food professional, Margery prepared food and drink not just for herself and her family. First, she was a brewer, "one of the greatest brewers in the town of N. for three or four years until she lost a great deal of money, for she had never had any experience in that business. For however good her servants were and however knowledgeable in brewing, things would never go successfully for them" (44). Margery's brewing skills were not enough to counteract what was probably poor business sense likely combined with undesirable microorganisms in the air of her alehouse, "For when the ale had as fine a head of froth on it as anyone might see, suddenly the froth would go flat, and all the ale was lost in one brewing after another, so that her servants were ashamed and would not stay with her." Margery then "thought how God had punished her before—and she could not take heed—and now again by the loss of her goods; and then she left off and did no more brewing" (44). On the flat surface of her ale, she read the writing of God's will, and she read her future.

In late-medieval England brewing was a vital enterprise; people normally avoided water, which was often contaminated, and thus drank ale as a regular part of their daily diet. Brewing, furthermore, was a small-scale, unorganized, local business in the hands of women. Ale was brewed with fermented malted barley, since beer (i.e., ale brewed with hops) only became common in England as the fifteenth century progressed. Hops contain natural preservatives that ale lacked, and thus before the advent of beer it was necessary to brew frequently that beverage that medieval people consumed in such vast amounts: ale deteriorated very quickly and it tasted best when produced locally (so much for local microbreweries being a contemporary fad!). Before the introduction of hops and beer in the fifteenth century, brewing was done primarily by women: "alewives" or "brewsters" (both terms referred to female brewers only), who sought to supplement the household income. Significantly, with the introduction of beer and the transformation of the brewing industry into a centralized, large-scale, profitable industry, women were squeezed out of it and men came to dominate it.[5]

After her ale-brewing failure, Margery undertook another food-based business: the grinding of grain (44–45). This business venture did not last long, either, though it was her failure as an alewife that most permanently left its mark on Margery's psyche and taste buds: in the rest of her book she no longer refers to ale but prefers wine—the eucharistic drink—and, on an occasion, even the still uncommon beer. She gives her good-quality wine to an old needy Roman woman, taking her sour wine in exchange, so as to better serve her and, through her, Christ; she herself receives very good wine from an abbot as a way of comforting her tears; a housewife steals wine from her husband's locked-up reserve in order to take care of Margery, who is "terribly thirsty" (since food was usually preserved by salting, it is believed that thirst in the medieval and early modern period was likely experienced more acutely than today)—"begging her to conceal the pot and cup, so that when the good man came back he might not notice it" (169). Margery's own "tears are angels' drink, and are truly to the angels like spiced and honeyed wine" (200).

In prebottling medieval times, the wine drunk in England was new and harsh. Honey and spices made this drink more palatable to medieval people, who tended to have a sweet tooth, anyway. So it is "a good hot drink of gruel and spiced wine" that busy, solicitous Margery offers Mary of Nazareth in order to comfort her after the death of her son Jesus: in her meditations on the Passion, Margery is actively involved in the care for both Jesus and Mary: "she made for our Lady a good hot drink of gruel and spiced wine, and brought it to her to comfort her, and then our Lady said to her, 'Take it away, daughter. Give me no food but my own child,'" to which Margery tried to console her: "'Ah, blessed Lady, you must comfort yourself, and cease from your sorrowing'" (236). The preparation and serving of this hot drink of gruel and spiced wine seal the reality of Margery's spiritual imagination, and affirm her ability to nurture in a bodily fashion the mother of God. Indeed, in a previous vision, Margery recounted how she had maternally nourished Mary of Nazareth herself with "good food and drink" from before Mary's own birth—by being Saint Anne's "maid and servant" when she was "great with child"—until she was twelve (52). And during Mary's pregnancy, Margery accompanies her "bearing with her a flask of wine sweetened with honey and spices." (53).

The preparation and ministrations of food complete and complicate Margery's relationship with Mary, usually described as being based on identification. Critics have related Margery's identification with Mary to the historical reverence for Mary the mother of God, characteristic of women in Margery Kempe's region, East Anglia.[6] Margery's *imitatio Christi*, her imitation of Christ, is thus also her *imitatio Mariae*, an imitation of Mary. Not only does Margery affectively identify with Mary as the mother of Christ—with the consequent abundance of tearful sorrow at the contemplation of his Passion—but Margery also is so identified with the role of mother that her maternal performance turns on Mary herself: by nourishing Mary "with good food and drink" while Mary was a child, by comforting Mary after the death of her son with "a good hot drink of gruel and spiced wine," Margery mothers Mary even as she becomes one with her. Margery did bear fourteen children, after all, and identifies her first major spiritual crisis as having taken place after giving birth for the first time—with the return to normality and divine grace being signaled by a return to food and drink, to the buttery.

Margery's maternal identification with Mary as Christ's mother and with Mary's own mother is composed of more than one layer. Though this second maternal role taken up by Margery, the role of Christ's grandmother, as it were, is not literally that of Saint Anne, Margery clearly represents a mother figure nevertheless. It is true that Margery's maternal relation to Christ is not particularly original, following a well-established devotional tradition. Caroline Walker Bynum has noted that both the medieval female laity and the medieval female religious acted out maternal roles in their spiritual activities, and that their maternal behavior toward Jesus Christ represents one of the ways in which women transposed their "ordinary nurturing roles over into their most profound religious experiences."[7] Yet in the passages cited above Margery is mothering not so much Christ, but Mary of Nazareth, Christ's mother, in a touching example of that mother-daughter bond so rarely represented in Western narratives—as writers and critics have rightly lamented.[8]

Margery takes care of Mary at her most vulnerable time with hot gruel, because Margery Kempe loved her wine, and she loved food just as much. This positive attention, this delight in food distinguishes Margery from those medieval women who fasted prodigiously and feasted on the Eucharist exclusively. Margery does not reject regular food, nor does she feel sick in its presence—on the contrary. Although like all Christians of her time she practiced periodic fasting and abstinence, there is no sense of self-starvation in Margery's writings. And this is what impelled me to reflect on wine, and stockfish, and stew: as the eloquent examples of Margery Kempe and Angela of Foligno make clear, it is not only in prayer and fasting, but also in eating and cooking that demonic temptation and divine grace, both leading to self-knowledge and conversion, can unfold in a woman's life, transforming it and conforming it to divine desire.

Food gave Margery physical and spiritual strength. Food is what she repeatedly shared with her friends, creating relationships, celebrating life. Eating alone—a common practice in today's busy world—is clearly regarded as undesirable in this book, and letting others eat alone is uncharitable at best. Though her fellow pilgrims often banned Margery from their table on account of her annoying habit of loud weeping and sobbing, so that "she ate her meals alone by herself," others, such as the Franciscan

Grey Friars, "took her in with them and seated her with them at meals, so that she should not eat alone" (109). Food is, in Margery's own words, where she can find "joy and comfort" (240). When she is faint, her fellow travelers put spices in her mouth (103). Margery is most explicit when she admits that the eating of meat is what she loves best in this world (50)—a heavy statement, given the connection between meat and sexuality (which meat was believed to excessively encourage) and the consequent need for its penitential renunciation. Margaret Ebner, for example, did not share Margery's carnivorous enthusiasm: "They wanted to give me meat, but in my mouth it seemed like something impure, totally unappealing as if it were uncooked. Then it was revealed to me by God that it was not His will that I eat it. Ever since then I have always done without meat."[9]

It is precisely the eating of meat and drinking of wine, that sweet spiced wine, that God intermittently asked Margery to give up: "But also, my beloved daughter, you must give up that which you love best in this world, and that is the eating of meat. And instead of meat you shall eat my flesh and my blood, that is the true body of Christ in the sacrament of the altar" (51). Through the sacrifice of meat and wine, foods that inspire desire and not revulsion, God pushes Margery both to become stronger and to prove that she is strong already; she abstains from meat and wine, for example, for four years before starting on her pilgrimage (97). "Vegetarianism," as Margaret Visser explains, "was for strong people. It was closely allied with fasting, where people retire from human fellowship (of which sharing a meal is a primary symbol) to think and pray and steady their resolve. The word 'fast' and the word 'steadfast' are both cognate with German *fest*—'firm.'"[10]

Food and drink, then, and abstinence from them—especially meat and wine, paired by Roland Barthes too as belonging to a "sanguine mythology"[11]—are some of the ways in which Margery presents herself to us as an everyday, plain, yet strong witness to God. Food and drink, material as well as metaphorical, also show a quotidian rather than a heroic Margery Kempe, a woman of God who, instead of sublime renunciations, lifelong trials, terrible penances, presents us with the small details of a domestic, undignified, humble life, whose difficulties are often quite similar to the ones many of us encounter on a daily basis. Her fasting is not self-destructive but self-empowering, both proving her strength and improving it: "For, my beloved daughter, this was the reason why I ordered you to fast, so that you should the sooner obtain your desire, and now it is granted to you. I no longer wish you to fast, and therefore I command you in the name of Jesus to eat and drink as your husband does" (60).

It is not only meat in general that Margery Kempe refers to. She sometimes speaks, specifically, of stew—a popular food staple in Margery's time, at least among those who could afford it. The regular, weekly gifts of hampers filled with all the ingredients necessary for a nourishing stew, "enough to serve her with two days' food," including a bottle of good wine, seal the friendship between Margery and her Italian companion Dame Margaret Florentyne: even though the two women could not speak the same language, Dame Margaret shared her lavish Sunday meal with Margery, serving "her food with her own hands" (130) at a time when our English mystic would have otherwise needed to beg for food—as she frequently did at other times during her travels. The stew, with its precious meat, became for Margery the opportunity to praise and thank God for the loving companions sent her way.

As a pilgrim and a beggar, Margery could ask and be gifted with food, yet she could not, for obvious reasons, reciprocate in kind. So what she does offer in gratitude for all she received from others is a prayer of self-giving. May her body, nourished by the stew of friends, become, through God's intercession, a sacrifice of stew: "If it were your will, Lord, I would for your love, and for the magnifying power of your name, be chopped up as small as meat for the pot" (181). She offers herself as gift of stew both for the love of God and, later, for the love and salvation of all human beings, when she quotes God's words to her: "Furthermore, daughter, I thank you for the general charity that you have towards all people now living in this world, and all those that are to come until the end of the world: that you would be chopped up as small as meat for the pot for their love, so that I would, by your death, save them all from damnation if it pleased me" (245). By becoming, at least metaphorically, "*as small as flesche to the potte*,"[12] Margery undergoes a profound transformation, even a sort of transubstantiation: from subject of religious experience to object of sacrifice, from object of love—Dame Florentyne's gifts of stew—to its subject through self-sacrifice. Instead of investing literal words with allegorical meaning, daily occupations with a supernatural interpretation, Margery performs the opposite task: it is the otherwise incomplete spiritual vision that she equips with a delightful measure of daily reality, a pot of stew. This constant anchoring to the solid domestic sphere manages to keep Margery's exceptional story naturally modest, simply understandable.

More amusing is the analogy Margery indirectly calls up between this offering of self for the love of humanity and an earlier episode in which the same expression is used in a rather different way. In the fourth chapter of her book, Margery undergoes a sexual temptation, "the sin of lechery," she calls it, with respect to "a man whom she liked." This man tells her that "for anything, he would sleep with her and enjoy the lust of his body," warning her to stay away from him because he would do anything to have his way with her. Margery falls for it, even though "he did it to test what she would do," and after a night when sex with her husband seemed "abominable," she goes in search of the man who had made her a much more attractive offer. Well, "he would not for all the wealth in this world," in fact, "he would rather be chopped up as small as meat for the pot" (49–50). The connection between meat and flesh is again invoked, though the context is now quite different: it is not sacrifice that impels the analogy, nor a movement toward the other, but rather a retreat from the other, away from Margery. Death, for this man, and a gruesome death at that, is preferable to having sex with Margery.

Meat and flesh can represent desire and its renunciation, strength as well as the weakness that often takes its place. That in medieval and early modern times meat was not always allowed, much less available, is also reflected in Margery's memoirs. So let us turn to another common medieval foodstuff, stockfish. Stockfish is dried cod, similar to the better known salted cod—popularly known as *baccalà* in Italy, *bacalhau* in Portugal, *morue* in France. Stockfish was an important part of the English diet during the Middle Ages, and large amounts of stockfish were imported into England at that time, mostly from Iceland and Norway (today the latter is still the prime producer of stockfish). Stockfish was so hard that, in addition to being soaked for several days, it had to be hammered with a special hammer for as long as one full hour! On the other hand, under the right storage conditions, it keeps for years preserving a high nutritional value. Before refrigeration, this was a considerable asset (though W. H. Auden commented, about dried fish, that "the tougher kind tastes like toenails, and the softer kind like the skin off the soles of one's feet").[13] Nowadays, stockfish and salt cod have been replaced in many households by canned tuna and frozen fish sticks (since the decline of religious observances, however, overall consumption of fish among Christians, despite the fact that Christ himself was piscivorous, has decreased considerably).[14]

Margery Kempe must have eaten her share of stockfish, during the many Wednesdays, Fridays, Saturdays, and Lents of her life. And she must have prepared and cooked quite a bit of it for her husband and fourteen children. So it is not strange to read two metaphors revolving around stockfish in her writings. The first, rather gruesome one, is from God's words to Margery regarding the dangers of the Christian life: "You shall be eaten and gnawed by the people of the world just as any rat gnaws the stockfish. Don't be afraid, daughter, for you shall be victorious over all your enemies" (51). In the next stockfish metaphor, on the other hand, God spoke of Margery's love in terms reminiscent of the warnings in a recipe for preparing stockfish: "Daughter, you are obedient to my will, and cleave as fast to me as the skin of the stockfish sticks to man's hand when it is boiled" (127)—or, to get a flavor of the Middle English original, "*Daowtyr, for thu art so buxom to my wille and clevyst as sore onto me as the skyn of stokfysche clevyth to a mannys handys whan it is sothyn.*"[15] The mingling of love and food is not new, nor is the central place food holds in religious belief and ritual. But as we read the autobiography of this brave and unconventional lady, the image of love as sticky stockfish skin jumps out of the page to claim a place deeper and wider than that of a trite simile. It is a reminder that spiritual hunger can motivate our actions much as physical hunger compels us to put food in our mouth. It confirms that the preparation of food involves a gift of self. As our fingers, hands, skin touch the various ingredients, getting them ready for the pot and for the table, an impalpable part of us—love?—cleaves to them, making cooking an intimate act of love. And Margery's stubbornly sticky skin of the stockfish physically reminds her reader of other, more pleasantly sticky effects of food. Cooking, and more commonly eating together binds people to their loved ones, and, in celebrating life, the breaking of bread joins us in our shared need for both food and one another—as the skin of a stockfish is bound, tied fast, connected to the hand that prepares (to eat) it. For as God says to Margery, echoing Isaiah 49:15–16, "I may not forget you and how you are written upon my hands and my feet" (65). It is at table, too, that God wants Margery to remember him as her lover: "keep me always in your mind as much as you can, and do not forget me at your meals, but always think that I sit in your heart" (224).

Food can be used to think of numerous social and cultural issues, ranging from health and politics to ethics and aesthetics and more. Through food, through Margery's stockfish and stew, we can sample cultures (England, for example) and get a taste of the past (the Middle Ages). By at least occasionally fasting, we can have an idea of what it feels like to go truly hungry—as much of the world's population does and has done through the ages (food supplies were most certainly precarious during medieval times). Eating binds us to our own past as well, since, as Joyce Carol Oates points out, "eating is one of the very few volitional human activities—perhaps it is the single one—that continues uninterrupted from birth to death, its source 'infantile' and its refinements 'adult.'"[16] We have a wealth of sources about food and eating—and starving—in the Middle Ages. Scholars have devoted many efforts to discovering who ate what and how. But I propose that in images of real food from holy women who, although they did not write specifically about food, still clearly loved and thought and prayed about their food, we can find reflections that menus and recipes may not be able to convey, at least not in the same way, and likely not to the same depths. These writings may be hard to find, for, as Buddhist Abbess Koei Hoshino has pointed out in an interview, "When we examine various religions we find that those engaged in ascetic practices are not those engaged in preparing the meals. Usually the ones who prepare meals do not do the spiritual practices. . . . It is only in the Zen sect that the priests also cook and consider it part of their spirituality."[17] But what the abbess is not taking into account is the experience of women like Margery Kempe and Angela of Foligno, holy women who gave themselves fully to their spiritual path after a life devoted to cooking and caring for a family, and who to some extent continued to take care of their own and others' bodies through meal preparation.

Margery Kempe's book shares with its reader a reverent attitude about food. In the continuity between its material and its spiritual aspects, food may fit in and complete a person's view of the world. Food may mean something beyond what we eat, food is about love and life and, yes, death, too. Years of feeding herself, her children, her husband, impressed this knowledge in Margery's mind, her body, and her soul. Margery sustained life through love and cooking, and the love she put into her preparation of food spilled on the food itself. Thus, it is fitting to conclude with a memorable scene recounted toward the end of her book but chronologically situated shortly after her conversion. I propose that we accept and read against the grain an anecdote that Margery's supporters instead dismissed as a slanderous falsity. Sitting at a rich table on a fish day, Margery chose to eat the delicious pike instead of the humbler red herring, exclaiming: "'Ah, false flesh, you would now eat red herring, but you shall not have your will.' And with that she set aside the red herring and ate the good pike" (288). Penance is eschewed in favor of pleasure. But rather than hastily reject the anecdote as false and even defamatory, we could instead choose to read this story as the portrayal of a table situation where, in tune with her previous movements between feasting and fasting, Margery identifies the excessive abstinence of red herrings as sinful, and enjoyment of the good pike as one of the gifts available in God's kitchen.

Margery Kempe's story and words are at once modern and alien to contemporary sensibilities. Like many married people today, Margery had to reconcile her relationship to her family of origin with her attachment to her family by marriage, the business of brewing and grinding with the work of family life, her love for the world with the love of God. Her choice of celibacy within marriage seems as odd today as it was desirable among holy women of her time. Her inner and outer travels brought her, as they may also bring us, to places of peace and places of strife, to spiced and honeyed wine and to parching, unquenchable thirst. Margery's relationship to food was no less complex. She willingly gave up what she loved best, meat, in honor of a God who gave her so much more—and this in spite of invitations to be content with earthly meat, and pressures to renounce the desire to become one with the divine (97). Margery took to heart the invitation to perform corporal works of mercy as she took care of and fed those who needed food and drink more than she. She cheerfully took on the humiliating task of begging for food, and was recompensed with hampers of stew ingredients and the friendship of like-minded women. Her connection to women continued in her visions, as she is given to nurture with food and drink Mary herself—who, like Margery, was a mother, and like Margery was a woman alone. Whether Mary appreciated the care received from Margery we do not know, but her son required much more of our English mystic than just a bowl of gruel—however spiced, however sweet. In Margery's visions of Christ's love, it is not enough to provide gruel and spiced wine. Margery herself must become food: although she is to suffer like a rat-gnawed piece of stockfish—perhaps unwittingly confirming that her ideas and her experiences are as desirable to the people in this world as stockfish is to a rat—Margery will remain stubbornly attached to her love, sticky as the skin of a stockfish, clinging to her maker. And if, in the end, she may even be asked to be cut up like meat for the pot, so be it, she readily says. The spiritual images of a woman who devoted years of her life to work and family propose a reverence before food that sees the divine in lowly activities even as it sanctifies the quotidian, through their common ability to effectively bind us to each other and to God.

8

How to Boil and Fry in God's Pots and Pans

Teresa of Avila's Kitchen Secrets

"**H**IS FRUIT IS SWEET to my mouth," the biblical bride exclaims about her beloved in the Song of Songs, and asks: "Strengthen me with raisin cakes, refresh me with apples, for I am faint with love" (Cant. 2:3–5). Her bridegroom responds just as sweetly: "How much more delightful is your love than wine"; "your lips drip honey, sweetmeats and milk are under your tongue" (Cant. 4:10–11). The connection between food, drink, and sex, through the survival they both signify and the sensual pleasure they both convey, is an old theme in the Judeo-Christian and, more generally, the Western tradition. The description of the shared goodness of body and drink—often quoted and reflected upon in commentaries of the Songs of Songs—justifies the soul's "Divine intoxication" and "heavenly inebriation" from "that Divine milk with which her Spouse continually nourishes her," in the words of Teresa of Avila's sixteenth-century commentary.[1] Milk and wine are the food of childhood and the beverage of adulthood, icons of pure nourishment and of sheer pleasure. In one of the essays in his *Mythologies*, French critic Roland Barthes claims that milk, and not, as one might assume, water, is the true cultural opposite of wine: "wine is mutilating, surgical, it trans-

115

mutes and delivers; milk is cosmetic, it joins, covers, restores. Moreover its purity, associated with the innocence of the child, is a token of strength, of a strength which is not repulsive, not congestive, but calm, white, lucid, the equal of reality."[2]

Milk and wine both flavor the body of the biblical bride: she tastes both childlike in her innocence and intoxicating in her sensuality, she is transformative like wine yet restorative like milk. The flavors of the bride's double fluidity blend together in this commentary to become one in their common ability to invite ecstasy and loss of self, to heighten that choice of powerlessness, of self-emptying, of kenosis, even, positively embraced in mystical texts as a necessary step if one is to achieve union with the divine. This union is as transformative as wine, as restoring as milk. Drunkenness is exalted in the Song of Songs and in Teresa's Counter-Reformation commentary as a sign of mystical ecstasy: "His will is that she shall drink, and become inebriated with all the wines that are in the storehouse of God. Let her rejoice in those joys; let her marvel at His wonders; let her not fear to lose her life through drinking beyond the capacity of her weak nature; let her die in this paradise of delights."[3] Breaking the rules of polite society and of Christian temperance, the woman in love drinks beyond her capacity, gets drunk, loses control, and in so doing gains access to divine delights. She is transmuted, disjointed, uncovered. She is in ecstasy.

This commentary on the Song of Songs, written between 1566 and 1567, is found amid the copious writings of Teresa de Ahumada y Cepeda (1515–1582). She called herself Teresa de Jesús when she entered the convent and has been better known as Teresa of Avila since her canonization in 1622—barely forty years after her death. Ironically, this, the highest official recognition of human holiness for the Catholic Church, took place only seventeen years after the recommendation by theologians that all her books should be burned! And Teresa's meditations on the Song of Songs were in fact burned in 1580. Having enjoyed wide circulation before then, however, four copies managed to survive.[4]

Teresa was born in central Spain, in the town of Avila, into a Catholic family with Jewish roots. Her mother died when Teresa was fifteen, leaving ten children behind. Teresa was then entrusted to the Augustinian nuns of Avila. She entered the Carmelite Monastery of the Incarnation in Avila as a rather unenthusiastic virgin at the age of twenty-one, against her father's will. Teresa underwent a sort of conversion as a mature adult, when at thirty-nine she intensified her spiritual practices and began to receive regularly the mystical graces for which she is well known—in part thanks to Gian Lorenzo Bernini's beautiful but also infamous statue, "The Ecstasy of Saint Teresa" (1647–1652), which can be admired in the Church of Santa Maria della Vittoria in Rome. I say "infamous" because this Baroque masterpiece effectively highlights the sensuality of Teresa's experience: half-open mouth, closed eyes, relaxed limbs, and bare feet (she is a discalced, or barefoot, nun) sensually peeking from her thick Carmelite's habit, with toes evocatively curled and spread. For this reason, Bernini's statue has been utilized at least as early as the eighteenth century by art critics and, later of course, psychoanalysts, as "proof" that mystical ecstasy is nothing but a form of sexual orgasm.[5]

Teresa de Jesús was a mystic and a writer, but also, most practically, a reformer and a foundress: in 1562 she founded in her hometown the first convent of Discalced Carmelites, the Discalced Carmelite Nuns of the Primitive Rule of Saint Joseph. The purpose of these new Carmelite convents and monasteries (for Teresa's reform affected both the men and the women of the order) was to return to a more primitive rule, inspired by Franciscan poverty as well as by the traditional Carmelite focus on the life of prayer. Teresa then went on to found seventeen convents—the last one, in Burgos, was established in 1582, the year of her death. Jesuit scholar Michel de Certeau explains Teresa's against-the-grain vocation by remarking that "the mystics do not reject the ruins that surround them. They remain there. They go there. A symbolic gesture: Ignatius of Loyola, Teresa of Avila, and many others wished to enter a 'corrupt' Order." But there is a spiritual as well as a practical reason for Teresa's counterintuitive vocation: "Not that they sympathized with decadence, but these disorderly, quasi-disinherited places—places of abjection, of trial (like the deserts where monks once went to battle against evil spirits) and not places guaranteeing an identity or a salvation—represented the actual situation of contemporary Christianity. They were the theaters of the present struggles."[6] This explanation should help us understand Teresa's pugnacious nature, her fearlessness, her effectiveness, in practical terms, but also the kind of spirituality that was at least in part shaped by her reforming practices, a spirituality known for graces and ecstasy and yet suspicious of graces and ecstasy, a spirituality founded on a contact with God that can be, certainly, full of pleasure—we might even call it, with the French, *jouissance*, a delight beyond words and tinged with eroticism—but also full of continual struggles, unrealizable demands, and enduring uncertainties.

Curiously, Teresa's oldest piece of writing still in existence is a 1546 letter concerning a delivery of wheat—the essential ingredient of the bread that was the staff of life in the Mediterranean basin.[7] But that is a coincidence, no doubt. Less coincidental is what Teresa makes of food in her writings. The best known of these consists of an autobiography, known as her *Life* (the first draft of which was finished in 1562), and a spiritual treatise, the *Interior Castle*, written fifteen years later in 1577. Teresa also wrote other books, including *The Way of Perfection* and *The Book of the Foundations*, as well as shorter texts and numerous letters. It is in the *Book of the Foundations*—an account of Teresa's foundation of convents throughout Spain first published, posthumously, in 1610—that we find what her foremost English translator, E. Allison Peers, refers to in a footnote as "perhaps the most celebrated phrase in the whole of St. Teresa's writings": "*Entre los pucheros anda el Señor,*" or "The Lord walks among the pots and pans."[8]

Teresa means exactly what the sentence sounds like, even out of context: God is found in lowly objects, in the menial kitchen jobs about which her nuns may complain because these tasks keep them away from those spiritual practices that are considered essential to the Carmelite life and to spiritual progress. On the contrary, says Teresa, obedience itself is what leads to spiritual progress; and in the colloquial style typical of some of her writings and to which I return below, Teresa tells her nuns that among the most spiritually advanced people she knows are some who spend "all their time in occupations imposed upon them by obedience and charity." This dedication does not prevent them from being "astoundingly" advanced in spiritual matters. "So come, then, my daughters," Teresa concludes, "let there be no disappointment when obedience keeps you busy in outward tasks. If it sends you to the kitchen, remember that the Lord walks among the pots and pans and that He will help you in inward tasks and in outward ones too." God's connection to kitchen utensils and activities, God's literal presence among the pots and pans, gives meaning, and should give pleasure, to those willing or obliged to play the role of Martha rather than of Mary, to serve at table rather than to sit and listen—oblivious to the needs surrounding them—to the words of God. (In the early days of one of her convents, Saint Joseph's in Avila, Teresa took turns with the other nuns in working for a week at a time in the kitchen: "it gave us no small happiness to see her in the kitchen," wrote her cousin and fellow Carmelite Maria de San Jerónimo after Teresa's death, "for she worked very gaily and took great care to look after us all . . . what she wanted was to give us good meals.")[9]

Teresa's pots and pans are vessels of food and vehicles of grace: using them for cooking and serving and washing them after is a priestly activity. Spiritual author Kathleen Norris remembers her first experience of Mass, finding it "enormously comforting to see the priest as a kind of daft housewife, overdressed for the kitchen, in bulky robes, puttering about the altar, washing up after having served so great a meal to so many people." Just as a priest prepares, serves, and cleans up after a meal, and in doing this obeys God and vocation, so the daily activities of homemaking also are acts of vocation, of priestly duty, and in their repetition, their intrinsically incomplete nature (dinner will have to be cooked again tomorrow, the table set, the dishes washed), they are liturgical as well: "like liturgy," Norris continues, "the work of cleaning draws much of its meaning and value from repetition, from the fact that it is never completed but only set aside until the next day." God walks among the pots and pans, Teresa says, because—and now I am quoting from Norris again, who is talking in a different context—"it is in the routine and the everyday that we find the possibilities for the greatest transformation."[10]

For those who have taken religious vows, obedience means conforming their actions to the orders of their superiors (with the implicit understanding that Christians all serve one another). For laypeople, on the other hand, obedience is a less explicit commandment, a more subtle virtue. It consists not so much in spoken orders but rather in conforming one's behavior to God (for those who practice religion) or to the needs of those who depend on us, our "neighbor" (if one is committed to making ethical choices, within a religious organization or outside of it). It is also in this physical obedience to others' call, and not only in lengthy meditation and contemplation, that spiritual growth can be achieved, implies Teresa. "The highest perfection consists not in interior favors or in great raptures or in visions or in the spirit of prophecy," says this woman ironically known not only for being a doctor of the church and a patron of Spanish piety but also for her favors, raptures, visions, and spirit of prophecy. The highest perfection, Teresa continues, consists in "the bringing of our wills so closely into conformity with the will of God that, as soon as we realize He wills anything, we desire it ourselves with all our might, and take the bitter with the sweet, knowing that to be His Majesty's will."[11]

Bitter as well as sweet is the flavor of obedience to God. Teresa picks up the metaphorical connections between the flavors of food and the experience of divine favors a few pages later, when she again discusses the inferiority of mystical graces with respect to the daily pursuit of virtue and love. In the end, she claims, it does not so much matter whether one's visions come from God or the devil—though this question was the subject of endless discussions among priests and inquisitors, theologians and spiritual directors. What matters for Teresa is not the origin of the vision but the humble spirit of the one who receives it. "Where there is humility," she says, "no harm can possibly ensue, even though the vision come from the devil; and where there is no humility, there can be no profit, even if the vision come from God." Teresa's practical approach deserves a practical simile: "For if what should engender humility in the soul, which knows it does not deserve such a favor, makes it proud, it becomes like the spider, which turns all its food into poison, instead of resembling the bee, which turns it into honey" (42). Much like bugs, women and men produce food for themselves and for others; but although bugs cannot choose what they will produce—spiders having no more control over their poison than bees over their honey—human beings, instead, can and should pursue humility and obedience in their spiritual practices. The poison of pride can then be forsaken in favor of a sweeter production: humble honey.

Teresa is too skilled a spiritual director and too practical an individual not to be keenly aware of the risks inherent in obedience. She frequently and humorously discusses the absurdity of excessive, unthinking obedience, and the funniest of these anecdotes involves cooking and eating—and, again, bugs. "A certain nun once brought her Prioress a very large worm," Teresa recounts, "asking her to look and see what a fine specimen it was. The Prioress laughingly said: 'Go and eat it, then.'" Well, the Prioress, had she read Teresa's previous examples of nuns jumping into ponds and wells after their superiors' rash jokes on obedience, would have known better than to issue her order (77). For the obedient nun took the worm, "went away and with great care started to fry it. The cook asked her what she was doing and she said that she was going to eat it, which she was in fact about to do. Thus the Prioress' very careless remark might have done her a great deal of harm" (92). There is probably nothing physically harmful about ingesting Spanish worms, however, and thus even in spite of this type of incident Teresa insists: "Still I much prefer obedience to be carried to excess, for I have a particular devotion to that virtue, and so I have done all in my power that others should have it" (92). Whether or not it involves frying, and possibly ingesting, worms, women and men must imitate the work of bees and become obedient makers of honey, lest we all become poisonous spiders instead.

The Book of the Foundations speaks of the convents Teresa reformed, and is addressed to nuns. Teresa's autobiography, an earlier literary effort and one more widely read still today, had a different addressee. Her *Life* is considered a rare example of female autobiography before the nineteenth century in which the reader can experience the presence of a strong sense of personal self—though some believe that Teresa's *Life* is not a true autobiography because it was written as an act of obedience rather than in order to show others her uniqueness as an individual. Composed at the command of Teresa's confessors, it can be called a judicial confession insofar as its purpose was to dispel fears that her prayers and extraordinary spiritual experiences might be diabolically rather than divinely inspired. In the words of a critic, "her confessors commanded her to write, in part because her activities continually attracted Inquisitional scrutiny, in part because her accomplishments were remarkable."[12]

The Inquisition looms ominously in the background of this book. Therefore, a few words must be said regarding Teresa's use of metaphorical language. Since she was writing under the command of her confessors and with the Inquisition as a potential audience (though she was never formally tried by the Inquisition, charges were brought against her several times), Teresa had to employ a plain style, described by many readers as conversational, spontaneous, and feminine, as natural and sincere. In fact, Teresa is now recognized as a skilled user of figurative language, and especially of metaphor—though her metaphors are made almost invisible by the much more apparent plainness of her style. Metaphors of food and cooking, in particular, are drawn from lowly aspects of daily life that pose little threat to the religious status quo incarnated in the Inquisition—much more interested in potentially heretical questions such as the individual's personal relationship with God, justification by faith, the inability to sin when recollected and absorbed in God, the authority for scriptural interpretation, and more.

In her portrait Teresa appears chubby, and a famous anecdote has her say that there is a time for penance and a time for partridge.[13] Her close collaborator María de San José Salazar describes Teresa as "more robust than thin and well proportioned in all ways," and reminds her fellow nuns that Teresa's "Constitutions" explicitly forbid conversation about food—about whether it was well or poorly cooked, too abundant or scant; María also remembers that, in their travels, Teresa and her sisters on many days "ate nothing but beans or bread and cherries and things like that," happily made dinners out of "lettuce, radishes, and bread," or else "nothing but apples and bread, sometimes cooked up and sometimes in salad," and at least on one occasion "found nothing to eat but some very salty sardines, and no one could improve this by giving us water."[14] Following the rules she herself set out, on the other hand, Teresa does not as a rule speak of her eating habits. Still, she uses metaphors of food in her *Life* to describe the soul's needs, wants, and joys. It may be surprising, for instance, to find the image of an overflowing cooking-pot in her description of the impetuous movements of the soul's love of God. In Teresa's words, "This love must flow into interior reflection, not boil over like a cooking-pot that has been put on too fierce a fire, and so spills its contents. The source of the fire must be controlled."[15] The author then goes on to use the powerful and well-exploited image of the fire, while the more lowly and expressive one of the cooking-pot gets abandoned—at least until the later composition of the *Book of the Foundations* and the finding of God among the pots and pans.

In another section of her *Life*, Teresa goes back to the kitchen in order to teach her readers to focus on other people's virtues and good qualities and to always remember their own shortcomings. Only in this way, she argues, can one progress in the life of prayer and of spiritual development. This advice she regards as especially important for those who "are very active with their intellects"—a type of work for which Teresa all too modestly affirms not to be well suited. Although it may seem to them "a waste of time," intellectuals, the author exhorts, should also take a break from their usual work in order to simply acknowledge and savor God's presence: "There is a time for one thing and a time for another, so that the soul may not be wearied with always eating the same food. The foods are very tasty and nourishing, and once the palate has grown used to them they bring great sustenance to the life of the soul, together with many other benefits."[16]

What is striking in this passage—written by a woman who has been described as a holy anorexic, a woman who sees "the very great trials of the religious life" as being "its penances, its poor food, and the yoke of obedience," a woman who writes in the same book, "this soul longs to be free. Eating is killing it, sleep brings it anguish," and later "how it pains a soul . . . to waste time attending to such bodily needs as those of eating and sleeping!"—is the positive, even the exalted representation of food and eating.[17] Variety in food is a good thing; its absence is metaphorically related to the soul's weariness. Food variety is likened to spiritual variety: if this metaphor benefits the representation of spirituality by giving it a simple material equivalent, by the same token food is elevated to the ranks of the spiritually profitable. The next sentence in the passage, however, is even more revealing: "The foods are very tasty and nourishing, and once the palate has grown used to them they bring great sustenance to the life of the soul, together with many other benefits." The custom of eating well, that is, brings not to surfeit, as one may surmise, or, worse, to the sins of intemperance and gluttony, but instead to sustenance and much more, "many other benefits." The life of the soul is enriched, in this case, not by fasting and abstinence, but by the bountiful consumption of tasty and hearty foods; the more one consumes these foods, and the more one stands in God's presence, the more sustenance and benefits are to be gained. The goodness of food and its spiritual pleasure are a mark of the connection food establishes with God and with divine understanding.

Obviously Teresa is not advocating, literally or metaphorically, epicurean feasts at every opportunity, nor the exaltation of gluttony. Yet she reads a particular meaning in food, a meaning that is not separation but connection, a meaning that brings pleasure and not pain. She is reminding those on a spiritual path to take a rest in the pleasure of God's presence, a pleasure as good and nourishing as the tastiest of foods. Teresa, in her life as a woman religious member of an austere order she reformed into even greater austerity, has given up the pleasure of food to a great extent: the constitution of the order stated clearly that, "Fasting must be observed, except on Sundays, from the Feast of the Exaltation of the Cross, in September, until Easter. No meat must ever be eaten, except in cases of necessity provided for by the Rule."[18] Teresa's was the sacrifice of a woman who, judging from some of the metaphors and images she uses, knew well the pleasure that this food can bring. And yet it is also clear that this pleasure is not perceived as being, in itself, sinful: she and her sisters are not vegetarians because meat is bad, but because meat is good. Only good things can be offered up to God in sacrifice. And hers is a joyful, not a resentful, sacrifice. The perils of gluttony in her autobiography are not at all the focus of her passages on food, on the contrary: food is good, and good food is better. Eating and drinking, like sleeping, are not annoying to her soul because they are evil or sinful, but because the intensity of her spiritual journey periodically requires a focused recollection.

Two pages after celebrating the tasty and nourishing foods metaphorically found in God's presence, Teresa returns to the metaphor of foods in the spiritual life—milk, bread, and other dishes—as she instructs her readers on the ways of prayer. In prayer, she claims, progress is intertwined with periodic returns to the beginning of the journey: "self-examination must never be neglected, however; for there is no soul on this path who is such a giant that he does not often need to turn back and be a child at the breast again. This must never be forgotten. Indeed I shall repeat it many times, since it is most important." Mother's milk, the infant's all, is more than food, it is life itself, and the conscious return to such a need is everyone's duty—because, as Teresa will explain later in life, beelike humility will help us produce honey rather than the spiderish poison that is the lot of the proud. "For there is no state of prayer so high," Teresa reminds her readers, "that it is not necessary often to return to the beginning, and the questions of sin and self-knowledge are the bread which we must eat with even the most delicate dish in this road of prayer." Delicate dishes may come our way, but the bread of self-knowledge is what the soul cannot do without if it is to survive. "Without this bread no one could be nourished, but it must be eaten in moderation. Once a soul finds itself exhausted and clearly understands that there is no good in it; once it feels itself ashamed before so great a King, and sees how little it pays towards the great debt it owes Him, what need is there to waste time on this?"

Teresa is a careful psychologist, she is an astute connoisseur of souls, and much as she focuses on self-knowledge as humility—no one can reflect on self and God and not come out humbler—this too must be tempered if it is not to result in self-hatred. There is a flavor, an experience, that is indeed "too sweet." So she advises, drawing still from an eating metaphor, that, "It will be better for us to go on to other dishes that the Lord puts before us, and that we should be wrong to neglect. His Majesty knows better than we what kind of food suits us."[19] If breastfeeding, the first and fundamental nourishment to which all must regularly return, has often led mystics to view Christ as our Mother—for we are nourished at the breast-like wound of his chest like babies at their mother's breast—the spiritual path is more generally likened to a banquet, or possibly a buffet, with many courses, between which the soul must move adeptly and tastefully. Though bread, as the most basic necessity of body and soul, figures in every course, still the eater, the spiritual traveler, must choose, or rather let God the host and chef choose, a balanced, nourishing, and delicious meal.

In Teresa's *Life* food appears as a figure of speech, as words precious and divine but also words that always stand for something else. Food is in her autobiography a metaphor that allows her to say the unsayable—unsayable not only because ineffable (a recurring theme of mystical writings), but unsayable also because dangerous, particularly in light of the interest the Inquisition had in her ideas and teachings. Teresa's spiritual masterpiece, *The Interior Castle*, also uses food metaphorically, and from its very beginning engages some of the topics of kitchen philosophies, of cooking and eating lessons, raised by other holy women writers.

In her very preface Teresa warns her readers that her language will be feminine: she speaks as a woman to other women, using "the language used between women"—this gesture would be greatly relished by those feminists who have theorized the existence of a female speech and a female way of writing. In Teresa's words, "The one who ordered me to write told me that the nuns in these monasteries of our Lady of Mount Carmel need someone to answer their questions about prayer and that he thought they would better understand the language used between women, and that because of the love they bore me they would pay more attention to what I would tell them."[20] She writes, and is read, as a woman, and she writes, and is read, out of love: women's language, the language used among women, is something Teresa elaborates on shortly into her text, when she writes that, "Learned and wise men know about these things very well, but everything is necessary for our womanly dullness of mind; and so perhaps the Lord wills that we get to know comparisons like these" (41). The comparisons Teresa is referring to are her plain examples, her extended metaphors, her careful explanations, but above all the oral style of her speech: though commanded to *write*, she subverts this order by choosing instead to *speak* to her sisters. Her writing will in reality be a way of speaking: "So I shall be speaking to them while I write" (34, "*iré hablando con ellas en lo que escribiré*").[21]

Teresa's choice of an oral language over a more traditionally written style (though naturally the irony is that she is in fact writing, even as she pretends to speak), echoes Hélène Cixous' connection between mother's milk and female voice that I evoked in the second chapter: "Between the command to *write* and the appreciation of the writing, both of which are masculine, the feminine act of *speaking* unfolds," explains De Certeau, for "the feminine spoken word insinuates itself within the masculine circumscription of writing."[22] It is but an impression, of course, an illusion, this conversation that Teresa is entertaining. It is an illusion of colloquiality that she preserves throughout the text with regular references to her read-ers', or her listeners', reactions, such as when she writes, "It seems to me I can see you asking what you should do" (140).

This women's language, this spoken word, leads to the use of images unusual enough for their author to require some distancing, a disclaimer of sorts: in discussing things that she has only recently come to under-stand, says Teresa, "the trouble is that . . . I will have to repeat matters that are well known; on account of my stupidity things can't be otherwise" (42). Teresa's regular and intense use of the humility motif has been noted time and again. Indeed, Teresa so overemploys the motif of women's physical weakness and intellectual inferiority that she ends up giving it new mean-ing: self-depreciation becomes in her writings not only the device of tra-ditional rhetoric (*captatio benevolentiae*, an appeal, that is, to the reader's benevolence with respect to the author's shortcomings), but also, less tra-ditionally, a way of exploiting stereotypes of women's language and of pro-tecting her right to write against inquisitorial intrusions: "if we consider these protestations within the context of her general rhetorical strategy, we can see that the 'coarse comparisons,' the ones that occur to Teresa's 'dull wit,' are not only a statement about ineffability but also a means of disavowing the presumption of exegesis," writes a critic, and "by allowing the reader to experience her frustration, indeed, her failure to find *le mot juste*, Teresa succeeds in explaining without teaching." Yet teaching is pre-cisely what she does, while preserving the illusions of chatty women's talk: "Teresa's rhetoric of feminine subordination—all the paradoxes, the self-depreciation, the feigned ignorance and incompetence, the deliberate obfuscation and ironic humor—produced the desired perlocutionary effect. Her words were taken as an ingenuous act."[23]

The building that gives the title to Teresa's *Interior Castle* cannot be represented in a picture, much as book covers and illustrations have tried: because the rooms contain each other, no two-dimensional image can adequately convey its architectural complexity. In this, the interior castle is not only "womblike,"[24] but it is also more like a food than like a build-ing. In fact Teresa describes the exchange between the soul and God as the eating of a delicious palmetto (*palmito* in Spanish, "a shrub commonly found in southern and eastern Spain that is recognized by its thick layers of leaves enclosing a succulent kernel"),[25] for God resides in that part of the human soul, of the interior castle, that is most like this food. "Well now let's get back to our castle with its many dwelling places," Teresa affirms. "You mustn't think of these dwelling places in such a way that each one would follow in file after the other; but turn your eyes toward the center, which is the room or the royal chamber where the King stays, and think of how a palmetto has many leaves surrounding and covering the tasty part that can be eaten. So here, surrounding this center room, are many rooms" (42).

Palmetto, or *palmito*, the only palm native to Spain, hides a tasty center under layers of inedible leaves. As such, this food offers an image of the divinity that the apparently loftier architectural metaphor is incapable of expressing: the women whom Teresa is addressing are more likely to have eaten a palmetto than to have entered a castle made of diamond—more than that, a castle that would involve miracles of engineering for its existence—and the simple language she has promised to speak demands understandable images. What this language allows Teresa to find, like the tasty part of the palmetto, is the presence of the other within one's self, the presence of God in the human soul, the otherness of the divine as a tasty morsel within the tough outer leaves of our human identity. And if God is a tasty morsel, "the soul becomes the place in which that separation of self from itself prompts a hospitality, now 'ascetic,' now 'mystic,' that makes room for the other," so that Teresa's castle becomes "the depiction of the soul as the place of the other."[26]

The place of otherness is the place of ecstasy and, in this book, it is also the place of hospitality and of drinking and intoxication. Let's proceed to the seventh dwelling places, the last, those where the soul comes into closest contact with God. In the second chapter a feminine and maternal God gives the soul milk as sustenance: "from those divine breasts where it seems God is always sustaining the soul there flow streams of milk bringing comfort to all the people of the castle" (180).

In the fourth and last chapter, however, the drink changes, as the soul is transformed from infant to adult, from baby at breast to woman in the bridal chamber: "But the soul is fortified by the strength she has from drinking wine in this wine cellar," writes Teresa, echoing the Song of Songs and her commentary on it, "where her Spouse has brought her and from where He doesn't allow her to leave; and strength flows back to the weak body, just as food placed in the stomach strengthens the head and the whole body" (192).[27] The references to wine and food combine in this passage to communicate a double message, one that, most openly, exalts intoxication for, with, and by God; but also, more practically, the passage is reminiscent of Teresa's frequent advice, to nuns prone to ecstasy, that they should be given more food and drink, and especially meat (normally forbidden by the Carmelite rule), in order to let them return to health. Teresa, known for her mystical trances and for being invoked by Sigmund Freud as "the patron saint of hysterics" and by Jacques Lacan as the epitome of woman's orgasmic *jouissance*, was instead a practical reader of ecstasies, which were more often than not brought on, in her view, by an amount of prayer and fasting excessive in view of some women's weak physical constitutions. (So also Teresa's contemporary Ignatius Loyola, 1491–1556, struggled with whether to eat meat or not: after deciding to abstain from it, and being "so firm about it that he would not think of changing it for any reason," he writes in his *Autobiography* that, "one morning after he arose some meat appeared before him," and though he had not until then desired it, "he also had a strong inclination of his will to eat it from that time on"; he tests his decision "that he ought to eat meat" by discussing it to his confessor, and though the latter suggests that "perhaps this was a temptation," Ignatius examines it "carefully," and concludes that "he could never be in doubt about it.")[28]

Teresa's more practical-minded side shines in one of the very last pages of the *Interior Castle*, where she shares her unique take on the perceived dichotomy between Martha and Mary often read in the Gospel episode dedicated to these two sisters, friends of Jesus (Luke 10:38–42). Contemporary theologians invoke Martha and Mary because, "the tensions embedded in this story raise more questions and interpretive problems than any other Lukan text involving women."[29] Martha's distraction with many things, in contrast to Mary's focus on one thing alone, the one thing needed, is one way in which the two sisters struggle with one another (or at least Martha struggles, while Mary seems oblivious to her sister's complaint). Hearing and doing are represented as being at odds, and Martha the doer is the object of Jesus' reproach: "Martha, Martha . . . " It is likely that many women and men will recognize their own thoughts in the consideration that, "although Martha is perhaps a negative model for Christians today, she is, nevertheless, an endearing model . . . She is harried with the busyness of the everyday, the stuff of ordinary days. This is what makes Martha a poignant model of spirituality: she is exactly like us."[30]

This episode of friendship and hospitality was a major theme in sixteenth- and seventeenth-century European painting. Tintoretto's "Christ in the House of Mary and Martha" (around 1566), Diego Velázquez's "Kitchen Scene with Christ in the House of Martha and Mary" (around 1620), Jan Vermeer's "Christ in the House of Mary and Martha" (around 1655), are only the best-known examples of a subject that fascinated northern and southern European painters alike in the years immediately following Teresa of Avila's life. Not that this theme is confined to sixteenth- and seventeenth-century Europe, obviously. But at that time and place, shortly after the Reformation, the implicit contradictions between Martha's active work and Mary's contemplative focus provided painters with a highly charged subject: the tension between the two sisters was a way of representing the conflict between the laity and the religious, but also, and more pointedly for that time, between the Catholic emphasis on works and the Protestant insistence on faith as the primary means of salvation. Salvation *sola fide*, through faith alone, is the choice that the story of Martha and Mary, when read as the expression of a dualism, seems to support—it is Mary who, in Christ's own words, has chosen the better part. Through centuries of exegesis, the story is still normally read as the embodiment of a conflict.

The paintings I just mentioned confirm the problematic nature of this episode. In Tintoretto's representation, Martha and Jesus both look at Mary, whose dress and position place her at the center of the viewer's gaze, as well. Velázquez positions the two sisters as far away from each other as possible: while a tiny Mary sits at the feet of Jesus in a distant, framed background (a mirror, likely), a large and sulky Martha uses a mortar and pestle at a work table that seems to extend beyond the painting. She is surrounded by eggs (symbols of resurrection), fish (a eucharistic food), garlic and hot peppers (Mediterranean favorites, though the peppers, an American import, were still fairly new at the time of the painting), and an elderly woman; the two sisters are divided, located in altogether different spaces—and despite Christ's preferential option for Mary's choice, the painting privileges Martha's role as cook. In Vermeer's representation the sisters are physically much closer to one another, belonging to the same plane, and though their conflict is still palpable, the perspective guiding the painting is illegible and its message, as a consequence, less understandable. Though all three images underline the age difference between the sisters through clothing, features, and positions, the mystery of the figure of Jesus prevents a facile reading of Martha and Mary as opposing personifications of the conflict at the heart of the Counter-Reformation.[31]

Though herself a central figure of the Counter-Reformation, in her interpretation of the Martha and Mary episode Teresa of Avila radically seeks to reconcile the two sisters and what they stand for, effectively undoing the opposition traditionally read into their story. "Believe me," Teresa tells the nuns in her customary colloquial tone in the *Interior Castle*,

"Martha and Mary must join together in order to show hospitality to the Lord and have Him always present and not host Him badly by failing to give Him something to eat." Martha's job is no less important, no less spiritual, no less necessary in the women's rendezvous with the God-man than Mary's spiritual conversations with Christ. "How would Mary, always seated at His feet, provide Him with food if her sister did not help her?" Teresa reasonably asks. Teresa takes Martha's mission seriously, as *the* scriptural story of finding meaning in the menial, and God among the pots and pans. Only after establishing the necessity of housework and the divine encounters it affords does Teresa draw an exegetical lesson from her material comparison: "His food is that in every way possible we draw souls that they may be saved and praise Him always" (192). But her conversation with the nuns immediately resumes, and Teresa goes on to address her interlocutors: "You will make two objections: one, that He said that Mary had chosen the better part. The answer is that she had already performed the task of Martha, pleasing the Lord by washing His feet and drying them with her hair" (192).[32] Teresa is here referring to the anointing at Bethany, described in John's Gospel (12:1–8), where, though Martha serves, she does not grumble about Mary; she does not refer to Luke (10:38–42), where Martha's complaint is clearly expressed.

Teresa connects the two episodes, and in so doing, not only does Martha's housework acquire a spiritual meaning, but also Mary's spiritual work is demonstrably founded on a previous physical chore. Mary's washing of Jesus' feet is analogous in Teresa's view to Martha's cooking and serving, and it is a chore whose bodiliness, with its pleasure and pain, gives new meaning to her spiritual and verbal connection with Jesus and with her sister. Teresa thus reads the Martha and Mary story in time, understanding it within a dynamic process of actions and changes, refusing to fix it, as painting inevitably does, into an iconic, immutable instant; decades and centuries later, viewers of her statue by Bernini will rarely be so generous. The episode of Martha and Mary is in Teresa's reading a narrative developing in time; only through time is their story understandable. Its potential conflicts, for Teresa, are not simply what they appear to be, and its joys are more abundant than they seem. The story of Martha and Mary is a narrative of friendship and sisterhood, of the labors of love, of hospitality and of the complexities, practical and spiritual, of welcoming God into one's kitchen.

9

How to Do Philosophy in a Busy Kitchen

Margaret Mary Alacoque, Sor Juana, Cecilia Ferrazzi

*H*ILDEGARD OF BINGEN was not the only one who imagined creation as a cooking spree and the cosmogony as akin to the making of cheese. A few centuries after Hildegard, a heretic from northern Italy, the miller Domenico Scandella, known as Menocchio (1532–1601), used the image of cheese in order to explain his unusual, materialistic theory on the origin of the world: "I have said that, in my opinion, all was chaos, that is, earth, air, water, and fire were mixed together; and out of that bulk a mass formed—just as cheese is made out of milk—and worms appeared in it, and these were the angels."[1] Rather than branding him as impious but innocuous—historian Carlo Ginzburg, to whom we owe the dissemination of Menocchio's tale, thinks that, had he lived a century or so later, the miller would have been considered mad and placed in an asylum—Menocchio was prosecuted by the Inquisition and after some years executed for his heretical beliefs. Among his varied and fantastic theological elaborations, Menocchio constantly reiterated that the world was not created by God, and he stubbornly insisted on the bizarre image of the cheese and the worms that are born of it. Menocchio, then, "used the familiar experience of maggots appearing in decomposed cheese to elucidate the birth of living things of which the first and most perfect were the angels." But more strikingly for our context, Menocchio likened the creation of the world to the coagulation of cheese, much like Hildegard of Bingen compared cheese making with the coming to life of human beings into the maternal womb. Menocchio's analogy may make sense to us today, for scientists have spoken of the earth's birth as a thickening of the nebula. But at Menocchio's time his culinary analogy inspired suspicion and fear. Ginzburg furthermore notes the disquieting similarity, the "astonishing coincidence," as the Italian historian calls it, between Menocchio's cosmogony and analogous ancient Indian myths of creation, surmising that together they might be evidence of the existence of "a millenarian cosmological tradition."[2]

Menocchio's tale is a story about, among other things, food and knowledge. Until the middle of the seventeenth century people could not make the distinction between the process of putrefaction and the process of fermentation, a fact that may have aided in the popular mistrust of cheese—in the most unflattering of objective definitions, "rancid mammary gland secretions."[3] The smell of cheese in the olden days was considerably more pungent than it is today: Claude Lévi-Strauss reminds us about the American soldiers in 1944 France, "the odor given off by Norman cheese dairies seemed to them the smell of corpses, and occasionally prompted them to destroy the dairies."[4] "The history of cheese is one of alternating acceptance and rejection," and "following a long and tortuous intellectual process, it finally established itself (except for a few persistent personal dislikes, idiosyncrasies and allergies) when a new image of the world began to spread, which was based on an unchallenged scientific paradigm."[5] Until then, the language of science and the language of mysticism and theology occasionally intersected on the subject of cheese and its iniquity. Bernard of Clairvaux, for example, in the twelfth century, associated butter with the food of pure infants and cheese with people of curdled and therefore hardened hearts.[6]

This same distrust we find in the writings of a French nun of the Order of the Visitation, who took her vows at the convent of Paray Le Monial in 1672: Margaret Mary Alacoque (1647–1690, canonized in 1920). Other than a four-year-long paralyzing illness during her adolescence and an early vocation to the convent, there are few memorable events in the life of this saint. The time when she lived, on the other hand, was tumultuous and transformative for the religion of her native France. The seventeenth century saw the dawn of the age of reason but was also the time when French women were bestowed the title of "the devout sex." It was an age of religious renewal and reform, from the popular success of Francis of Sales's pious spirituality, founded on the practice of everyday virtue (I have described the metaphorical fruit in his *Introduction to the Devout Life* at the end of chapter 4), to Vincent de Paul's assistance to the poor largely through the work of charitable women.[7]

But while the other two seventeenth-century women discussed in this chapter strove for intellectual and administrative accomplishments, and embarked in what were for their age uncommon adventures and singular lifestyles, Margaret Mary was a traditional mystic who devoted herself to penitential practices. These, in turn, did not fail to bring her those exceptional states associated with medieval mysticism: levitation, ecstasy, apparitions, and revelations. Most important among these events was Margaret Mary's vision of the heart of Jesus with a crown of thorns— now a familiar image of Catholic devotional iconography, but at first ardently opposed. Though the cult of the Sacred Heart can be traced to writings from the early centuries of Christianity (Margaret Mary Alacoque did not invent it), its unique devotional and visual forms were theologized and championed by this woman, thus known as the Messenger of the Sacred Heart. The cult as Margaret Mary developed it spread slowly: the papacy promoted it in the eighteenth century, and it was not until 1871, with the building of the Basilica of the Sacred Heart in Paris in expiation for the bloody violence of the Commune (when the royal troops repressed the revolutionary government established by the people of Paris), that this cult was officially accepted as a mainstream devotion.

Margaret Mary Alacoque's autobiography, written at the request of her spiritual director, describes at length and in depth her pleasure-filled encounters with Jesus. The heart is for this mystic a privileged means of communicating with God, the channel of exchange between human and divine, and ultimately the place of salvation. As well as about the heart of Jesus, however, Margaret Mary speaks of her insurmountable aversion for cheese, an aversion that was so well known to, and shared by, the rest of her family that, upon her entrance into the convent, her brother had it included in Margaret Mary's religious contract that his sister was not to be asked to consume any cheese product.[8]

But in one so given to self-mortification, a disgusting encounter with cheese could not be long in coming. After she was asked to eat cheese by her superior (in violation of the family contract), Margaret Mary struggled for three days about what to do with a piece of cheese, and then, after three or four hours spent asking for strength of the Blessed Sacrament, she succeeded in eating it. And she continued eating cheese for about eight years, she tells us, because, as Jesus told her, "love should not have any reservation," and though each time she ate cheese was for her as repugnant as the first, Margaret Mary's sacrifice of her disgust for this food was amply repaid with almost unbearably pleasurable graces and favors. Shortly before telling of her first cheese-eating episode, in fact, Margaret Mary describes her "insatiable hunger for humiliations and mortifications, even though my natural sensitivity suffers from them intensely." Instead, "it was after this first sacrifice that all the graces and favors of my Lord doubled, inundating my soul."[9] We saw how Angela of Foligno ingested human filth (the water used to wash a leper's sore) in order to express her solidarity, to overcome the limitations of her sensibilities, and to give in to the pleasure of the abject, of the abyss. But for Margaret Mary the object of disgust is simpler and more easily available, living as she did in a country that boasts of having a different cheese for every day of the year. Cheese is part of the convent's daily fare and Margaret Mary's sacrifice, unlike Angela's or Catherine of Siena's, can be a continuous one. Margaret Mary's nausea becomes part of her regular spirituality. Her sensual rejection and consequent forced consumption of a particular food, she sees as a sign of divine grace.

"Food loathing is perhaps the most elementary and most archaic form of abjection."[10] An emotion belonging to the cultural and social sphere, disgust (the very word ties it to food, through the Latin word *gustus*, meaning taste) is a reaction to a food's meaning more than to its physical properties. Disgust for cheese was not unique to Margaret Mary Alacoque's tastes. Color, the German doctor Johann Lotichius wrote in his 1643 *De casei nequitia* (On the vileness of cheese), is the only difference between cheese and dung.[11] Cheese and dung are both located, to use psychoanalytic terms, on "the other side of the border, the place where I am not and which permits me to be."[12] Cheese was for Lotichius the marker of distinction between the uncouth, peripheral mountain people who consumed such brutish food and the urban city dwellers: cheese "was the border between barbarism and civilization."[13] Cheese represented a border, then, but paradoxically cheese, because it is abject, also "disturbs identity, system, order," it "does not respect borders, positions, rules," it is the "in-between, the ambiguous, the composite."[14] Neither solid nor liquid, neither fresh nor altogether rotten, cheese is a strange food, prone to eliciting disgust—an emotion "rarely discrete or silent," an emotion often described as menacing to the sense of self, as a real and symbolic threat to an identity that is always precarious to begin with.[15]

Not coincidentally, perhaps, among the very first examples of disgust given by Julia Kristeva in her classic book on the subject, *Powers of Horror*, is the skin that forms on the surface of boiled milk.[16] Milk is both within and outside the human body, milk is for animals as well as for humans. *Powers of Horror* is indebted to the anthropological theories of Mary Douglas, who in *Purity and Danger* suggests that "Reflection on dirt involves reflection on the relation of order to disorder, being to non-being, form to formlessness, life to death," and at the beginning of her very first chapter describes the abject practices of Catherine of Siena—for whom "sound hygiene was incompatible with charity, so she deliberately drank off a bowl of pus."[17] Cheese "has always provoked uncontrollable revulsion and passionate devotion," it has been claimed, because it "can mirror the inexhaustible variety of human attitudes to life."[18] The encounter of cheese with Christian mysticism, then, which according to Kristeva "turned this abjection of self into the ultimate proof of humility before God,"[19] was a meeting waiting to happen—in the space of a woman's mouth, Margaret Mary Alacoque's.

For very different reasons, a contemporary of Margaret Mary Alacoque, another nun who lived in the seventeenth century, in a different continent, Sor Juana Inés de la Cruz (born as Juana Ramírez de Asbaje, 1648 or 1651–1695)—"the most famous nun of the colonial period"[20]— also avoided cheese. She too, like Menocchio a century earlier, linked food, and particularly cheese, with the acquisition of knowledge—though Sor Juana's link was a negative one. As a child, Sor Juana "would abstain from eating cheese," even though she "was as greedy for treats as children usually are at that age," because she "heard tell that it made people stupid, and the desire to learn was stronger in [me] than the desire to eat—powerful as this is in children."[21] Today we may not see cheese as a treat for a child (with the possible exception of string-cheese sticks: with numerous strings that can be pulled apart before being eaten, they gratify the children's desire to play with their food, and this playfulness is accentuated by the jokes on the wrapper). But a treat is precisely what the renounced cheese represents for little Juana. The reason she gives it up, though, is neither self-mortification nor abject disgust, but rather it is for that love of learning, which is the core of her life. Just as we still speak of devouring books, of being hungry for knowledge, thirsty for learning, so also in Sor Juana's words about cheese the desirability of food is compared, and given up in favor of, the will to study. Eating and learning are joined together, for this nun, by desire—the force that motivates both.

Margaret Mary Alacoque was a religious visionary, Sor Juana was a literary star: the latter's visions asserted a poetic rather than a divine experience, and her claims to truth involved more secular realities—the right of women to read and write, for example—than those of the writers who accompany her in these pages. For Margaret Mary Alacoque, cheese signals disgust, the obverse of pleasure—not only its opposite, however, but also that with which pleasure and desire are sometimes layered; her ability to overcome this disgust is the measure of her love of God. For Sor Juana, cheese signals meaning: the meaning of what she does not want—stupidity—and of what she does seek out—knowledge; the meaning of food exploration as a scientific quest, founded on her renunciation of vilifying victuals; and the meaning of a woman's life and writings, her right to pursue lifelong learning, her right to, literally, choose how and what to mean.

Food and learning are again united later in the same text where Sor Juana connects cheese and stupidity, namely, in her justly famous "Poet's Answer to the Most Illustrious Sor Filotea de la Cruz." The context is a discussion of heretics, about whom Sor Juana writes through vivid and scientific metaphors of eating and digesting. Though learning "can be the best nourishment and life for the soul," Sor Juana claims, these people are harmed by it: "For just as an infirm stomach, suffering from diminished heat, produces more bitter, putrid, and perverse humors the better the food that it is given, so too these evil persons give rise to worse opinions the more they study." They are sick, and as a consequence "their understanding is obstructed by the very thing that should nourish it"; so, "the fact is they study a great deal and digest very little, failing to measure their efforts to the narrow vessel of their understanding."[22] Eating and learning are comparable activities: both so require the involvement and the preparation of the eater and the learner that good results are only possible if the person eating, the person learning, is ready, healthy, and whole. Just as no one with a sick stomach can profit from good food, and indeed the better the food, the worse its effect on the sick, so also no one who is evil can profit from study—and indeed the more they study, the less their understanding thrives.

But the bonds between food, learning, and identity are best expressed in an earlier passage of this document. Shortly after remembering how she had learned geometry by spinning a top on flour sifted on the floor, Sor Juana goes on to explain in detail why the kitchen is a good place to be for a philosopher and a scholar:

> Well, and what then shall I tell you, my Lady, of the secrets of nature that I have learned while cooking? I observe that an egg becomes solid and cooks in butter or oil, and on the contrary that it dissolves in sugar syrup. Or again, to ensure that sugar flow freely one need only add the slightest bit of water that has held quince or some other sour fruit. The yolk and white of the very same egg are of such a contrary nature that when eggs are used with sugar, each part separately may be used perfectly well, yet they cannot be mixed together. I shall not weary you with such inanities, which I relate simply to give you a full account of my nature, and I believe this will make you laugh. But in truth, my Lady, what can we women know, save philosophies of the kitchen? It was well put by Lupercio Leonardo that one can philosophize quite well while preparing supper. I often say, when I make these little observations, "Had Aristotle cooked, he would have written a great deal more." And so to go on with the mode of my cogitations: I declare that all this is so continual in me that I have no need of books.[23]

Sor Juana's cooking as she describes it in this passage is playful, experimental, and proves that much can be learned by playing with food. She effectively illustrates what and how by playing with language. Sor Juana refers to scientific observations as inanities: *frialdades* is what she calls her reflections, a word derived from *frío*, cold, as her editors point out, and meaning "chills"—therefore particularly ironic in the context of cooking in butter and oil. She assumes the presence of laughter in a context dangerous to her very safety, addresses a man as if he were a woman, and claims female ignorance and stupidity well knowing she is a genius. She even cracks a joke about Aristotle's written output: "*Si Aristóteles hubiera guisado, mucho más hubiera escrito*," "Had Aristotle cooked, he would have written a great deal more." Sor Juana was among the most illustrious forerunners of feminism and the first to defend women's rights in Latin America. She eloquently describes the kitchen as an ideal place of learning—before rhetorically putting down this type of learning as "women's stuff."

Sor Juana Inés de la Cruz wrote her "Poet's Answer to the Most Illustrious Sor Filotea de la Cruz" as an epistolary, autobiographical response to a criticism of her secular intellectual and literary work by the Bishop of Puebla (a man of power who used "Sor," or Sister, "Filotea de la Cruz" as a pseudonym to mask his rank and gender). Through carefully crafted rhetoric, full of irony, hyperbole, and humor, Sor Juana's letter vehemently defends women's right and duty to lifelong learning and teaching—a pursuit, a vocation, even, that demanded, in her view, the single rather than the married life, especially given what she calls her "absolute unwillingness to enter into marriage." The only honorable single life at that time unfolded in the convent; Sor Juana, the precocious child of a single mother, raised in Nepantla, near Mexico City, preferred the comfortable Hieronymite convent of Santa Paula in Mexico City (where she lived from the age of ten) to the much stricter Discalced Carmelite convent (like Teresa of Avila's) that was her first religious home—and which she left within a few months on account of an illness. Sor Juana is known for her literature, not for her holiness, and unlike the heretics she chides in her text, her studying, in and outside the kitchen, brought her internal understanding and public glory, though mixed with suspicions, in life as well as in death.

Returning to her "Answer," it is clear that Sor Juana wants to impress upon her addressee a simple yet controversial reality: her learning, connected with food and sacrifice since her childhood, is unstoppable, even in the absence of books—which for three months she had been forbidden from reading by a superior, possibly in anticipation of her permanent silencing to come. She cannot stop learning because, in the observation of all that is around her—and particularly in the kitchen—she finds instruction in the ways of knowledge and in the ways of God. That might well be because "the function of uniting and separating elements," such as, in Sor Juana's accounts, eggs, syrups, butter, and sugar, "is essential to alchemy, to chemistry, to cooking, and . . . to philosophy."[24] Chemical and philosophical thinking is analogous, as Sor Juana well realized, to the work of a cook: like chemists and like philosophers, cooks separate and mix, reduce and expand, break into fragments and put back together into a whole. (As a young man, the Austrian philosopher Ludwig Wittgenstein—reputed to live almost exclusively on oatmeal—declared that he could do his best work and his best thinking while peeling potatoes.)[25]

In the words of Kathleen Myers, a scholar of Sor Juana, "Most religious women who wrote *vidas* describe visionary and at times mystical experiences of knowing God. Sor Juana is content to know God through the study of his creation"—a study that, in the kitchen and elsewhere, should be not only allowed but encouraged because "the lack of individual will in the manifestation of her talent," as Myers puts it, is "a key indication of its divine origins."[26] It is not surprising, then, that, in addition to writing in all the genres of baroque literature, Sor Juana is believed to also have compiled a cookbook (attribution remains uncertain): of its thirty-seven recipes, twenty-seven are for sweet foods, maybe because, as one editor claims, the convent relied on the production of sweets for some of its economic sustenance—like the convents encountered in chapter 5.[27] But, taken as she was with poetry and philosophy, with science and perhaps with cooking, Sor Juana did not dedicate a sufficient portion of her talents to the praise of God and church, some of her antagonists claimed.

And so there is no happy ending in Sor Juana's extraordinary tale. Known as the Phoenix of America and as the Tenth Muse—complimentary titles focusing on her intellectual rather than spiritual accomplishments—this prodigiously learned individual and one of the very first women to publish in the New World, was silenced in 1693–1694, when she was pressured to renew her religious vows, give away her massive library (among the largest in the Americas), and officially renounce her literary and intellectual pursuits (though she may have continued writing in secret, as some documents suggest). The tensions between Sor Juana's role as intellectual and her vocation as a woman religious inform much contemporary scholarship of her life and work, as well as María Luisa Bemberg's beautiful movie on Sor Juana, *Yo, la peor de todas* (*I, the Worst of All*, 1990). In Myers's words, "in spite of church efforts to make Sor Juana a *perfecta religiosa*, she represented the possibility of a more multivalent role for women and individuals."[28] Yet feminist theologians have been able to reclaim Sor Juana's religious accomplishments as more than mere façade to protect her secular pursuits. When, a year after her silencing, Sor Juana died in an epidemic at the convent, she left behind a legacy that "speaks of the birth of a people" and constitutes "a vital historical resource for feminist scholarship"—and particularly, some claim, for Latina feminist theology.[29] Though not a traditional mystic, Sor Juana brings together some of the vital questions that animate my discussion: she is a consecrated, celibate woman with a bent for cooking and for writing about food. Sor

Juana, then, well illustrates the importance of examining the connections between women and eating, between spiritual and bodily nourishment, and, particularly, between holy women and food practices. These connections are complicated by the fact that Sor Juana's holiness was always clouded by what were, for that time and place, her far more extraordinary intellectual abilities; her writings nevertheless continue to teach her readers that the "philosophies of the kitchen," her "*filosofías de cocina*," provide a privileged space for women to think and to write, and that the kitchen is as good a place as any for peeling apart philosophical arguments and for mixing them with theological matters.

Back in the old continent, and more precisely in Italy, food features prominently as an instrument of divine knowledge in the story of another silenced holy woman of the seventeenth century, a woman from whose deposition to the Inquisition I now cite:

> Before the plague came, my sister who is still living, then called Maria [as a Carmelite, Maria had later changed her name], put a needle shaped like a fishhook into her mouth and swallowed it, holding it in her stomach for a whole week and feeling great pain. Many remedies, including holding her upside down, were tried, but none of them worked. At last turning to prayer, I prayed to God for my sister, who was in danger of dying. And I heard an internal voice that told me to take some lasagna noodles with a few greens and cook them in a pan with a little butter. That's what I did, my sister ate it right away, and two hours later she evacuated the needle, which was stuck in her intestine. I pulled out the needle, but because [part of] the intestine was outside and bleeding heavily, they summoned the barber, who touched the intestine with a hot piece of iron, and she was safe and sound.[30]

We are in Venice, in the years 1664–1665, and Cecilia Ferrazzi (1609–1684), a single woman in her fifties, is being tried by the Venetian Holy Office. Arrested while she was on a boat on the Grand Canal, she has been accused of "pretense of sanctity." Cecilia requests and is granted the opportunity to tell her own story, rather than just answer the questions asked of her by the inquisitors. Unable to enter a convent because orphaned and penniless, Cecilia, after spending a few years in the home of affluent relatives and friends, in 1648 started taking care of young women who were "in danger," as she herself had once been, of falling into prostitution for lack of a protective home. By the time the Inquisition turned its ominous eyes to her, Cecilia Ferrazzi was a successful single woman in charge of about three hundred girls and women, all between the ages of five and thirty. What worried the Inquisition was not so much the accusation, on the part of some girls, that Cecilia was authoritarian or that living conditions were less than ideal. The much more dangerous practice to which Cecilia dedicated herself was to hear the confession of the virgins in her care and to absolve them.

In the words of Cecilia's editor and translator, historian Anne Jacobsen Schutte, "In seventeenth-century eyes, preserving girls' virginity was a perfectly appropriate job for a woman; mediating their standing with God was a responsibility reserved to ordained men."[31] Cecilia dictated her autobiography hoping to convince the inquisitors of the falsity of the accusations leveled against her, but, by responding to their questions, she provided further trails for the inquisitors and evidence for her guilt. In 1665, Cecilia was convicted of "pretense of sanctity," namely of faking holiness and of claiming that God had given her special graces. Two years into her seven-year jail sentence, Cecilia was transferred to house arrest in nearby Padua, and in 1669, as a sixty-year-old woman, she was finally allowed to return to Venice. We know nothing about the last fifteen years of her life, except that she died when she was almost seventy-three, in 1684.

Food recurs frequently in Cecilia Ferrazzi's story, and it is usually linked, by herself or by her accusers, with supernatural events. Cecilia suffered since childhood from stomach troubles, which prevented her from consuming a regular diet. The extraordinarily little food that painfully entered her body is matched by the extraordinarily large excretions that with even greater pain came out of it: gallstones as large as eggs! Meat (which in Italian means flesh, too) was for Cecilia a devilish temptation of adolescence, as were the apples and oranges offered her, also by the devil, while she was on her way to Mass. In the passage quoted at the opening of this section, Cecilia refers to her younger sister Maria: we can only wonder what possessed Maria to put a needle shaped like a fishhook in her mouth—poor food preparation on her part or the fishmonger's? Penance, perhaps? Punishment?—but we must admire her sister's practical solution. By Cecilia's preparation of lasagna noodles with buttered greens ("*un poco di lasagne con un poco di verze e che le cucinassi nel tegame con del butiro*"[32] —"*verze*," the word used for greens in the Italian original, are a type of cabbage: an effective natural laxative, if one wants to be practical about it), and with the later intervention of a barber, the sister is returned to safety and health.

The choice of greens is far from casual, nor is it limited to their laxative effects: aside from the fact that tomato sauce on pasta did not become
widespread until the nineteenth century, and thus Cecilia's lasagna would
definitely be seasoned with something quite different from what most
Italians would put on it today, greens hold a special place in Cecilia Ferrazzi's life. She claimed to have been born with greens in her mouth, and
someone attributed this to the fact that her mother ate only greens when
she was pregnant with Cecilia.[33] Greens, as we have seen with Matrona of
Perge and Angela of Foligno, were symbolic of the simple life, of the pure
food that God will make available against all odds, and against temptations by demons. Despite her own periodic inability to eat regular food
and her frequent bouts of vomiting (problems she attributed to a purely
physical illness) and rumors that she lived on communion alone (these,
clearly connected with her accusation of false sanctity), Cecilia—born
with life-giving greens in her mouth—was comfortably at home among
kitchen remedies: she took care of an infant girl by feeding her "a bit of
cooked apple moistened with sweet almond oil" and for another she made
"some pap with holy water"; the wine she poured in a bottle turned from
cloudy to delicious and replenished itself, lasting for no less than seven or
eight months and quenching the thirst of several women during that
entire time.[34]

Her kitchen doings did not go unnoticed, and God rewarded Cecilia's
kitchen solicitousness with a culinary miracle that confirmed both her
cooking and her spiritual talents, anchored them solidly to real, daily food,
and infused this very food with a supernatural grace. At the time when the
following episode took place, Cecilia was living at the house of Signora
Marietta Cappello, a noblewoman with whom she lived for nine years—
the second half of the twenty-year-period she spent as guest-servant after
the death of her parents. Cecilia regarded Signora Marietta as her superior to whom she owed complete obedience. One day, when Signora
Marietta was on a business trip to her villa, Cecilia was left alone with her
husband Paolo, ill with dysentery and near death.

[Signora Marietta] sent from the villa a basket containing some thrushes,
which I showed [Signor Paolo] to cheer him up, and he ordered me to prepare one of them for his dinner. But because I was so busy, being alone in the
house, I forgot to pluck and cook it. While I was feeding him for he could-
n't even put his hand to his mouth, he asked me whether the thrush was
cooked, but so as not to disturb him, I didn't answer. But going into the

kitchen, I knelt down in the middle of it, begging the Most Holy Mother's pardon for my negligence with tears running down my cheeks. And as I knelt there, he called me, asking whether the thrush was cooked. And I, not knowing what to say because I couldn't bear to tell him that it wasn't even plucked, told him 'Right away, sir.' And at the entrance to the kitchen, I met a little boy, handsome and graceful, who held in his hand a skewer with a roast thrush—exactly what he had ordered. Taking the thrush from the boy, I immediately carried it to the sick man and put it in his mouth a little piece at a time. He ate it with the greatest pleasure, thanking the Lord because it was so good. And I considered myself unworthy of having received so great a favor from the Lord.[35]

The culinary appreciation of songbirds was a late-medieval and Renaissance passion, but for Cecilia Ferrazzi these thrushes are much more than a gastronomic exploit. The story underlines the lowliness of Cecilia's social status: she risks much by forgetting to prepare the labor-intensive thrushes, and is ashamed to admit her negligence (a negligence, she notes, due to the great amount of housework she had to do, and not to self-indulgence, laziness, or unwillingness to work). Her humble request for forgiveness, her turning to the Holy Mother, her desire to please her master, are all rewarded with a gastronomic miracle: a thrush appears in the hands of a boy, plucked and deliciously roasted on a skewer. Some witnesses denied this story, others said they did not remember it. Did Cecilia consciously invent it, in her fabrication of a saintly life? Is the story a part of her fiction of sanctity? Or, rather, did Cecilia struggle to create for herself a new saintly role—neither wife nor mother, much less nun—a role that was both private and public?[36] If so, then food—roast thrushes and vegetable lasagna most notably—is more than miraculous prop, more than a superficial, though necessary, physical sign of divine grace. Cecilia's are gastronomic miracles: she is not dealing with simple bread loaves such as Mary of Egypt's, here, but with elaborate, refined dishes. In the case of the lasagna with greens the miracle is an effect of Cecilia's culinary skills, and in the case of the roast thrush the culinary result is itself the miracle. In both cases grace is mediated by a woman ready and willing to cook, a woman so skilled in the kitchen arts that it is through these very arts that she invited God to make himself known to her—and, through her, to those around her. The kitchen thus becomes a place for theology and for sanctity, a place where a woman teaching holiness and effecting miracles can be more readily accepted than elsewhere. It is a place where God might more easily come to help with the cooking and sit down to share a meal.

The kitchen is where manual labor nourishes the bonds of community and nurtures the life of the mind. The place of cooking is a room where scientific meanings are produced and understood (by watching eggs harden and melt), mystical connections are made and strengthened (by eating cheese or renouncing it), divine pleasure is shared and increased (by serving a divinely roasted thrush). It is by Sor Juana's culinary reflections at the stove, amid sizzling butter and bubbling syrups, that I am most inspired, as I read and wonder about all these holy women who turned the kitchen into a theological space, a mystical room. It is Sor Juana, not a mystic, barely even a holy woman writer, who most vociferously, most persuasively claims a place for women and a place for the kitchen in holy and spiritual lives. Her kitchen is both literal and figural, and the places she claims for women and for kitchens, for women in kitchens, subvert the stereotype of what women and kitchens are for. When a woman is in the kitchen, says Sor Juana, she may in fact be cooking, but even as she cooks she is developing understanding, expanding her learning, elaborating philosophies. Like Sor Juana, the cook might make theological as well as scientific considerations—"anybody following any recipe in the kitchen," it has been rightly noted, "is in effect performing a scientific experiment."[37] Even as she cooks, Angela of Foligno might add, she has the opportunity of expressing her desire, and her willingness to fight for her lover. Even as she cooks, Margery Kempe would chime in, she learns of God's overwhelmingly sticky love and of her own ability to meaningfully give in to that ultimate connection—with others and with the divine. That Sor Juana was silenced well expresses the dangers of the kitchen and of what may take place in it. That Sor Juana was not the only holy woman to be silenced makes us wonder what it is about the kitchen that can cause trouble and exude danger.

"I am a woman, ignorant, weak, and frail," complains Julian of Norwich. "Everything is necessary for our womanly dullness of mind," writes Teresa of Avila. "What can we women know, save philosophies of the kitchen?" echoes Sor Juana. These self-deprecating gestures were spoken both as common formulas and with the awareness that writing about one's unmediated experiences could be dangerous to one's safety and to the circulation of one's writings. Sor Juana was not a mystic, yet in her love of learning and of food, and in the threats she posed in emerging from the crowd, she was not alone. Sor Juana was silenced, ordered to get rid of her library and scientific instruments, and ordered to stop writing. Teresa of

Avila was repeatedly admonished by the Inquisition. Other holy women certainly had it worse: the Inquisition went relatively easy on Cecilia Ferrazzi, but Marguerite Porete, whom we met in the introduction and who was burned at the stake, was not so lucky: mystic writings in general have aroused suspicion. Some have been ignored: Margery Kempe's book was not discovered until the 1930s, Marguerite Porete was not identified as the author of *The Mirror of Simple Souls* until 1946. Others, such as Thérèse of Lisieux's autobiography, have been heavily edited and only recently made available in their entirety to the public. The private, personal qualities of contemplative prayer make it seem harmless and distant from direct criticism of the status quo, of institutional abuse, of social injustice and ideological trickery. But the integrity brought on by the unmediated contact with God makes the mystic, and more generally those who entertain a close relationship with the divine, hard to control. Talk of food, of kitchen philosophies, hazelnuts, palmettos, and lasagna, of greens simply washed and greens cooked in butter, both ground the mystic in the language of women—to whom and of whom they speak—and in some cases even provide a sense of safety, a screen, an excuse to speak, a sense of innocence, of unimportance, of harmlessness, as well as of authority. After all, to borrow one last time from Sor Juana, "What can we women know, save philosophies of the kitchen?"

10

How to Feed the Spirit on Corn Pudding and Pork Fat

ELIZABETH SETON'S CULINARY CONVERSION

*M*OTHER'S FOOD IS BEST. From the milk of her breasts to the nutritious fares that build our growing childish bodies, from the delicacies she has time to prepare once the nest is empty to the more insipid dishes she cooks when her aging taste buds reject the intense flavors of youth, mother's food is best: it is familiar, it is comforting, it is, above all perhaps, safe. Fairy tales warn readers and listeners against accepting, requesting, or stealing food from women outside one's immediate family: everyone knows the effect on Snow White of the apple she took from the enchantress and bit into, the consequences of Rapunzel's mother pilfering the ogress's rampion, as well as the risks Hansel and Gretel ran for nibbling on an inviting gingerbread house. Themselves the victims of family hunger (their mother sends them away because there was not enough food in the house for all and is swiftly punished with death), the children escape ingestion thanks to Gretel's feminine kitchen connection: by shoving the witch into the oven and locking her in, Gretel cooks her before the witch could cook Hansel.

Women's food, offered, accepted, or stolen, is a hazardous object of consumption, related to the dangerous transformations effected in the kitchen—and not just because of the cooking fire, literally burning or metaphorically passionate. Witches deal with herbs, potions, and mysterious concoctions, and among the most popular stereotypical images of the sorceress is the picture of a woman deliberately stirring the steaming contents of a simmering cauldron—much like a careful female cook.

Not only in fairy tales are kitchens dangerous places, and mother's food preferable to all other. Some unappetizing examples of dangerous, magical kitchen doings are found in Bishop Burchard of Worms's eleventh-century book of sins and penances, a book called *Penitentialia*. The bishop's text provides appropriate penances for superstitious practices such as women's serving their husbands fish that they killed by placing it, while still alive, inside their genitals—the purpose of which practice was to increase the husband's passion and potency. This same objective, or we might call it a hope, impelled other women to have bread dough kneaded on their naked rear ends. In both cases, sexuality gets manipulated through food. More specifically, this misogynistic book imagines woman's sexual dissatisfaction, her disturbing desire, as the cause of disgusting cooking practices—particularly revolting because undetectable: how is the eater to know what happened in the kitchen to that fish, to that bread now sitting so invitingly on his plate? More optimistically, these admittedly extreme customs are examples of women's influence on and power over the world around them—and particularly their family—through the double practice of food preparation and distribution. And the proximity between food and magic is clear in the use of herbs and roots, utilized to flavor dishes but also to make potions and poisons.[1] Healers and witches, often women, have traditionally worked through food and drink, the ingredients of which had to be selected, gathered, and prepared according to very precise rules and regulations. These ingredients consisted in large part of plant matter and animal flesh.

In today's industrialized nations, patients often seek out alternative health practitioners—chiropractors and naturopaths, for instance—for ideological rather than financial reasons. In fact, health insurance companies (for the privileged ones who enjoy their protection in the United States) are generally more willing to pay for regular doctors, however more costly, than for alternative medical treatments. In premodern times, though, the services of doctors were prohibitively expensive for most people, who turned to monks and folk healers for an affordable alleviation of their ailments. With the rise of a medical profession reserved for men, traditional health practitioners were increasingly relegated to a secondary, private, and frequently secret practice of the healing arts, knowledge of which was usually handed down from mother to daughter. It was often these women who were accused, particularly from the fourteenth century on, of being witches—for healing without permission, for making someone sick, for causing an undesired passion, for preventing or interrupting a pregnancy, and more. Feats such as these were ostensibly accomplished to a large extent through those kitchen arts of which women were the repositories—for example, by mixing a certain ingredient in a dish or by dissolving a powder in water or wine: handling food and drink was women's prerogative, one of the few instances when women could operate freely and affirm themselves, their abilities, their desires.[2]

Whether it was used for healing or hurting, for medical or supernatural purposes, there has always been more to food than meets the eye—or the taste buds, for that matter. Since an apple a day is powerful enough to keep the doctor away, for instance, and since an apple can cause the loss of Eden, what else is food capable of doing? This question animates holy women's reflections about the binding powers of food, the variety of its meanings, its potential for a spectrum of pleasures.

The lifestyles of the women in God's kitchen are as varied and interconnected as the meanings and the pleasures of the food found in their writings. First married and then single, at one time mothers and later free of family ties, late medieval and mystical, Angela of Foligno and Margery Kempe had much in common. Also from that period of flowering mysticism, Marguerite Porete and Julian of Norwich—guiding voices, if not subjects in this book of specific chapters—fit well together, for their visionary experiences and extraordinary writings. As a Carmelite and a leader, a teller of her own life and a fellow fighter, Teresa of Avila was a model for Cecilia Ferrazzi, who, though different in many ways, was a contemporary of Sor Juana; like Sor Juana and Teresa of Avila, Cecilia was celibate and consecrated, like them she was suspect to church authorities. Sor Juana and Cecilia both struggled throughout their lives with an orthodoxy that eventually, though in different ways, changed their behavior and crushed their aspirations. (Clinging to radical obedience, subtle in her use of language, Teresa was more successful in her self-definition.)

Still it might seem strange and anachronistic to proceed from these writers to a late-eighteenth- and early-nineteenth-century American woman—a saint, certainly, but by no means a traditional mystic: no visions motivate her actions, no spectacular graces decorate her existence. She was a doer, one who without apparent regrets chose the active over the contemplative life, Martha's less appreciated lot over Mary's better part. One for whom indeed the conflict between action and contemplation was never even a lifestyle option. Indeed, to the eyes of a contemporary observer, Elizabeth Ann Bayley Seton (1774–1821)—the first United States–born person to be canonized by the Roman Catholic Church (1975) and a patroness, in the United States, of parochial schools—could well embody an illustrious and spiritually fortified version of what has come to be known as the fulfillment of the American dream. She was enterprising, energetic, unafraid, and willing and capable of going from one job to another, of moving from one place to another, of making the most of the opportunities life offered her—despite a broken family of origin and an early widowhood, despite ill-health and homelessness, unemployment, geographical displacement, religious prejudice.

By any standard, Elizabeth had a busy, effective, productive, and varied life. Though the description of mysticism is a complicated and political one, only the most generous of such definitions would be able to include among the mystics this practical, sensible woman, more given to the care and education of children than to those disciplining practices that led some of her more contemplative predecessors to visions and ecstasies. Yet in her writings Elizabeth Ann Bayley Seton shares with us some mystical moments of union with God as well as many homemaking details connecting her daily activities to her spiritual growth. Her kitchen doings and the flavors of her vocation link her—for the meanings of her life and the pleasures of her spirit—to the mystics who preceded and followed her.

As was the case for many medieval mystics, the holy Eucharist was the focus of Elizabeth's spirituality as well: after her initial fear of idolatry, the enthusiastic frequency with which Elizabeth Seton approached the Eucharist became striking at a time when frequent communion was not the norm: "that *he is There* (oh heavenly theme!) is as certainly true as that Bread naturally taken removes my hunger—so this Bread of Angels removes my pain, my cares, warms, cheers, sooths, contents and renews my whole being." Like Angela of Foligno, Elizabeth performed a quasi consecration—when her dying husband, on Christmas Day, expressed a desire for the sacraments but no priests were available: "Yes he said 'and how I wish we could have the Sacrament'—Well we must do all we can, and putting a little wine in a glass I said different portions of Psalms and Prayers . . . and we took the cup of Thanksgiving." Like Catherine of Siena, Elizabeth did not hesitate to criticize clerics for their wrongdoings—even, for example, an ill-prepared sermon: "O, Sir, that awakens my anger! Do you remember a priest holds the honor of God on his lips. Do you not trouble, you to spread His fire He wishes so much enkindled? If you will not study and prepare when young, what when you are old? There is a Mother's lesson!" She uses her maternal authority in the absence of a priestly one, and like Teresa of Avila, she had a passion for obedience: "I am so in love now with rules that I see the *bit* of the bridle all gold, or the *reins* all of silk."[3] Like Thérèse of Lisieux, Elizabeth also took Jesus as her primary spiritual director. Like all of her fellow holy women discussed in these pages, food figures in the life and writings of Elizabeth Seton as a bond to her physical world and at the same time a connection to the spiritual dimension of life on earth.

God's generosity to this American saint was matched by the abundance of food on the American table during her lifetime: during Elizabeth Seton's years, the belief that Americans were better fed than their European counterparts and that their land generously provided them with all the food they needed and wanted was very much an integral part of American folklore: "It was natural, said the Philadelphia physician John Bell in 1793, that Americans, living amidst 'superabundance,' should be 'great eaters'" (a painfully prescient assertion, in retrospect, given today's figures for obesity in the United States).[4] So Elizabeth, a child of her land, can exclaim: "Oh, Food of Heaven, how my soul longs for you with desire!" (72).

Elizabeth Ann Bayley was born in New York City in 1774. Her Episcopalian family was prosperous: her father was a well-respected physician as well as the first professor of anatomy at Columbia University medical school; her mother died when Elizabeth was only three years old, and her father remarried within a year of his wife's death. Her relationship with her father was not always easy, and the fatherhood of God helped Elizabeth understand and in part redress the imbalance of that other paternal connection.

In an 1803 entry of her Italian journal—which she kept in order to share her experiences with her sister-in-law Rebecca Seton, her "Soul's Sister"— paternal love, mystical union, and food memories blend in Elizabeth's description as "one of those sweet pauses in spirit when the Body seems to be forgotten" (115). This pause consists of a pleasant reminiscence of a wagon trip to the woods in 1789, when Elizabeth's father was in England, and she, feeling unloved by her earthly father (he seems to have been quite inept at expressing love for either of his wives, nor was he much better with his three daughters), turns to her heavenly father for paternal protection. She is almost thirty, and thinks back to the time of her adolescence:

Italian Journal (December 1803)
in the year 1789 *when my father was in England* one morning in May in the lightness of a chearful heart I jumped in the waggon that was driving to the woods for brush about a mile from Home the Boy who drove it began to cut and I set off in the woods—soon found an outlet in a Medow, and a chesnut tree with several young ones growing round it, attracted my attention as a seat, but when I came to it found rich moss under it and a warm sun—here then was a sweet bed. the air still, a clear blue vault above, the numberless sounds of spring melody and joy—the sweet clovers and wild flowers I had got by the way, and a heart as innocent as a *human heart* could be filled with even enthusiastic love to God and admiration of his works—still I can feel every sensation that passed thro' my Soul—I thought at that time my Father did not care for me—well God was my Father-my All. I prayed-sung hymns-cryed-laughed in talking to myself of how far He could place me above all Sorrow—Then layed still to enjoy the Heavenly Peace that came over my Soul; and I am sure in the two hours so enjoyed I grew ten years in my spiritual life—told cousin *Joe* to go Home with his wood, not to mind me, and walked a mile round to *see* the *roof* of the *Parsonage*, where lived-the Parsons *son* of course-there I made another hearty Prayer-then sung all the way Home-with a good appetite for the *samp and fat pork.* (115)

And that is how the reminiscence ends, with the image of samp (a porridge made from coarsely ground corn) and fat pork and Elizabeth's hearty appetite for these dishes. ("For most Americans," we might remember so as to best understand this passage, "abundance meant lots of meat—mainly pork and, to a lesser extent, beef—accompanied by breads made from corn (maize), rye, and, increasingly, wheat.")[5] In the connection Elizabeth establishes between mystical experience, fatherhood, and food, she renews the observation of more contemporary religious thinkers: for instance, that "God's is no fatherhood as we have learned it from our fathers; it is not a fatherhood of power, but of equality. It is not a fatherhood of authority, but of unity."[6] As divine and biological fatherhood reflect and complete one another, so also Elizabeth perceives no contrast between a highly spiritual experience, one that concentrated ten years of growth and development into two hours, and the bodily desire for food.

As one of her biographers puts it, "One of the happy by-products of Elizabeth's grasp of the complex interweaving of the earthly and the heav-

enly, the human and the divine, was the way she could talk about the profoundly spiritual in the homeliest of terms, thus putting it in the reach of
all, as God intended."[7] Indeed, Elizabeth's craving for corn pudding and
fat pork arises at the height of an event described, in her own words, as
"one of those sweet pauses in spirit when the Body seems to be forgotten."
The body might be forgotten, but its love for samp and fat pork demands
to be remembered—and it succeeds. Hers is a personal meditation, a food
mnemonics, that encourages a communal sort of history, one that, by
making of food an agent of memory, highlights the continuity between
our body and our soul, between the little facts of everyday life and the
spiritual path holy people choose for themselves.

Elizabeth Ann Bayley married William Magee Seton, six years her elder,
in 1794 in New York, when she was twenty years old, and gave birth to and
raised five children: Anna Maria, born in 1795, William, in 1796, Richard
Bayley, in 1798, Catherine Josephine, in 1800, and Rebecca, in 1802. She
stuck with her husband when his initially prosperous import business
started declining in 1797 and when his good health deteriorated. Elizabeth
then moved with him and their oldest child to Italy in 1803 in order to try
and improve his physical condition through a better climate (the other
children were left in the care of Rebecca Seton, Elizabeth's "Soul's Sister").
Once in Livorno, however, where they arrived on November 19, the family was quarantined because of the New York yellow fever epidemic. The
cold, damp, and smoky conditions in the lazaretto, located on a canal a few
miles from the town of Livorno, were hardly beneficial to William's health,
and he died in Pisa on December 27, 1803, just days after leaving the
lazaretto that had been the three Setons' home for a month.

In a letter to Rebecca Seton, written two days into her sea journey,
Elizabeth writes of her experiences on the boat to Italy: her husband
William, she thinks with dismay, "has more appetite than I wish as it
brings on fever invariably " and "is pondering over his molasses and spoon
not very well able to keep his legs but not at all sick." Little Anna, her
eldest daughter and the only child to travel to Italy with her parents, "has
been very sick but after relieving her stomach has fallen asleep." Elizabeth
herself, on the other hand, ever cheerful, feels quite differently: "I am as
usual sober and quiet made my breakfast with great relish and it still sets
very comfortable" (97). Among the fevers, nauseas, and retching of her
loved ones, Elizabeth must continue, with enjoyment, to feed and to eat.
Among the fasting and eucharistic feasts of her fellow holy women, Elizabeth enjoys regular food—distinctively flouting the threefold pattern,

characteristic of the medieval period but found in later centuries as well, according to which "women fast, women feed others, and women eat (but never ordinary food)."[8]

Repeatedly, Elizabeth Seton breaks this monotonous model and, less and less in the course of her life will she find herself able to fast, consumed instead with the ascetic care of children and fellow nuns. A few years later, in 1807, Elizabeth will write to her Italian friend Antonio Filicchi—whom she addresses as "My dear Brother": "My Health is very much as when you left me—when I eat and drink, and laugh I am as well and gay as at fifteen" (199). "One who is cheerful and gay while at table benefits from his food" (Sir. 30:25), might be an appropriate biblical motto for Elizabeth. For, despite her modesty and simplicity, there is little doubt in the reader's mind of this woman's courage, strength, and physical, intellectual, and emotional health. The balance between the needs of the body and the needs of the soul is a striking achievement in the work of Elizabeth Seton. There is no dualism there, but rather a continuity in which she finds no paradox. This continuity is often conveyed in terms of food: in her relish for food Elizabeth finds spiritual and physical comfort, as well as the expression of her "soberness and quiet."

In her Italian journal Elizabeth also talks of the foods available when she arrived with her husband and daughter at the lazaretto near Livorno: "3 warm eggs, a bottle of wine and some slips of Bread" sent by the Capitano (105). He continues to favor them by also sending, for example, "chestnuts and fruits from his own table"—a relative feast, as little Anna Maria acutely observes, wondering why the European victims of a shipwreck housed in the same building "have not Bread" (113). No matter: William can touch neither eggs nor wine, and must rely instead on "our little syrrups, current jelly, drinks, etc. which he must have every half hour on board Ship" (105). Unfortunately, these are not available at the lazaretto, causing everyone great distress: "I had heard the Lazaretto the very place for comfort for the Sick—and brought Nothing . . ." writes Elizabeth (105). Fortunately, dinner came at sunset from the Filicchis, Elizabeth's Italian friends and protectors, a family who will later play a fundamental role in Elizabeth's conversion to Catholicism. The next morning William and little Ann had milk with bread (warm milk continues to be William's main source of nutrition), while Elizabeth breakfasted, more interestingly, on "a crust and glass of wine" (106).

Food, though simple and scarce, is the only material consolation in a room of cold bricks and walls, with mattresses spread on the bare floor and not even a fire to warm them up—hardly a healing environment for a tubercular man traveling to Italy in search of health improvement. When an elderly servant sent by the Filicchis, Louie, came to stay at the lazaretto so as to prepare the family meals, Elizabeth remarks with amused interest that he "makes excellent soup—cooks all with charcoal in little earthen pots" (108).

But the irony of their condition is painful even for this exceptional woman: "Consider—My Husband who left *his all* to seek a milder climate confined in this place of high and damp walls exposed to cold and wind which penetrates to the very bones, without fire except the kitchen charcoal which oppresses his Breast so much as to Nearly convulse him—no little syrup nor softener of the cough—Bark and milk, bitter tea, and opium pills which he takes quietly as a duty without seeming even *to hope*, is all I can offer him from day to day." These offers William appreciates, and lets his wife know: "Night and day he calls me '*his Life his Soul his dearest of Women his all*'" (110). Elizabeth's homemade medications, however, are limited to bark and milk, bitter tea and opium pills; what Elizabeth knows would help (cough syrups, cough softeners) are not obtainable, and, ironically, the only heat—that of the kitchen stove—is also the source of chest oppression due to its smoke. (Elizabeth herself, like her daughter, keeps warm by jumping rope, or hopping "on one foot five or six times the length of the room without stopping—laugh at me my Sister," she tells Rebecca Seton in her diary, "but it is very good exercise, and warms sooner than a fire when there is a warm heart to set it in motion" [112]).

Tuscany is known for its excellent food products and its simple but delicious peasant cuisine. And especially Livorno, a new city by Italian standards, and not known for its art and architecture, is nevertheless regarded as one of Italy's gastronomic capitals for seafood. But for the Setons' stay in the Livorno lazaretto, there is no Tuscan sun to flavor the bitter dishes; food is neither pleasure nor pastime much less a cultural connection, but rather food is necessity, medicine, and even salvation itself. Simple foods such as bread, milk, wine, and soup, are not very different from the more medicinal syrups and jellies, bitter tea and opium: to survive, the family must ingest them just as Elizabeth must prepare and serve them.

Metaphors of healing foods are not uncommon in spiritual writings, and Elizabeth's food, like that of her fellow holy women, is often metaphorical, symbolic, theological: she speaks of the Bread of Angels and is devoted to the Eucharist. But the workings of her memory, stimulated by a transatlantic journey from which she returns widowed and on the brink of conversion, impel her to make considerations and connections that are at once more practical and more tasteful, at once culinary and theological. She remembers about traveling the changes brought on by physical and spiritual displacement, she gives thanks for the grace of her own appetite and supports its absence in others. In making dinner for her darling children by boiling raisins in rice, she blends an ingredient from her Tuscan past—the raisins Antonio Filicchi brought to her, now living in New York, as a gift from Italy—with the cooking style of her present. And we have already read the most unusual of her food memories, when Elizabeth remembers with relish the savory conclusion of an adolescent experience of most intense spiritual growth (ten years concentrated in two hours): she leaves her prayerful spot in the woods with "a good appetite for the *samp and fat pork*" (115).

Ill themselves after William's death, as well as unable for a time to find a safe passage back to America, Elizabeth and Anna Maria stayed on in Tuscany until April 1804 (they arrived in New York on June 4), and came to love the relatively exotic country where William had lost his life. In Italy, they were exposed to Catholicism through their Italian friends, the Filicchis, William's business partners. After a period of doubt and soul searching, Elizabeth converted to the Roman Catholic religion in 1805: the year after her return to New York, Elizabeth was confirmed into the Catholic Church. With her conversion to Catholicism—and thus her belonging to a minority religious group still very much discriminated against in the upper-class New York society that was her home (the Episcopalians among whom she was born were the dominant religious and political group)—came a new interpretation of the rules of fasting, as she details in her Italian journal in April 1804:

> All the catholic religion is full of those meanings which interest me so— Why Rebecca they believe all we do and suffer, if we offer it for our sins serves to expiate them—you may remember when I asked Mr.H-what was meant by fasting in our prayer book, as I found myself on Ash Wednesday morning saying so foolishly to God, 'I turn to you in fasting, weeping and mourning' and I had come to church with a hearty breakfast of buckwheat cakes and coffee, and full of life and spirits with little thought of my sins, you may remember what he said about it being *old customs* etc. well the dear Mrs. F. who I am with never eats this Season of lent till after the clock strikes three (then the family assembles) and she says she offers her weakness and pain of fasting for her sins united with our Saviours sufferings—I like that very much. (134)

She likes it but has difficulty with it, and, given how expensive and difficult it is to buy fish (so much that her "Bread and Water Spirit is ashamed to partake of it"), Elizabeth even obtains a dispensation from Friday abstinence—a dispensation she does not plan on using. "I am a poor creature," she writes Antonio Filicchi with surprising frankness, "before I was in the blessed Ark could fast *all day* on Friday, now can hardly wait from one meal to the other without faintness" (188).

But what Elizabeth learns about Italians' relationship with food is obviously not only focused on fasting: when Antonio visits her in New York in 1805, his wife (the Mrs. F. of the quotation above) has him bring Elizabeth raisins and figs (though what Elizabeth does with the raisins, which Tuscans might embed in biscotti and other baked goods, is rather American: "I boil them in rice for [my Darlings] and it makes an excellent dinner")—and Elizabeth reciprocates, or at least wishes she could reciprocate, with "some fine *Apples*" (175).

Elizabeth's conversion isolated her further from her family and friends, though she managed to survive the financial difficulties of a thirty-year-old widow with five children by opening first a school for boys—which had to be closed down because of rumors that she was trying to proselytize into the Catholic Church—and then, in 1808, a Catholic school for girls in Baltimore at the invitation of some local priests. Elizabeth stayed in Baltimore, at the Paca Street School, only one year; the school was then moved to the more rural Emmitsburg, a small town near the Pennsylvania border, and renamed Saint Joseph Academy (which eventually became Saint Joseph's College).

Elizabeth Ann Seton's writings make it clear that she was passionately in love with her children: her greatest spiritual turmoil was brought on by the premature death of her oldest child, Anna Maria, in 1812, when the girl was only sixteen. Elizabeth was a true working mother, whose vows of poverty had to be modified so that she could properly handle her children's affairs even as she headed her new religious community. Her two boys went to the nearby Catholic seminary of Georgetown in 1806, when William was ten and Richard eight, in order to strengthen their faith and perhaps encourage a vocation to the priesthood (neither of them became a priest). After the family's move to Maryland in 1808, the boys were living in Catholic academies located near their mother. Her three girls, on the other hand, remained with Elizabeth until separated by death.

One of Elizabeth's editors described her difficulties with an exquisite understatement: "That the community's head was a recent convert widow, with five children still dependent on her, further complicated matters" (29). In this respect, it is worth contrasting Elizabeth's experience with that of the Italian mystic Angela of Foligno, known for her seemingly cruel prayer for the death of her family (mother, husband, children) so that she may be free to follow God's path for her: her life is so embedded in the rules of homemaking as to require a way out in order for her to be who God is demanding that she is. Analogously, for Margery Kempe the need to separate from her husband surely must go beyond the sexual chastity she protests to seek. Elizabeth on the other hand, although she was also, like Angela, a widow (husbands are most often an impediment to the official recognition of women's holiness), managed to successfully combine her motherhood with her religious vocation. Her situation is at once simpler and more complex. It is more complex biographically, because her children stay with her throughout her journey—they do not die like Angela's unspecified number or mysteriously disappear from the story like Margery's fourteen. Elizabeth's situation is simpler spiritually, because it never seems to be a question for her of what to do with her children, or with their eating and feeding needs: her ministering to her biological children, as well as to her symbolic ones, is from the beginning and very much remains a part of Elizabeth's identity and of her spiritual path. And so, while Angela is known as the master of theologians, Elizabeth Ann Seton is commonly referred to as Mother Seton: mother of five children, mother of the women religious in the communities she founded, and mother to the many women and men who for two centuries have been praying to God through her maternal intercession.

Elizabeth Seton's first job as wife and biological mother was a productive one, with the birth of five children in seven years, and her second job as a nun and spiritual mother was no less prolific. In 1809 Elizabeth took vows as a Sister of Charity of Saint Joseph, and began to be called Mother Seton. Elizabeth began a sisterhood modeled after the Rule of Saint Vincent de Paul for the Daughters of Charity in France; it was called the Sisters of Charity in the United States. More schools and communities later arose out of these original ones, so that Elizabeth's offspring grew in very many ways. After three years of illness, Elizabeth Ann Seton died of tuberculosis in 1821, on January 4—which is also now celebrated as her feast day (Saint Elizabeth Ann Seton shares her day of death and also her feast day with another holy mother and cook for God, the Blessed Angela of Foligno). By the time of her death, there were twenty houses of her new order.

The poet Charles Simic writes of a friend who finds the obsession with food to be the best available evidence for the existence of the soul: one's body can be satisfied after a meal even when one's soul is not. Simic's own rather non sequitur conclusion is that his friend's conundrum is a sign of happiness, and that "When our souls are happy, they talk about food."[9] This is true of many holy women writers as well: that their happy soul, that is, sometimes speaks with God and of God in the vocabulary of cooking and eating, of food and drink. By linking food with memory and repetition, with contemplation and liturgy, Jesus' encouragement at the Last Supper to eat and drink "in memory of me" establishes the holiness of serving, of feeding, of eating. Though herself a devoted participant in the Eucharist, Elizabeth Ann Seton remembers her food and its sacramental nature in more personal terms as well. The corn pudding and pork fat of Elizabeth's reminiscence, recalled at a time of nutritional distress about her husband (in 1803 she wrote about an idyllic 1789 experience while at the Livorno lazaretto, in the midst of great suffering over her husband's ill health and her own inability to comfort and feed him), are central to this woman's writing and life project. Their memory is exemplary of Elizabeth's spirituality and of the inevitable sanctification of embodiment that the celebration of her life should bring on. Food, as we have seen through numerous examples, is very much a part of Elizabeth Seton's spiritual and earthly journey, be it the food desired for herself and consumed at the end of a highly spiritual experience—the samp and pork fat eaten as an adolescent and vividly remembered (like Proust's far more famous *madeleines*) many years later, in a different continent, at a different stage of life—or the food desired for her husband yet not available at the beginning of another spiritual experience—her trip to Italy as the inception of her conversion to Catholicism. In Italy, Elizabeth's remembrance of foods past, of her adolescent connection between spiritual quest and gastronomic desire, heightens the pain of her present inability to feed her beloved in the satisfying and healing way that God once fed her. It is the absence, rather than, as in Proust, the presence, of past tastes and familiar foods that triggers culinary, and mystical, memory. And yet, with the intensification of the pain of absence comes also a deepening of the meaning of this pain through its memory. Nowhere is food more meaningful for Elizabeth Seton, never does it elicit such deep pleasure for her, as when it is remembered and relished as the sign of an enduring, sacramental bond between present and past, self and other, human and divine.

11

How to Indulge
in Divine Delicacies

GEMMA GALGANI'S TASTY TREATS

*T*O FEAST ON THE EUCHARIST and to fast from daily fares:
these are but the most dramatic and better-known features of a
relationship—that between women, food, and holiness—involving uneven measures of personal choice and religious tradition, mouths
moving in speech, prayer, and eating, as well as numerous voices heard,
read, and written along with dishes prepared and consumed. Christian
holy women's religious and culinary beliefs and practices are shaped by
connections, meanings, and pleasure. Silent and vocal prayer advances the
understanding of (and the connections between) self and other—also a
relationship of serving and feeding. Mystical and contemplative union
with God brings (often pleasurable) graces—honeyed or sugary as the
sweetest of dishes. Prophetic and visionary experiences confer authority
(through their exceptional meanings) otherwise to be found, for long centuries and in limited ways, primarily in homemaking skills. Not only is this
true for religious women: the bond with food is a problematic one for
women in general: "There is no area of a woman's life quite like her relationship to food. It is an area fraught with fascination and contradiction,
with longing and disgust, with resolution and strange capriciousness. For

most women, food is a major preoccupation. An obsessive engagement."[1] Obsessive and laden with attraction and opposition, desire and revulsion, resolution and strange whims, is how the relationship between women and food has been described. But similar levels of contradiction and dualism, of hesitation and doubt, also permeate the engagement between food and Christianity. Meat, for example, is a suspicious food because it was linked for early Christians with blood, violence, paganism, as well as with sexuality and the flesh in general. Saint Jerome overtly advises those seeking perfection to refrain from consuming meat: "*si vis perfectus esse, bonum est carnem non manducare*," "if you want to be perfect, it is good not to eat meat." And thus, starting in the fourth century, every Christian was obliged to follow the rules of abstinence for at least part of the year (during Lent and Advent, for example, and on certain days of the week).[2]

Meat is not the only suspicious food, however: the pleasure found in *any* food is an object of distrust, and food temptations need to be overcome. In order to do this, Catherine of Genoa seasoned "any food she had a particular liking for" with "hepatic aloe and ground agarico" ("*dell'aloe epatico et agarico pesto*"): hepatic aloe is an especially bitter and opaque species of aloe, used in herbal medicine, while agarico is a sour-tasting poisonous mushroom.[3] Though Catherine's may be a rather extreme way of mortifying the sense of taste, all Catholics are called to find penance in their daily life, including food, and still today they are bound to abstinence and fasting during Lent, in preparation for the lavish banquet that is the Resurrection.

The Protestant tradition has its dietetic counterpart in certain of its groups—such as the ascetic Lutheran sect portrayed in Gabriel Axel's *Babette's Feast* (1987), set in late-nineteenth-century Denmark. In this movie, images and sounds underline the meanings of food through the connections it strengthens and the pleasure it gives—even in spite of the eaters themselves, reluctant to savor it and suspicious of its effects. Based on a 1953 short story by celebrated Danish writer Karen Blixen, a.k.a. Isak Dinesen (1885–1962), the movie tells the tale of two unmarried sisters, Martina and Philippa, and their French cook Babette Hersant. For fourteen years Babette serves them in exchange for little more than room and board—and a sorry board at that: their diet consists in stockfish and brown ale-bread soup—her only remaining tie with France is a lottery ticket that a friend plays for her every year. When she wins ten thousand francs at the lottery, the sisters fear that Babette, now rich, will leave them.

But instead Babette pleads with them to let her cook, in their father's honor, a true French dinner for them and their old friends. Afraid that this dinner will be a witches' Sabbath, the eleven friends vow not to talk about or enjoy the food and drink. At dinner, they are joined by the nephew of one of the old ladies; having been stationed in Paris, he recognizes in the unique *cailles en sarcophage* the signature dish of a celebrated Parisian woman chef. Babette reveals to Martina and Philippa that she was that chef and that she had spent her entire lottery winnings on the dinner, because she is an artist and longed to do her best. Philippa tells Babette that in Heaven she will be the great artist that God always intended her to be. Though Philippa does not say as much, we can easily imagine Babette as the star chef in God's kitchen.[4]

Who among the female characters in the movie is most like the mystics that are the subjects of these pages? Martina and Philippa are the ascetic ones, who best conform to the popular image of the mystic: dedicated to prayer and care of the poor, virginal so as to best serve the father/Father, rejecting all worldly pleasure and all earthly love and ambition, in the joyful expectation of the spiritual fulfillment that is to come. Babette, on the other hand, has been a wife and mother and is the practical Martha to Martina and Philippa who, like Mary, have chosen, according to Luke's gospel, "the better part" (Luke 10:42). Babette is the one who satisfies the hunger of the villagers, their appetite for more than the subsistence fare that was their daily lot—the staleness of the bread having infected their spiritual relationships as well. The fish the community ate, before Babette's arrival, was long dead, hanging on sticks left to dry in the northern wind (this is the stockfish we have encountered in the story of Margery Kempe). What Babette cooks, on the other hand, turtle and quails, starts out alive and loved: Babette calls the birds she will cook *"mes petites cailles,"* "my little quails"—a term of endearment in French (and a reference to the quail sent by God to the Israelites in Exodus 16).

Alive as her food, and equally nourishing, is Babette's transformative, eucharistic gift to the community—a gastronomical gift of sensual delight and of life's sweetest graces, a connection with the divine that is also a connection between Babette and the holy women who, like Margery Kempe, Cecilia Ferrazzi, Elizabeth Seton, and the others, preceded her in doing God's work through the making and tasting of food. It is with the delightful flavor of sweetness that God returns the mystics' hospitality to him in their heart. Like God, Babette shows gratitude with a lavish feast for the hospitality that the two sisters had shown her fourteen years ear-lier. So lavish, in fact, that her tale could be seen as a story of death and resurrection, leading the twelve Danish villagers from sin to salvation, from captivity to freedom, from spiritual death to life—through the feast, Babette's "last" supper, prepared in a kitchen where it is not so difficult for the viewer to see God's hand also at work, chopping and blending, pour-ing and mixing, and making all things new.

Just a few years after the setting of Axel's film, in a European kitchen farther south, God was working through the hands of another woman in the kitchen. We do not know whether Mea, a cook for the prosperous Giannini family in Lucca, Tuscany, was as skilled and as inventive as Babette. Probably not, given that she was feeding on a daily basis a large family of a dozen children plus half a dozen or so adults. In one of Gemma Galgani's letters to her beloved spiritual director, Father Ger-mano, we read: "Dear Dad, today finally your dear angel has also appeared. How beautiful he was! . . . Imagine: he came into the kitchen while Mea, the cook, was making meatballs! I was there watching her make them, and I was thinking . . . I was thinking . . . of Jesus."[5] Mea does not even notice the angelic visitor and keeps on making her inspiring meatballs. But Gemma sees both the meatballs (*le polpette*) and the angel (not her own guardian angel this time, who spends much time with her, but another, Father Germano's), and as her life comes to a close—at the time of the meatballs, she has less than two years left—angelic visits while she is in the presence of food increase in both frequency and meaning, even as her appetite for and consumption of food diminishes. In Lucca, visitors to her shrine can see Gemma's favorite spoon, with a hole through the spoon's cup, and her readers are familiar with her request to be denied the taste of food. She asks her director in a letter: "*Are you happy that I ask Jesus the grace to not let me taste, for as long as I live, any fla-vor in any food?* Daddy, this grace is necessary to me."[6] In return, she shares with her spiritual father the certainty of her ability to keep food down, to not throw it all up anymore.

Gemma's relationship with food was complicated, tinged with anorexia and flavored by her sweet tooth. Like her near contemporary Thérèse of Lisieux (who had the sweetest of saintly teeth), Gemma Galgani (1878–1903) lived during the golden age of feminism, of psychoanalysis, and of sweets, and through the emergence of a mass consumer culture: the lowering of sugar prices and the development of new food technologies turned sweets and chocolate—treats for the rich during the preceding centuries—into industrialized modern commodities available to larger numbers of people than ever before. In the medical field during the late nineteenth and early twentieth century, the nutritional properties of sugar were at the center of much studying, particularly in France. At that time, France was indeed developing a conscious, and complex, relationship to food and drink as part of its national identity. There, consumption of sugar was 2.64 pounds per person per year between 1815 and 1824, but rose to 26.4 pounds per year between 1885 and 1894—Thérèse's years (between 1920 and 1924 consumption of sugar in France again increased to 52.8 pounds per year). In Europe, the industrialization of the sweets industry, aided by the increased extraction of sugar from beets (which made European nations less dependent on the import of cane sugar), started around 1750 and developed in the course of the nineteenth century: European chocolate was first produced industrially in 1802, candies in 1878, cookies in 1888. And though it is commonly assumed that human beings have an innate preference for sweet foods (an instinctive incentive to consume mother's sweet milk), in France at the turn of the century the working and peasant classes had to be taught to like sweets, because they traditionally mistrusted them.[7] Though studies have focused on France, similar claims may be made about Italy, and indeed I still clearly remember my paternal grandmother (born in the late 1800s—she refused to remember the precise date) repeatedly reminding us children that sugar must be avoided because "sugar gives you worms": "*lo zucchero fa venire i vermi.*" (How and where, exactly, we never asked.)

Unlike the protagonists of some nineteenth-century literature, Thérèse of Lisieux and Gemma Galgani were certainly not forced to enter the convent—in fact, they spent inordinate amounts of energy trying to let themselves into one despite forceful opposition from those around them. Marriage was not an option they considered, having chosen since childhood Jesus Christ as their spouse. Thérèse was born in early 1873 and died in late 1897; Gemma was born in the spring of 1878 and died in the spring of 1903. Both lived their entire lives in predominantly Catholic countries, France and Italy. Both came from large families and both lost their mother at an early age. Both were beautiful, ideal images of nineteenth-century women, and of both we have several photographs that played an important part in the quick spread of their cult. The interpretation of these saints' beauty as an expression of their spiritual elevation might be an exception, if it is true that female beauty "is almost never perceived as a manifestation of, an appearance by a phenomenon expressive of interiority—whether of love, of thought, of flesh," having instead the role of "a *garment* ultimately designed to attract the other into the self."[8] Both Gemma and Thérèse longed for daily Communion. Both left numerous personal letters as well as autobiographical writings. Both lived short, spiritually full lives, and died of tuberculosis—that most romantic, transcendent of diseases—at almost exactly the same age: Gemma had just turned twenty-five, Thérèse was three months away from her twenty-fifth birthday. The ethereal beauty of both, literally consumed by illness, seems to have peaked at the moment of their death, according to those who witnessed it. Despite the shortness of their lives, by the time they died both had developed a reputation, and the self-assurance, of sanctity. Both were canonized in the first half of the twentieth century, and not long after their deaths: Thérèse in 1925 and Gemma in 1940.

Gemma Galgani and Thérèse of Lisieux clearly had much in common. But at least as much, and probably more, separates these two saints. Thérèse was a Carmelite nun from the age of sixteen. Gemma longed for her entire life to enter the convent, and specifically, in her last few years, a Passionist convent, yet she was never allowed on account of her poor health (and, she significantly believed, of her poverty). Thérèse had four loving sisters who were all, like her, nuns, and who with her father formed a close-knit family who adored her from birth on. Gemma lost her father not long after losing her mother, the brother and sister to whom she felt close died young, and the remaining siblings teased her about the more visible of her religious experiences. Gemma was an ecstatic and a stigmatic—the first of the twentieth century. Thérèse's extraordinary spirituality manifested itself in much less dramatic forms: a cult of the small, the ordinary, the childlike. Gemma's writings were published after her canonization by the press of the Passionist Order, and through the twentieth century few people remembered or read them. Thérèse's *Histoire d'une âme*, translated into English as *The Story of a Soul*, received an enthusiastic welcome when it was first published in 1898, the year after Thérèse's death, and within a short time several editions and translations in thirty-five different languages were published, with millions of copies bought and read throughout the world. Thérèse was proclaimed in 1997 doctor of the church: she is the third woman, after Teresa of Avila and Catherine of Siena, to receive this honor. Gemma's writings have been criticized for their immature peevishness. Gemma, we are told, is simply childish while Thérèse heroically made childhood the basis of her spiritual doctrine.[9] Also importantly, while both women went through an extraordinary amount of suffering in their lives, Thérèse turned this suffering into child-like joy, while Gemma experienced it as the very adult pain of an often neglected lover.

Both women, at least beginning in adolescence and for the rest of their short lives, ate little. Both would have perhaps lived longer had they eaten better and, more generally, taken better care of themselves. Why then look at food in their writings from a positive perspective? Why disregard their obsession with the Eucharist and focus instead on the more rarely mentioned details of nonsacramental foods and drinks? In part it is because the study of spirituality should engage the quotidian, the mundane, especially when we are trying to understand the lives of women often so inextricably entangled with the details of daily life. Perhaps because these mundane details, not as layered with centuries of religious tradition as the Eucharist, provide a more spontaneous view of the women involved, paint a picture less determined by external interpretations of the spiritual meal. And perhaps also because these seemingly meaningless details bring Gemma and Thérèse together without overlooking their differences—and their seeming meaninglessness may help us understand the seeming meaninglessness of these women's suffering. Finally, and more hypothetically, because together—and sweet treats bring Gemma and Thérèse together in novel and thought-provoking ways—these two saints remind us, like Agatha's two breasts and Lucy's two eyes, of two things. First, they remind us of the return of the repressed, in psychoanalytic terms, namely, the reappearance of the ignored and the unspoken—the other breast that comes back in artistic representations, the food given up in fast and abstinence that reappears in the details of autobiography. Second, and less obviously, they remind us of the insufficiency, the inappropriateness of forcing a unifying narrative in the study of women's language, along the lines of what feminist theorist Luce Irigaray has elaborated as the "two lips."[10]

The image of the two lips, drawn from female anatomy, founds Irigaray's claim that women's sex, and women's language, is not "one," cannot be reduced to that logic of the one that in turn homologates, and thus transforms the other (women, for example) into a copy of the same (of men, in that case)—and a pale, deficient copy at that. The paradigm of the two, of the lips and of the labia, of the breasts as well, is modeled on a relationship in which the other is accepted and respected, in which difference is recognized. Just as for Thérèse herself, as we will see, "one"—of anything—is not enough, so also in our reading of holy women a focus on the two, an acceptance that contradictory elements cannot always be conflated and reduced into a comfortable narrative, can give us the understanding that one cannot give us: the ability to follow Gemma's and Thérèse's dual claim when, anticipating Irigaray's own plea for women's divinization, they tell themselves and us of their sinfulness, yes, but also that they will become saints, great saints, and, possibly, even divine.[11]

Gemma Galgani was born in 1878 in Camigliano, a suburb of the Tuscan town of Lucca, the fifth of eight children. One month after her birth the family moved to Lucca. Her father was a well-to-do pharmacist, and she was tutored at home through elementary school. Starting in 1889 she continued her studies at the institute of the "Zitine," newly founded by Blessed Elena Guerra, though in 1893 she had to leave it because of her poor health. Her childhood was brusquely interrupted by the death of her mother when she was eight years old, then of her beloved older brother Gino, who was a seminarian, in 1894, and finally of her father in 1897. The latter death led to the family's financial collapse and general disintegration. In 1889–1890 Gemma was miraculously healed of spinal tuberculosis, and her mystical experiences began. Impoverished, in 1900 she was taken in by the Giannini family. This large household consisted of husband and wife, eleven children (aged two to twenty-two) and one more on the way, an aunt, a priest, a cook, a nanny, and an elderly male servant. It was Signora Cecilia, the unmarried aunt, who more than anyone else took Gemma under her wing.

Given her youth, beauty, poor health, and extraordinary spirituality (she received the stigmata for the first time in June 1899, and every week thereafter, between Thursday night and Friday), Gemma quickly became the center of this group's curious attention. What she wanted and desperately asked for throughout her short adult life, however, was to be concealed and locked away in a convent, to be preserved from the inquiring eyes and hands of the curious ones surrounding her. Her position at the Gianninis was between that of a permanent guest and an unpaid servant, even though the family's matriarch always vehemently denied that Gemma did anything other than contribute to the household like everyone else in it. The Passionist Father Germano Ruoppolo visited the Giannini residence one day in 1900 and became interested in Gemma's experiences—the stigmata and other bodily phenomena that testified to her participation in the Passion, as well as her numerous and vivid visions of Jesus, Mary, her guardian angel, Saint Paul of the Cross (1694–1775), and Saint Gabriel of Our Lady of Sorrows (1838–1862). Father Germano then became Gemma's spiritual director, the one she chose and trusted infinitely more than her original spiritual director, Monsignor Volpi— who was from the beginning suspicious of the graces that filled Gemma's prayer life.

In 1902, Gemma had to leave the Giannini home because her health had deteriorated so much that she posed the danger of contagion. She died of tuberculosis, the white plague, derelict and abandoned, in a room in Via della Rosa, just around the corner from the Gianninis' Lucchese home, on Holy Saturday of the year 1903. In 1905, the first Passionist nuns arrived in Lucca to found the convent that Gemma had so much desired and worked for during her life. Gemma was beatified in 1933 and canonized in 1940, the first saint and the first stigmatic of the twentieth century. Gemma's surviving writings consist of an *Autobiography* in the form of a letter of general confession, written in 1901 and addressed to Father Germano; a *Diary* that records the events that happened between July 19 and September 3, 1900; numerous letters addressed to Father Germano, to her ordinary confessor Monsignor Volpi, and to members of her family, to members of the Giannini family, and to other acquaintances; and the *Ecstasies*, which are the words Gemma said while in ecstasy, written down not by Gemma herself but by the women around her.

Lucca is known for its olive oil and wine, it produces a variety of cold cuts and cheeses, and its cuisine does delicious things with spelt and wheat, but Gemma, though deeply tied to Lucca in physical and spiritual ways, is not a child of her hometown as far as food is concerned. It is true that she receives that angelic visit in the Giannini kitchen while Mea was making meatballs. But, like Julian with her hazelnut, Gemma does not say that she ate those meatballs. Indeed, Gemma's references to food are mostly to say that she cannot eat, that God doesn't allow it, or that occasionally she is allowed to keep down some food. Gemma even asks her spiritual director, Fr. Germano, for permission to ask God not to let her taste "any flavor in any food."[12] It is difficult not to think of anorexia in Gemma's life, particularly as in her case the diagnosis would not be anachronistic: it was precisely in the late nineteenth century that the term "anorexia nervosa" was used for the first time, and Gemma is not immune to the neurotic behaviors that might allow us to characterize her as mentally (but also physically and socially) ill. The control that she exerts on her body by not eating, for example, must be understood in the context of a life where she had no control over where and what her body would be—homeless and penniless, rejected by the convents she desired to enter, Gemma could not choose her abode. Nor could she control the tuberculosis that was to take her life at such a young age: she is the object of consumption rather than its subject. While certainly Gemma's relationship with food could not be called exemplary, it would also be misleading to reduce its spiritual complexity to a bodily pathology dictated by self-destructive, individualistic mental processes. Gemma places herself, and readers familiar with the history of spirituality can also easily place her, in a genealogical line of Christian holy fasting that in turn had pre-Christian roots in fasting as an expression and exorcism of pain, as a purification of the soul that aids contact with the divine, as a philosophical choice indicating the liberation of the soul from the body, a return to the soul's original purity, and ultimately the refusal of any fleshly bond.[13]

Gemma's writings are no cookbooks. Others are the concerns that consume her: following Jesus so as to connect with God, a quest for meaning in the religious life, the pursuit of ecstatic pleasure. But occasionally Gemma speaks of treats, and speaks of them with delight, with unsuspected indulgence—perhaps because they remind her of Jesus' own *dolcezza*, that sweetness that is always on her lips. In a letter to Fr. Germano, Gemma writes that her benefactress Cecilia Giannini takes good care of her by remaining by her side while she suffers, and that in some ways Signora Cecilia prefers Gemma to the others in the family—particularly because she gives her "chocolate and a lot of wine." Although she says she does not deserve any of this, and should instead be treated "like the chickens," in Signora Cecilia's treats Gemma tastes a love otherwise absent from her family life (chocolate was also a favorite Catholic drink because, though nutritious, it was liquid and therefore not believed to break the obligatory fast of Lent, Fridays, and the hours before taking the Eucharist).[14]

Just about one year later, on November 17, 1901, Gemma tells her confessor that the next day she will send him tobacco and mints—sharing with the most important man in her life the flavor of the God-man's bittersweet delights. And a few months later still, on January 28, 1902, Gemma asks Fr. Germano to add in his letter a line for Sister Maria, so that the nun will bring her mints, *"mentini,"* this time.[15] More mysteriously, on July 20, 1902, Gemma tells Fr. Germano that her guardian angel, with whom she has daily conversations, has given her to drink "a few drops of a white liquid in a little golden glass, telling [her] that is was the medicine with which the doctor of Heaven healed his patients."[16] Symbol of purity and thus also of virginity, whiteness reflects in food and drink the condition that Gemma regarded as essential for the salvation of her soul and the integrity of her body. Liquid, unlike food, is an instrument of salvation much like, in the form of chocolate and wine, it was a bearer of love and privilege. In her *Diary*, in the entry dated August 20, 1900, Gemma had already written that her guardian angel, when she felt unwell after eating, gave her "a cup of coffee so good that I was healed instantly."[17] As the name of that most popular of Italian desserts, *tiramisù*, suggests (a creamy sweet spiked with both alcohol and espresso), coffee picks you up, its healing and strengthening properties having been long touted by its supporters.

Chocolate, mints, coffee, wine, white medicine . . . none of this is regular food, all of it is special, a treat, whether it is the highly symbolic and intoxicating wine, the coffee that had been so problematic in the eighteenth century, the still-expensive and exclusive chocolate. We know too little about each of these foods in Gemma's story to interpret them individually, but together they produce questions, if not answers: Does Gemma hope to salvage the tattered dignity of the homeless orphan that she was through these luxury items—among the few foods she associates with desire rather than sickness? Is she reclaiming the treats of a childhood that was never hers? What does she communicate with these choices, how do they help her establish her identity, regain her well-being, express her desires? Does she give up food and take up sweets the way she renounces marriage and embraces divine ecstasy? Could we see, between these two choices, a relationship of analogy rather than sublimation? Gemma Galgani's foods appear as a still life: a handful of appetizing delicacies on an otherwise empty table, their dramatic chiaroscuro staring at Gemma's hungry soul. At once alive and dead, *natura morta*—as the still life is called in Italian—is literally "dead nature," suggesting the transience of nature, of food in particular, and the need for mimesis and metaphor in order to represent it. In traditional painted still life items such as exotic fruit point to the patron's wealth, while in Gemma's textual still life the treats she evokes signal, in their scarcity, the pleasure and desire of a life she ultimately rejects. Gemma's mention of treats such as chocolate and coffee, wine and mints, in her otherwise bare foodscape, highlight the writhing image of her self-starvation, even as they show her to be a young woman hungry for that sweetness that only divine contact was able to give her: "I thank you, Jesus, for letting me taste this sweetness; but I am ready to be deprived of it forever, forever."[18]

There is safety and there is danger in Gemma's bond with food: the safety of those who gave her healing treats, the danger of the lack of nourishment from more substantial fares. Eating is for her nourishment and poison at once. Gemma's choices are both familiar and alien when compared to those of many of today's young women—and, perhaps, akin in more constructive ways to the choices of children, as well. Chocolate and wine, mints and coffee counterpoint presence and absence in Gemma's journey; they are an equivalent of junk food, the only food she seems to desire and is able to keep down. If it is true that, "food belongs to the adult world and is symbolic of the adult's control over children," that, "by disordering and confusing the conceptual categories of the adult world children erect a new boundary over which adults have no authority," and that, "by eating that which is ambiguous in adult terms the child establishes an alternative system of meanings which adults cannot perceive,"[19] then we might be able to imagine an alternative or a complementary reading to Gemma's anorexia—a rejection of bourgeois food in favor not of self-destruction but of an alternative pleasure. The pleasure of mints and chocolate is fleeting, as Gemma knows well, that of God less so. Food is as rare in Gemma's writings and life as it is important to her mission: aware that each of her suppers might be the last one, the pain of its abundance underlines the necessity of its absence. The displacement of food into the sacraments is the measure of God's ability to provide her with eternal delight.

If Gemma Galgani's language and behavior can at times be called childish, her existential choice is thoroughly adult: unlike Thérèse of Lisieux, Gemma seems to know the pleasures of a bride. Gemma even longs to be Christ's *lover*—possibly the only Italian mystic to have so boldly expressed her desire to unite with God: "You will always be my father, and I will always be your faithful daughter, and, if you like, I will be your lover . . . " ("*Mi sarai sempre padre, ed io sarò sempre tua figlia fedele e, se ti piace, sarò tua amante . . .* ").[20] Thérèse on the other hand makes of childhood her chosen path, and when she calls herself Christ's bride, there is no hint of the pleasures of the wedding chamber. The two women live out their earthly singleness and divine marriage in very different ways—ways that embody and are embodied in the contradictions of the relationship between women and sweets, between these women and their sweets. Sweets connote childish pleasures on the one hand and erotic delight on the other: candy bars are treats, while chocolate truffles are aphrodisiacs. Ravenous yet unable to eat, Gemma prefers to indulge in the taste of her bridegroom through the sweetness of eroticism: "O love, o endless love! . . . See: your love, my Lord, penetrates me, it passionately enters my body. When, when will I unite myself with you, my Lord, you who keep me united with you here on earth with such force of love? . . . Do it, do it! . . . Let me die, and die of love!"[21] "*Ch'io muoia, e muoia d'amore*": these are the words of a passionate lover, not of a child. Because, unlike Gemma, Thérèse chooses instead the sweetness of childhood in order to be one with her beloved—and the sweetness of her childhood, as we will soon see, is best expressed in the sweets that dot the account of her early years.

12

How to Savor Sweets, Play with Food, and Dress a Salad

FLAVORING THE SPIRIT
WITH THÉRÈSE OF LISIEUX

D O WOMEN CRAVE SWEETS because they themselves are sweet? Or is eating sweets what makes them sweet? Jean-Jacques Rousseau, in his epistolary novel *La nouvelle Héloïse* (1761), claimed that sugar and milk products are naturally preferred by women's taste, they are like "the symbol of female innocence and sweetness"—while men prefer stronger flavors and alcoholic drinks (more generally, Rousseau claims, food preferences are a sign of a people's character: Italians are soft and effeminate because they eat vegetables, while the English consume so much meat that it makes them inflexible, harsh, and almost barbaric).[1] Some years later, in 1825, Brillat-Savarin read the same gender into the most popular of sweeteners, claiming that, "there is not a woman, especially if she be well-to-do, who does not spend more for her sugar than for her bread."[2] In turn-of-the-century America, candy eating was a feminized activity, and candy was shaped and marketed for women as the target consumers: an article from the *New York Times* said, in 1899, that "Three-fourths of the candy made is consumed by women, and half the other fourth by children, leaving men a pitiable fraction of the total amount."[3] In the assessment of a contemporary food writer, "Salt is the masculine presence in the tabletop constellation, sugar the feminine one. Sugar is not only sweet itself but a flatterer in other foods, heightening and mellowing flavors without introducing any taste of its own."[4] Indeed, when chocolate is considered an addiction, it is one favored by women, born in the cyclical nature of their body: "Most chocoholics are women and many of them crave chocolate most intensely just before their menstrual period."[5]

Some foods have been traditionally perceived, and some continue to be perceived, as more masculine, others as more feminine, and folk associations, as well as some of the metaphors that shape our language, reflect these distinctions. While the king eats "four-and-twenty blackbirds" his queen sups on bread and honey in her parlor; and if it weren't for the ogre's wife, Jack would have been gobbled up by the master of the castle at the top of his beanstalk. Linguists have developed a more specific association between women and dessert dishes in Standard English, such as cookie, cupcake, cheesecake, tart—some of which words are also used to describe the female genitals. Desserts are peripheral, and their frivolous, inessential qualities get metaphorically transferred onto the women to whom such toothsome items refer.[6] If we then relate women's existential and erotic sweetness with the sweetness of God and with the gendered perception of mysticism and, more generally, religion—because Christianity was described as early as the second century as the religion of "slaves, women and little children," and nineteenth-century Europe witnessed what has been called the "feminization" of Catholicism[7]—we are left with a series of sweet and sexy associations, or path-crossings, that are just too delicious to ignore.

Popular culture confirms some of the connections—religious, alimentary, linguistic—I just invoked. "What are little girls made of? Sugar and spice, and everything nice: That's what little girls are made of." The flavors of sugar and spices—pleasurable, even sinful and decadent, but also frivolous, dispensable, optional—coincide with the taste of girls (boys, on the other hand, being made of "snips—or frogs—and snails, and puppy dogs' tails," do not sound nearly as appetizing, nor, obviously, as sweet). Is this sweet identification not in fact extended beyond the childhood of "little girls" to the youth of nubile women? (I underline "young" because the combination of female maturity and the unmarried state is most commonly cooked up as a figure with very different flavors: the embittered or soured spinster.) Sweetness makes girls and young, unmarried women sexy and childish at once, for sweetness points to both the treats of child-hood and the eroticism of adults. Thus the infantilization of women, their alleged childishness, is in turn complicated by the association of sweetness with sensuality, as the pleasure of eating sweet foods has a sensual equivalent in erotic practices.

Nutritious fares are to reproductive sexuality, we might say, as sweets are to eroticism: sweets and eros are the most sensuous though perhaps the least necessary aspects of two basic physical needs—food and sex. They are the place where need is sublimated into something else, something more, where energy is expended for the attainment of a greater pleasure than nature herself would necessitate or provide. Clearly sweetness and pleasure are not the prerogative of women, but both are recurring concepts in the representation and self-representation of women, including holy women. Sweetness and pleasure make a contradictory claim to both female innocence—obedient childhood—and female guilt—transgressive sexuality.

The bride of the Song of Songs favored sweet flavors and, like her, Elisabeth of Schönau and Margaret Ebner encountered sugary sweetness in God their lover. For centuries convent confections have displayed a predilection for the making and baking of sweets. This divine sweetness surfaces time and again in holy women's texts, and several centuries after Elisabeth and Margaret, in the neighboring country of France, Thérèse of Lisieux (1873–1897) joins her mystical predecessors at this sweet intersection of affective and gustatory delight—and not only because of the luscious treats that appear throughout her writings. Most symbolically, Thérèse belongs among the sweet-toothed mystics because of the many accusations that she was herself too sugary sweet, a flatterer, with no taste of her own: her language is sugary, her story is sugary, her spirituality is sugary—and this gooey textual, biographical, and religious syrup has seeped into the language, story, and spirituality of those devoted to her cult.

The metaphoric potential of sweetness has been amply mined by Thérèse's friends and foes alike. In *The Eagle and the Dove*, the 1943 biographical study of Teresa of Avila (the eagle) and Thérèse of Lisieux (the dove) British writer Vita Sackville-West writes that, "The infantilism of Thérèse, the treacly dulcification, the reduction of the difficult to the easy, which inspire so enthusiastic a devotion and response in some, provoke an equivalent exasperation in others . . . There is, to some minds," Sackville-

West continues, "something infuriating about the imagery and phraseology we encounter, as nauseating as a surfeit of marshmallows." A few years later, Thérèse's biographer Ida Görres alludes to "the rosy, saccharine glaze" and "the honeyed insipidity of the usual representations of her," and Louis Bouyer notes that, in order to discover the true Thérèse, we need to "extract her from all this sugar."[8] A different flavor of saintliness is explored by Dorothy Day, who was born in the year of Thérèse's death and who wrote Thérèse's biography in 1960. As the founder of the Catholic Worker movement explains, Thérèse performed no miracles in her lifetime, her claim to sanctity being that "she was just good, good as the bread which the Normans bake in huge loaves, and which makes up a large part of their diet." Good as the bread of her land, and good as its drink, continues Day, "Good as the pale cider which takes the place of the wine of the rest of France, since Normandy is an apple country." In addition to flavor, Dorothy Day also refers to size—another frequent metaphor in the description of the saint of the Little Way: "'Small beer,' one might say. She compares to the great saints, as cider compares with wine, others might complain. But it is the world itself which has canonized her, it is the common people who have taken her to their hearts."[9] Predictably good as French bread, clean as apples and dull as cider, common as the people who made of her a saint. "Small beer," or even, one might add, "small fry." But through her simple and influential theology, the "Little Flower of Lisieux"—as Thérèse is known to her English-speaking devotees—was able to redeem the apparent futility of her short life, and particularly of her premature death, with the lasting and toothsome grace of endurance.

The Little Flower made virtue out of necessity and sainthood out of her smallness—out of the fact that, as one of her biographers put it, when we read her life we feel as if we "were being forced to look through the wrong end of a telescope."[10] Nineteenth-century France was rich in, and fascinated by, flamboyant religious phenomena: in 1830 Mary of Nazareth showed Catherine Labouré how to make a miraculous medal, in 1846 she appeared to two shepherds at La Salette, in 1858 Mary showed herself to Bernadette at Lourdes. During the last decades of the century, theologians and doctors were busily trying to distinguish or conflate the experiences of mystics and the symptoms of hysterics; at the same time writers and artists were turning en masse to religious images and symbols in order to express spiritual and scientific questions and discomforts.[11] Whether Thérèse can be considered a mystic is a matter of debate.[12] An inclusive definition of mysticism would count her in—she lived a contemplative life as a Carmelite, and the closeness of her connection with God, as she tells it in her autobiography, was exceedingly intimate. She speaks with God as with a dear friend, with Jesus as with a trusted bridegroom. But Thérèse's life does not include those extraordinary graces that filled the prayer life of both classical mystics such as Angela of Foligno and Teresa of Avila, and more recent ones such as Gemma Galgani; her sanctity is founded on the ordinariness of her calling and of her daily existence—an ordinariness she willfully raised to the level of extraordinary grace.

Born in Alençon, in northern France, in 1873, the last of five girls, Thérèse Martin moved to Lisieux following the death of her mother in 1877. After the entrance in the Carmel of her two oldest sisters, Thérèse decided that she, too, would become a Carmelite; through her insistence, and backed by her father, she entered at fifteen, in 1888. In the words of Hans Urs von Balthasar, "her call is absolute, more powerful than her own will, more powerful than her own self; it is the very source of her being. She has been chosen and cannot pay more heed to human arrangements than to God's will. And, even if it means getting churned up between the wheels of ecclesiastical clockwork, she must still go on."[13] In January 1896, ill with tuberculosis, Thérèse completed the first version of her autobiography, the part called Manuscript A. It was addressed to her sister Pauline (Mother Agnes), who at the time was prioress of the Lisieux Carmel and who had asked Thérèse to write down her childhood memories. Autobiography was a literary form appropriate for women and ideal for Thérèse. Her "little way" was made of nothing, it consisted in raising up to sanctity the small domestic virtues that characterized her life: "a man would never have been canonized on the basis of what Thérèse did."[14] In September of 1896 Thérèse completed Manuscript B, addressed to her sister Marie (Sister Marie of the Sacred Heart). Finally, Manuscript C, addressed to Mother Marie de Gonzague, was turned over to the prioress in January 1897. Thérèse died on September 30 of the same year, of the tuberculosis that had dramatically revealed itself during Holy Week of 1896, the blood on her handkerchief announcing, in Thérèse's elated words, "the Bridegroom's arrival."[15] She was happy to have died at twenty-four because this spared her the disappointment of not being able, because of her sex, to become a priest (twenty-four being the minimum age for the priesthood).[16]

Life at the Carmelite convent was dedicated primarily to prayer and work. It was a harsh life: housecleaning and laundry were demanding tasks; the convent, following the directives of Teresa of Avila, was not heated, and the rule included wearing sandals without socks. Food was, to put it generously, simple. Meat was allowed only in case of illness. Fasting was frequent and severe: Thérèse first coughed up blood on Good Friday of 1896, after God gave her "the consolation of observing the fast during Lent in all its rigor" (210–11). Thérèse's relationship with food, in the convent, was a painful one, particularly as she had difficulty digesting the milk and legumes that, with bread, were the staples of convent diet.

Even among the mortifications of convent life, at least in the first part of her stay, for Thérèse food preserves the aura of that familial love so central to her joyous vocation—and so absent from Gemma Galgani's story. In a letter to her father written from the convent, Thérèse writes of her "sweet mission" and thanks her "King" for "an avalanche of pears, onions, prunes, and apples, which came from the turn as from a horn of plenty. Where did all this come from?" Thérèse wonders, twice puzzled: by their provenance and by their ease in joining the Carmel: "The strange thing is they had less trouble entering [the convent] than your Queen, who was obliged to go to Rome to have the door opened for her" (she is referring to her trip to Rome, when she asked the pope for permission to become a Carmelite before the minimum age). Thérèse especially appreciates the most humble of her father's gifts: "The enormous onions delighted my heart; they made me think of those of Egypt. We shall not have to sigh for them as the Israelites did. I thought again of those from Lyons that cost fifty *centimes* and are so big."[17] With the adjective that describes her most distinctive flavor, Thérèse identifies her mission as "sweet," and then explicitly compares herself to, even identifies with, the produce—pears, onions, prunes, and apples—stating that it was easier for her father's gift to enter the convent than it was for his little queen—her father's other, more costly gift to the Carmelite Order. Humble food, bearing paternal love and divine abundance, is transfigured into religious figures of sorts—who enter the convent with greater ease than Thérèse herself—in a process characteristic of Thérèse's "little way, a way that is very straight, very short, and totally new" (207). It is in small and apparently insignificant things such as onions—a scriptural vegetable, by Thérèse's own avowal, reminiscent of the onions the Israelites had enjoyed in Egypt and missed after the conclusion of their captivity (Num. 11:5)—and through small and insignificant people such as herself, that the love of God, and of Jesus her bridegroom, is to be found.

A letter to Céline well illustrates Thérèse's worldview and her regard for the holiness of the ordinary. Thérèse describes one of her favorite fruits, "a beautiful peach, rosy and so sweet that no confectioner could imagine so sweet a flavor." Its beauty and sweetness impel her to ask her sister, "Tell me, Céline, was it *for the peach* that the good God created this lovely rose color, so velvety, so pleasant to see and touch? Was it for the peach alone that he used up so much sugar?" But she answers herself, attributing the significance of fruit to the ability of the peach to bind us to God, and writing, "Of course not, it was for us and not for the peach. What belongs to it, what makes the *essence* of its life, is its *kernel*, we can take away all its beauty without taking away *its being*."[18] After comparing herself to produce—both gifts of her earthly father to the Carmelite convent—Thérèse describes a piece of fruit as both a gift from her heavenly father (who indulges his daughter's sweet tooth with a sugary peach) and as an instance, a symbol, of the self-sacrifice that brings about life rather than self-destruction: we may eat the flesh of the peach, we are indeed encouraged to eat the flesh of the peach, because it is beautiful, rosy, sugary (adjectives that have been employed for Thérèse herself), but our eating does not consume the essence of the peach—nor does tuberculosis consume Thérèse's: human beings will not, they cannot destroy the kernel of the peach, where its essence resides. Physical death, Thérèse never tires to remember and to remind us, is but a prelude to true life, her peachy body but a shadow—though a sweet one indeed—of her immortal soul.

Weeks before her death, no longer able to enjoy the taste and texture of fruit in her mouth, Thérèse will say, "I get so much pleasure out of touching fruit, especially peaches, and I like to see them near me."[19] She does manage to eat one grape, because it is a gift from Jesus, but then recalls that, "The first time I was given grapes in the infirmary, I said to Jesus: 'How good the grapes are! I can't understand why You are waiting so long to take me, since I am a little grape, and they tell me I'm so ripe!'"[20] Thérèse will leave the convent the way she entered it: as a piece of fruit.

Like the letters, the first part of Thérèse's autobiography, recounting her childhood, abounds in images of food—of sweet foods, to be precise. These occurrences are particularly notable because, as frequent as they are in the first part of *Story of a Soul*, Manuscript A, they all but disappear in the much shorter Manuscripts B and C—where the still regular references to sweetness, food, and nourishment are usually metaphorical and almost always general. The first part of *Story of a Soul*, Manuscript A, embodies the encounter of memory, food, and narrative. It presents the child Thérèse as a latent expression of her adult vocation: Thérèse the Carmelite, clearly, but, more importantly, Thérèse the Saint. Foods and sweets in particular for this little girl, connect her with those she loves on earth and help her express her longing for heavenly bonds, express the meanings she ascribes to her vocation, and vividly share with her reader the sensual and spiritual pleasures this vocation has brought her.

On the evening of the day of her sister Léonie's First Communion, Thérèse recalls, "they put me to bed early as I was too little to stay up for the banquet, but I can still see Papa coming at dessert time, carrying a piece of cake to his little Queen" (21). Thérèse, as usual, refers to herself as Queen and her father as King, and his particular action in these circumstances, bringing to Thérèse the best of what she is missing out by not participating at the banquet because of her age, is emblematic of their relationship in general. For in spite of the pain of being orphaned of her mother at a young age, Thérèse was loved, cosseted, and fawned on. The special delight she receives from sweets, and the attention she gives to it in her writings, define her as childlike, infantilize her in a self-conscious, self-chosen way. Her second mother Pauline, the sister who took special care of her after her mother's death and to whom this first part of Thérèse's autobiography is addressed, also delighted Thérèse with treats—this time, clearly invested for Thérèse with sisterly, maternal, sacramental value: "Then you gave me a piece of chocolate that you had kept for three months. Can you imagine what a relic that was for me!" (22).[21] This interpretation of a chocolate bar ("*une tablette de chocolat*") as a relic ("*relique*") is indicative of the sort of significance Thérèse conferred on her foods, as it sacralizes a treat that, though certainly edible, hardly figures in the West among those foods endowed with a celebrated, privileged symbolism (though we might remember the social symbolism of sugar, beloved of the French bourgeoisie and still despised by the working classes during Thérèse's own time). This chocolate-bar-turned-relic absorbs the qualities of its giver (her motherliness, her painful absence) by its extended, three-month-long contact with her, and its value as physical sweet is redoubled by the emotional sweetness and the sacred bodiliness it conveys to its new owner.

Of a visit to an aunt who was a nun in Le Mans—reminding us of sweets and convents—Thérèse recalls with gusto a story of candies gained and lost:

> I remember nothing about the visit except the moment when Aunt handed me a little white toy mouse and a little cardboard basket filled with candies, on top of which *were enthroned* two pretty sugar rings, just the right size for my finger. Immediately I exclaimed: "How wonderful! there will be a ring for Céline also!" I took my basket by the handle. I gave the other hand to Mama and we left. After a few steps, I looked at my basket and saw that my candies were almost all strewn out on the street like Tom Thumb's pebbles. I looked again more closely and saw that one of the precious rings had undergone the awful fate of the candies. I had nothing now to give to Céline and so was filled with grief! I asked if I could retrace my steps, but Mama seemed to pay no attention to me. This was too much and my *tears* were followed by loud *cries*. I was unable to understand why she didn't share my pain, and this only increased my grief. (23)

One might, superficially though with some profit, interpret this story as an advice against using open cardboard boxes as containers for candies, against choosing brittle treats such as sugar rings for a two-year-old, and against entrusting a toddler with the care of her own fragile and precariously packaged gifts—admittedly valuable advice for the prevention of temper tantrums such as little Thérèse's reaction. Thérèse, however, significantly and romantically interprets her adventure as a fairy tale (later in the book she speaks of "my little story which resembled a fairy tale"), equating her fate to that of Tom Thumb, actually Perrault's "Le Petit Poucet" (212; the only thing the English and the French tales have in common is a smaller-than-life protagonist). Like Thérèse, Petit Poucet is the youngest of a large brood of children. Youth and smallness—Petit Poucet was physically tiny and Thérèse makes of smallness her vocation and her theology—bring them together and define their quest. But while Petit Poucet purposefully dropped first pebbles, then breadcrumbs, in order to later be able to retrace his steps after being abandoned in the forest by his impoverished, starving parents—his story evokes the ghost of European famines, like Hansel and Gretel's—Thérèse's strewing of candies on the street was unintentional, an accident experienced and described as far more terrible than, though also predictive of, the many losses Thérèse was to experience in her short life. In *La prima estasi* (the first ecstasy), her narrative meditation on the life of Thérèse of Lisieux, Italian novelist Elisabetta Rasy aptly describes this experience of candy loss as "A sense of fading, of loss, as painful as a hemorrhage," seeing in it a sort of preview of Thérèse's tubercular fate to come.[22] Thérèse's transformation of the story into a fairy tale, and of herself into Petit Poucet, ascribes intentionality to accident and a divine design of fullness to a life full of loss.

Broken sugar rings notwithstanding, Thérèse's attachment to her sister Céline continued to express itself in sweet ways: "I remember I really wasn't able to be without Céline. I'd sooner leave the table without taking my dessert than not to follow her as soon as she got up" (26). Sweeter than dessert is Céline's presence to the child Thérèse, but rather than use this by now bland metaphor, Thérèse, ever a taste-full writer, employs a table memory—the sacrifice of dessert in exchange for her sister's company—to express a desire (being with her sister) that was stronger than a pleasure (eating her dessert). Stronger than pleasure and stronger than table manners: Thérèse gets up before she is finished, and, also, Thérèse plays with her food. She dawdles, she procrastinates, she observes, she recycles: when Thérèse has food placed in front of her, there are, we will see, many things that she wants to do with it—and not simply, not immediately, not necessarily eat it.

Thérèse spent a lot of time playing with food—in both material and spiritual ways. Food establishes her childishness, or childlikeness, or, ideally, her childhood, and its sanctity (according to Christ's injunction, "unless you turn and become like children, you will not enter the kingdom of heaven" [Matt. 18:3], often recalled by Thérèse in her writings). Since Thérèse did not know how to play children's games and repeatedly mentions her difficulties in trying to mingle with her peers, she played with food and her father instead, preparing "mixtures with little seed and pieces of bark," mixtures she would then bring "to papa in a pretty little cup. Poor Papa stopped all his work and with a smile he pretended to drink." But then her father, after the short pretense, asked her if he should throw out Thérèse's precious mixture: "Sometimes I would say 'Yes,' but more frequently I carried away my precious mixture, wanting to use it several times" (36–37). In this scene, Thérèse's imagination, with her father's complicity, transforms (transubstantiates?) inedible objects into nourishing food. Elsewhere, and this time with her sister's complicity, Thérèse, exhibiting what she later calls her vocation to the priesthood, directs the metamorphosis of regular food into holy food. Thérèse tells stories of "blessing bread": if Céline was unable to bring back blessed bread from Mass, when Thérèse was too young to attend, a way was soon found. "'You haven't any blessed bread? Then make some!' No sooner said than done. Céline got a chair, opened the cupboards, took the bread, cut off a slice, and then very *gravely* recited a *Hail Mary* over it, and then she gave it to me. After making the sign of the Cross I would eat it with *great devotion*, finding it *tasted* the same as the *blessed bread*" (26–27). A play consecration, or perhaps simply reminiscent of the blessed bread called *antidoron* and *eulogia* treasured in chapter 1, this scene repeats itself a few years later when, pretending with her cousin Marie to be hermits, Thérèse recounts: "one day, the younger hermit forgot herself completely: having received a piece of cake for lunch, she made a big sign of the Cross over it before eating it, causing people to laugh" (55).

Playing with food, however, was not always to be so joyous. Just as Thérèse had earlier wondered, in her letter, about the theological status of the peach, she now remembers an episode with another fuzzy fruit: when "Céline was given a beautiful apricot" she tells little Thérèse, "We are not going to eat it; I will give it to Mama." But this was not likely to help their mother: "Alas, poor little Mother was already too sick to eat the fruits of the earth; she was *to be satisfied* only in heaven with God's *glory* and was *to drink* the mysterious wine He spoke about at the Last Supper, saying He would share it with us in His Father's Kingdom" (33). We don't know what then happened to the beautiful apricot, whether Céline and Thérèse resignedly ate it, probably thinking of the sugary peach made for us by God, or whether the apricot was thrown out after having been offered, uselessly, to their sick mother. But in all cases, in sickness or in health, fruit is for Thérèse a treat to be shared with her family: when Céline is gone on a three-day-retreat, and Thérèse is separated from her for the first time in her life she "kept a small bunch of cherries that papa had brought me in order to eat them with her." But Céline does not come back that night, and their father consoles Thérèse's sadness "by saying he would take me the next day to the Abbey to see my Céline and that I would give her another bunch of cherries!" (57).

During her own retreat at the age of eleven, Thérèse remembers, "Marie and Léonie came each day to see me, along with papa, who brought me all sorts of pastries. In this way, I didn't suffer the privation of being far from the family, and so nothing came to darken the beautiful heaven of my retreat" (75). Pastries replace family love, fill the emptiness of privation, and light up the potential darkness of Thérèse's spiritual journey. Louis Martin's Queen continues to be spoiled through special and playful foods, the vivid memories of which flavor her fasting lifestyle and season her memory and her self-representation—as a child, as an innocent, as a saint. Another time, the sight of food—sweet food, once again—reminds her of the transitory nature of life on earth. Thérèse enjoyed going fishing with her father, her King, bringing their lunch in a basket; but when she opens the basket, "The *beautiful* bread and jam you had prepared," Thérèse says (she is addressing her sister Pauline), "had changed its appearance: instead of the lively colors it had earlier, I now saw only a light rosy tinge and the bread had become old and crumbled." The emotional effects of this color change are devastating: "Earth again seems a sad place and I understood that in heaven alone joy will be without any clouds" (37). If treats, and particularly treats lovingly prepared by practically perfect Pauline, can't be trusted to retain their color and appeal, reasons Thérèse, then there really is no hope for happiness in life on earth. Dorothy Day perceptively says of this passage that, "Eating and drinking with others is a communion, and the fact that our Lord left Himself to us in bread and wine makes eating a divine as well as a human act, so when the Little Flower talks about her distaste for the picnic lunch, one may well see that there was a natural melancholy of temperament there, a sadness of the body as well as of the soul."[23]

Still with her father, Thérèse, upon encountering an invalid on crutches who would not accept her alms, reflects: "Papa had just bought me a little cake, and I had an intense desire to give it to him, but I didn't dare. However, I really wanted to give him something he couldn't refuse, so great was the sympathy I felt toward him." A spiritual solution promptly presents itself to this six-year-old: "'I'll pray for this poor man on the day of my First Communion.' I kept my promise five years later" (38–39). Once again aided by the workings of memory, and an extraordinary memory at that, sweets impel her to prayer and thus effect that union that money instead risks undoing. The bond of food works with strangers as well as with family, and the spoiling of Thérèse started early in the morning; it started with sweets. On Sundays, for example, her older sister "Pauline spoiled her little girl by bringing her some chocolate to drink while still in *bed*" (41)— and ideally chocolate was meant to be consumed in bed, for its essence "was fluid, lazy, languid motion . . . meant to create an intermediary state between lying down and sitting up."[24] The doting sister receives her reward soon thereafter. Anticipating her own life of penance at the Lisieux Carmel, Thérèse makes sure she offers sweet delights to Pauline before she enters Carmel, so that in the last few weeks Pauline spent at home, "every day, Céline and I brought her cake and candy, thinking that later on she would never eat these anymore" (59). True enough, as is true of Thérèse herself: life in the convent, with its strict and penitential vegetarian diet, did not tolerate the presence of candy and cake.

Other than the description of her relatives looking to her, from her sickbed, like a row of onions, and some general metaphors, the foods I have discussed thus far are representative of the foods that Thérèse brings up in Manuscript A. There is no mention of stews, eggs, potatoes, and other such foods more typical of the late-nineteenth-century diet of the French middle class. All the foods Thérèse mentions in this manuscript are sweets or bread, perhaps because she constructs herself as once a child and always childlike, or perhaps because they best counterpoint that adult vocation that is so inextricably tied to her lover: "O Jesus, unspeakable *sweetness*, change all the consolations of this earth into *bitterness* for me" (79). As always, Jesus obliges her. Once he and Thérèse are forever united in the Carmel, all other sweetness ceases, its role in Thérèse's sweet-toothed life having been made unnecessary and unwanted by the ubiquitous, jealous sweetness of her lover's presence: "Later I will tell you, dear Mother, how Jesus was pleased to realize my desire, and how He was always my ineffable *sweetness*" (79–80). In *Story of a Soul*, once Thérèse enters the convent, sweet foods no longer appear as memory, only as metaphor. Part of the explanation can be found in Manuscript C, the last part of Thérèse's autobiography: souls must sooner or later "recognize that a little bit of bitterness is at times preferable to sugar"—though a few lines down Thérèse is "very happy to be able to follow the inclination of my heart and not serve up a bitter dish" (240).

The most prominent image of food in this last part of the book hovers between metaphor and reference to actual victuals. Thérèse is tired of being praised and considered perfect—indirectly identifying the sweetness of praises with that of sugar.

> Sometimes there comes to me a great desire to hear something else besides praises. You know, dear Mother, that I prefer vinegar to sugar; my soul, too, is tired of too sweet a nourishment, and Jesus permits someone to serve it a good little salad, well seasoned with vinegar and spices, nothing is missing

except the *oil* which gives it added flavor. This good little salad is served up to me by the novices at a time when I least expect it. God lifts the veil which hides my imperfections, and then my dear little sisters, seeing me just as I am, no longer find me according to their taste. (244)

"I prefer vinegar to sugar"?! Thérèse's tastes have evidently changed in the convent, where sour replaces sweet, and the salad of criticism sates Thérèse's surfeited palate. The novices' open criticism of Thérèse "is a delightful banquet which fills my soul with joy," and after one particularly stinging critique "my soul enjoyed the bitter food served up to it in such abundance" (244–245). "Sugar and spice and everything nice" are not enough anymore. Thérèse confesses to being sick of sweetness, ready to sample a different dish—and, especially, to become one: if Thérèse, as food, is not to the novices' taste, it is probably because, no longer a child, her sweetness has gone sour. Hagiographical accounts of her life cover up this sourness with abundant layers of sugar and syrup, much like Thérèse's profound religious doubts for the last year and a half of her life (the entire length of her sickness) are glazed over with the sweet story of the eternal child, forever faithful, unwavering in her belief.

Thérèse is the saint of childhood and of death. Her chosen name is perfectly expressive of this dual vocation. Unlike her namesake, Teresa de Jesùs (Teresa of Avila), Thérèse is not content with one holy referent for her name, and selects two: she is Thérèse of the Child Jesus *and* of the Holy Face, at once newborn and dying, alive and agonizing, sweet and bitter (the devotion to the Holy Face, championed in nineteenth-century France by the Carmelite nun Marie de Saint Pierre, refers the suffering face of Jesus during his Passion, and is usually linked to the medieval tradition of the imprint left on Veronica's veil when she wiped the face of Jesus with it on his way to Calvary). As Thérèse had written in a letter to her aunt Guérin: "Does the truth not come out of the mouth of children? Well, one must forgive me if I tell the truth, since I am and want to always remain a child."[25] At no other time in her life does Thérèse bring these two aspects of her spirituality, sweetness and childhood, so close together as when she is near the end. "The only happiness on earth," she writes in her last letter to her sister Léonie, "is in applying oneself to find delicious [*délicieuse*] the part that Jesus gives us." And she concludes that same letter excusing herself because she needs to rest: "I will write to you more at length another time, I cannot now: I am a baby who needs a nap" ["*bébé ayant besoin de faire dodo*"].[26]

Thérèse's return to infancy at the height of her sickness, at the approach of her death, is marked by physical needs (food and rest) and baby talk (*dodo, lolo*), two elements that bring together, like Thérèse's name does, the beginning and the end of life. Her needs underline the bodiliness that precedes the physical growth in childhood and the bodily corruption in death; her speech is transformed into the babble that preludes the child's development of language and, in death, silence. Indeed, in her last letter to Fr. Roulland (one of the two missionaries Thérèse considered her "brothers"), Thérèse writes: "For the past five or six weeks I too have been a baby, because I am surviving just on milk [*je suis aussi un bébé, car je ne vis que de lolo*], but soon I will sit at the heavenly banquet, I will slake my thirst with the waters of eternal life."[27] In this simple sentence Thérèse effectively summarizes the connection between her feeding needs and her thirsting desires, noting how even that spiritual childhood, which she so energetically developed in the course of her life, the babble of which she can hardly avoid near death, must be outgrown, its sweetness a bit reluctantly abandoned in favor of water that is, yes, eternal, but, regretfully, without the color and flavor of peaches, cherries, sugar rings, and chocolate.

So, in the course of one of her last conversations, Thérèse exclaims, "It's quite unbelievable! Now that I can no longer eat, I have a desire for all sorts of things, for example, chicken cutlets, rice, tuna fish." Noticeably, there is nothing sweet in her list. "I have an appetite that's making up for my whole life," she says, "it seems to me I'm dying of hunger."[28]

In the account of her early childhood, there is an episode, apparently trivial (and in this typical of *Story of a Soul*), that Thérèse defines as "a summary of my whole life." Léonie, regarding herself as too old to play with dolls anymore, offers Céline and Thérèse a basket full of doll's clothes, with materials to make more clothes and even her own doll on top. "Céline stretched out her hand and took a little ball of wool that pleased her. After a moment's reflection, I stretched out mine saying: 'I choose all!' and I took the basket without further ceremony" (27). This anecdote expresses not only Thérèse's childish greed, but also her fear of doing things half way—"I don't want to be a *saint by halves*," she insists—of not doing everything right, and, above all, I think, her fear of not having everything she wants. When she writes to her sister Marie "I feel within me other *vocations*. I feel the *vocation* of the WARRIOR, THE PRIEST, THE APOSTLE, THE DOCTOR, THE MARTYR," Thérèse also explains that her "dream is a folly, for I cannot confine myself to desiring *one kind* of martyrdom. To satisfy me I need *all*."[29] She is practicing, and representing, what Luisa Muraro calls "an excessive feminism," typical of the late twentieth century yet also at work in the writings of this saint: an attitude that is transgressive of historical limitations and cultural paradigms.[30] In this sense, perhaps, the taste request Thérèse had made in Manuscript B, the shortest and most poignant part of *Story of a Soul*, has been fulfilled for her at the end. In her declaration of love to Jesus, Thérèse exclaims:

> I feel, O Jesus, that after having aspired to the most lofty heights of Love, if one day I am not to attain them, I feel that I shall have tasted *more sweetness in my martyrdom and my folly* than I shall taste in the bosom of the *joy of the Fatherland*, unless You take away the memory of these earthly hopes through a miracle. Allow me, then, during my exile, the delights of love. Allow me to taste the sweet bitterness of my martyrdom. (197)

This "sweet bitterness" ("*les douces amertumes*")[31] is the oxymoron that solves Thérèse's quandary and allows her to be a child and dying, to have the pleasure and the pain of beginning and ending: she is to the end "Thérèse of the Infant Jesus and the Holy Face," of Jesus' embodiment in birth and in death. But also, to the end, she preserves her sensitive palate and recognizes flavors for what they are. As she tells one of the nuns who is caring for her during her last weeks of life, "You know that you're taking care of a 'baby' who is dying. And (pointing to her glass) you must put something good in the glass, because 'baby' has a very rotten taste in her mouth."[32]

Thérèse died on September 30, 1897. At the beginning of September, Sister Geneviève, who was taking care of her in the Carmel infirmary, wrote to Thérèse's aunt Madame Guérin:

> Here's what my little patient said just now: "*I'd love to have something, but only Aunt or Léonie could be able to get it for me. Since I'm eating now, I'd really love to have a little chocolate cake, soft inside.*" I mentioned a chocolate patty to her. "*Oh! No, it's much better; it's long, narrow, I believe it's called an éclair.*" I understood she thought it was made out of chocolate in the middle. In any case, it has a lot of chocolate on the top, this would amount to the same thing. She said: "*Only one, however!*" Thank you. Thank you.[33]

A chocolate éclair is not exactly what one expects to find at the deathbed of a Carmelite nun—even a French one. But it made me happy to read this letter. Because I can hope that, maybe, Thérèse did not lose her sweet tooth after all, and that maybe, in the end, she could once again enjoy the sweets that, by flavoring her life as it was being lived and when she later remembered it, made her hardships more palatable, her sufferings less hard to swallow.

Thérèse's fellow Frenchman Pierre Bourdieu (1930–2002), a renowned sociologist, has devoted his most famous book, *Distinction* (1984), to showing that French people (and, by implication, the rest of us) are made by their tastes, that taste classifies them and defines their identity: the distinctions people make, as an expression of our taste, tell the world who we are.[34] Bourdieu is talking about taste in general and not only of food, and of social classes more than single individuals, but his claim might nevertheless help us knead together the connections between women, sweets and holiness encountered in this chapter and, occasionally, in earlier ones as well: we might say that Thérèse's "sweet bitterness" tastes a lot like the impossible flavor of convent confections, sexy yet celibate, indicating at once self-enclosure and communication, language and silence, personal preference and bourgeois status. Thérèse's "sweet bitterness" is also the contradiction of representing physical celibacy as mystical marriage, of Gemma's anorexia and her satiation in God's love. It is the interplay of hagiography and the culinary arts, that which cooked up the bitter martyrdom of Saint Agatha into the sweetest of cakes—a taste for which may signal celibacy as much as perversion, excess as well as sacrifice. If artistic representations can double up Agatha's single mutilated breast, and convent chefs can in turn multiply that breast into countless sweets, so also for Thérèse two, or more, is better than one, and rather than choose between the flavor of her childhood and that of her adulthood, between the sweetness of her family's past treats and the present bitterness of life at the convent, Thérèse manages to have both, and once again, as she once did with a basket of doll's accessories, to "choose all."

Conclusion

❧

EATING AND COOKING LESSONS

READING ABOUT FOOD makes me hungry. Just as often, however, reading about food makes me want to cook. Though I bake bread every week, wash lettuce on a daily basis, and regularly prepare most of the other foods mentioned in the writings of holy women—lasagna with greens, meat stew, dried fish, a variety of cakes, and even, occasionally, a simple cheese—God has not (yet) walked among my pots and pans as among Teresa of Avila's, nor have philosophical epiphanies like Sor Juana's taken place at my small and heavily used stove. In the hope of learning new culinary secrets and homemaking skills, however, I keep seeking to discern, through the pleasure of the kitchen and the connections that cooking and eating bring into my life, the meanings of what I do in my favorite room of the house and of what others before me have done in theirs.

If you want recipes to whet or sate your appetite for the foods of holy people, I can recommend such inspiring books as *Cooking with the Saints* and *A Continual Feast*, as well as, for more scriptural meals, *Food at the Time of the Bible*.[1] There are certainly many cooking and eating lessons there. But we are readers and not only eaters, we are seekers as well as cooks. . . . "Cooking," English philosopher Alfred North Whitehead said, "is one of those arts which most require to be done by persons of a religious nature," and "a good cook," his wife added, "cooks to the glory of God." His South

189

African colleague Martin Versfeld has indeed added that, "It takes a saint to be a cook."[2] More practically, American farmer and essayist Wendell Berry has said some persuasive things about the politics, aesthetics, and ethics of food, about the risks of degradation and abuse inherent in the industrialization of food, about the urgent need to eat responsibly, to consume with knowledge and understanding: because, to recall the words of the medieval nun Hildegard of Bingen, "Why will a person chew on a grape and still wish to remain ignorant of the nature of that grape?"[3]

Though Hildegard was speaking in metaphors, Berry echoes the German visionary's intent when he reminds us that, "eating takes place inescapably in the world, that it is inescapably an agricultural act, and that how we eat determines, to a considerable extent, how the world is used. This is a simple way of describing a relationship that is inexpressibly complex. To eat responsibly is to understand and enact, so far as one can, this complex relationship."[4] Who could better express this inexpressible relationship than the mystics, the real professionals of the ineffable?

So, what are some of the eating and cooking lessons to be learned from the words of the holy women who have dwelled on the topic of food?

Not altogether inexpressible, yet certainly and irreducibly complex, the cooking and eating lessons of holy women do not let themselves be too quickly summarized. Most generally, they tell that food and the spirit are not so far from each other that we cannot learn from their encounter. They show that the history of spirituality and the history of food share the hardened bread of the holy women of Byzantium and of the poor; that these histories converge in the medieval obsession with spices and holy women's spicy encounters with God. The writings of these holy women follow the vicissitudes of the apples of Eden and of homemade cheese, and let us marvel at the sweetness of Sicilian convent confections and of Agatha's martyrdom. These women's stories draw from the material abundance of the early American table and the spiritual riches of its first canonized saint, Elizabeth Ann Seton. They gather in the sugary flavor of France's sweetest saint, Thérèse of Lisieux, at the height of the bourgeoisie's love affair with sugar in Europe.

The lessons to be learned are not only historical, of course—for there are plenty of spiritual and intellectual instructions as well. Some are tough, others tender; some are raw, others a bit overdone. Most obviously, and hopefully not too superficially, Elisabeth of Schönau's exaltation of honey and cinnamon in medieval Germany fills the sweetness of life with divine meanings, conferring upon all that is sweet, but also spicy, a divine spark. In a similar sweetness another medieval nun, Margaret Ebner, also finds knowledge and understanding, though she might have to suffer more, and bite harder, to obtain grace—her apples are crunchier than Elisabeth's liquid honey, because they are sour as well as sweet. In Angela of Foligno's lettuce-washing episode, no less crispy, those who struggle to balance the life of the mind with the physical demands of the body (one's own or the body of those who depend on us) may find a model of the dauntless strength, the defiance even, possible and needed in the face of what often appears to be a task beyond our forces and an enemy bent on humiliating us. In Counter-Reformation Spain, Teresa of Avila reminds us to seek the metaphorical kitchen rather than the swooning ecstasies for which she is better known if we want to find God. Grace is not served on silver platters, but it is more likely found in the courage to jump, if obedience demands it, from the frying pan into the fire. Through humble example rather than pedagogical distance, the American Elizabeth Ann Seton—after spitting out of her mouth the silver spoon with which she was born—shows her readers how to find consolation in memory, and meaning both in comfort and in the pain that makes such comfort necessary. Back in Europe, in turn-of-the-century Italy, Gemma Galgani's pull between the dangerous pleasures of union and the lonely safety of a middle-class table might reveal the way we too are torn for love sometimes between comfortable and riskier choices: her own silver spoon really has a hole in it, for she would prefer no flavor at all to the bad taste that most earthly foods leave in her mouth. And in Gemma's contemporary Thérèse of Lisieux some readers could find a rather spunky predecessor in the all-too common quest to sweeten the bitter pills that inevitably come our way.

After all, as my grandmother was fond of saying as she merrily poured three or four spoonfuls of sugar in her cup of espresso, "*La vita è amara, il caffè lo voglio dolce*": "Life is bitter, I want my coffee to be sweet."

Sweet is the contact with God, but sweet is also the wisdom this contact brings on. The links between understanding and food have been underlined by the treatises of Hildegard of Bingen in medieval Germany as well as by the baroque self-reflections of Sor Juana Inès de la Cruz in colonial Mexico: cooking processes, if undertaken with an inquisitive attitude, can bring knowledge and intellectual satisfaction. There is learning and there is wisdom to be found even at the most modest of stoves, at the most lonely or crowded of kitchens. As Simone Weil put it, more metaphorically than some of her predecessors, a few decades ago—Simone Weil, who had to leave the Spanish Civil War because, clumsy as she was, she burned her leg with boiling oil in the makeshift kitchen (not a good cook for God, this one):

> One can only verify whether the behavior of the soul as regards this world bears the mark of an experience of God.
>
> In the same way, a bride's friends do not go into the nuptial chamber; but when she is pregnant they know she has lost her virginity.
>
> There is not fire in a cooked dish, but one knows it has been on the fire.
>
> On the other hand, even though one may think to have seen the flames under them, if the potatoes are raw it is certain they have not been on the fire.[5]

Even for this most incompetent of cooks, God can roast potatoes as a mark of divine presence that is as certain as a swollen belly.

So also, for the linguistically astute reader, Margaret Ebner's apples are crisp, tasty lessons in reading symbols of oppression as symbols of exaltation, the apples of female weakness (and pain) as the apples of women's knowing and learning (and pleasure). Angela's cooking lesson includes a language demonstration on how to answer back, how to mean more than you say, and how to have the last word. Teresa of Avila's bugs, as food (the worm) and as producers of food (the bee and the spider), as signifiers of misreading ("Go and eat it, then!" said the impetuous mother superior to a nun who showed her a big worm) and of the production of meaning (the bee makes honey the way the spider makes poison), shape her connection between God and the kitchen as the emptying out, the pouring out, of that which exceeds language—God—into that which is below language itself—bugs. Gemma's lesson, like Agatha's, is about binding opposites to signify excess where there would otherwise be scarcity. Thérèse's strategy of compromise, the connection between flavors she establishes—her embrace of the bittersweet convent after a youth spent enjoying the sugar of family life—is a writing lesson on eating and autobiography, on how to represent one's past as one's present, and on how to have it all: Thérèse has her cake, or éclair, and eats it, too. There's an eating lesson!

I have been talking about connections, meanings, and pleasure. The reader's tools are not the same as the cook's, much less the saint's, but these common pursuits may bring reader, cook, and saint together in the shared attempt to reach beyond the self toward the Other—whether our other is God, a hungry neighbor, or a book to be read or written. It is with this Other that, in the disciplined practice, learned in the kitchen and at table, of separating in order to better mix, of admitting ignorance in order to better know, of waiting in order to better enjoy, we learn to make connections, discern meanings, experience pleasure. The taste of an attempt at this is what I hope to have given you in these pages. Whether the result is sweet or sour, bitter or insipid, might well be a matter of personal taste—and about taste, the Romans wisely said, there is no arguing.

Notes

❧

Introduction

1. Letter of Hildegard of Bingen to Daniel, Bishop of Prague, dated 1153–1154, in *The Letters of Hildegard of Bingen*, ed. Joseph L. Baird and Radd K. Ehrman, 2 vols. (New York: Oxford University Press, 1994), 1:107. Throughout this book, I refer to holy women primarily by their first name: for many of them we do not have a last name, only the name of the town they are from, and thus, for the sake of uniformity, their first name will be my main way of calling the women in God's kitchen.

2. Margaret Ebner, *Major Works*, trans. Leonard P. Hindsley (New York: Paulist Press, 1993), 122.

3. Carla Lonzi, "Itinerario di riflessioni," in *E' già politica. Scritti di Rivolta Femminile 8*, by Maria Grazia Chianese et al. (Milan: Rivolta Femminile, 1977), 13–50; Luisa Muraro, *Lingua e verità in Emily Dickinson, Teresa di Lisieux, Ivy Compton-Burnett* (Milan: Libreria delle donne, 1995), 32–33; Muraro, *Il Dio delle donne* (Milan: Mondadori, 2003), 98–99; Luce Irigaray, *Speculum of the Other Woman*, trans. Gillian Gill (Ithaca: Cornell University Press, 1985), 191; Irigaray, "Divine Women," in *Sexes and Genealogies*, trans. Gillian Gill, 55–72 (New York: Columbia University Press, 1993), 63.

4. Peter Burke, "How to Become a Counter-Reformation Saint," in David M. Luebke, ed., *The Counter-Reformation: The Essential Readings* (Malden, Mass.: Blackwell, 1999), 130–42. Of great interest are also the essays in *Women and Faith: Catholic Religious Life in Italy from late Antiquity to the Present*, ed. Lucetta Scaraffia and Gabriella Zarri (Cambridge, Mass.: Harvard University Press, 1999).

5. Elizabeth Johnson, *Friends of God and Prophets: A Feminist Theological Reading of the Communion of Saints* (New York: Continuum, 1998), 18.

6. Adrienne Rich, "When We Dead Awaken: Writing as Re-Vision," in *On*

Lies, Secrets, and Silence: Selected Prose 1966–1978 (New York: W. W. Norton, 1979), 33–49, 43.

7. Rudolph Bell, *Holy Anorexia* (Chicago: University of Chicago Press, 1985); Caroline Walker Bynum, *Holy Feast and Holy Fast: The Religious Significance of Food to Medieval Women* (Berkeley: University of California Press, 1987).

8. Marguerite Porete, *The Mirror of Simple Souls*, trans. Ellen Babinsky (Ramsey, N.J.: Paulist Press, 1993), 158–59.

9. Julian of Norwich, *Showings of Love*, trans. Julia Bolton Holloway (Collegeville, Minn.: Liturgical Press, 2003), 15.

10. Julian of Norwich, *Showings*, trans. Edmund Colledge and James Walsh (New York: Paulist Press, 1978), 149, 130. Julian's original language may be found in *The Shewings of Julian of Norwich*, ed. Georgia Ronan Crampton (Kalamazoo, Mich.: Medieval Institute Publications, 1993), 43.

Chapter 1

1. Elisabeth Schüssler Fiorenza, *In Memory of Her: A Feminist Theological Reconstruction of Christian Origins* (New York: Crossroad, 1984).

2. Ben Witherington, *Women in the Ministry of Jesus: A Study of Jesus' Attitudes to Women and Their Roles as Reflected in His Earthly Life* (Cambridge: Cambridge University Press, 1984), 40–41. More on this parable may be found in Warren Carter, *Matthew and the Margins: A Sociopolitical and Religious Reading* (Maryknoll, N.Y.: Orbis Books, 2000), 290–91; and Herman Hendrickx, *The Third Gospel for the Third World*, 4 vols. (Collegeville, Minn.: Liturgical Press, 2000), 3A:293–95.

3. Simone Weil letter to Joë Bosquet, in *The Simone Weil Reader*, ed. George A. Panichas (New York: David McKay Company, 1977), 90.

4. Claude Lévi-Strauss, *The Raw and the Cooked: Introduction to a Science of Mythology: I*, trans. John and Doreen Weightman (New York: Harper & Row, 1969).

5. Grace M. Jantzen, *Power, Gender and Christian Mysticism* (Cambridge: Cambridge University Press, 1995), 196–97.

6. Alice-Mary Talbot, ed., *Holy Women of Byzantium: Ten Saints' Lives in English Translation* (Washington, D.C.: Dumbarton Oaks, 1996).

7. Pseudo-Athanasius, *The Life of Blessed Syncletica*, trans. Elizabeth Bryson Bongie (Toronto: Peregrina Publishing, 1996), 60.

8. Benedicta Ward, *Harlots of the Desert: A Study of Repentance in Early Monastic Sources* (Kalamazoo, Mich.: Cistercian Publications, 1987), 103.

9. Ibid., 34.

10. "Life of Abba Cyriacus of the Laura of Souka," in Cyril of Scythopolis, *Lives of the Monks of Palestine*, trans. R. M. Price, 245–61 (Kalamazoo, Mich.: Cistercian Publications, 1991), 257.

11. Talbot, *Holy Women*, 85.

12. Ibid., 85–86.

13. Massimo Montanari, *The Culture of Food*, trans. Carl Ipsen (Oxford: Blackwell, 1994), 33–34.

14. Talbot, *Holy Women*, 89–90. Further page references to this book will be given in parentheses for the remainder of this chapter.

15. In Montanari, *The Culture of Food*, 16–17.

16. Hildegard of Bingen, *Scivias*, trans. Columba Hart and Jane Bishop (New York: Paulist Press, 1990), 121.

17. Elisabeth of Schönau, *The Complete Works*, trans. Anne L. Clark (New York: Paulist Press, 2000), 75.

18. Angela of Foligno, *Complete Works*, trans. Paul Lachance (New York: Paulist Press, 1993), 53.

19. Marguerite Porete, *The Mirror of Simple Souls*, trans. Ellen Babinsky (Ramsey, N.J.: Paulist Press, 1993), 100.

20. Margaret Ebner, *Major Works*, trans. Leonard P. Hindsley (New York: Paulist Press, 1993), 109, 92, 119.

21. *Saint Bride and Her Book: Brigitta of Sweden's Revelations*, ed. Julia Bolton Holloway (Cambridge: D. S. Brewer, 2000), 37.

22. Teresa of Avila, *The Life of Saint Teresa of Avila by Herself*, trans. J. M. Cohen (London: Penguin Books, 1987), 94.

23. Elizabeth Ann Seton, *Selected Writings*, ed. Ellin Kelly and Annabelle Melville (Mahwah, N.J.: Paulist Press, 1987), 105–6, 70. Elizabeth Seton's spelling and punctuation differ from contemporary Standard English. Her editors have not corrected these variants and I have left them in my quotations.

24. Thérèse of Lisieux, *Story of a Soul: The Autobiography of Saint Thérèse of Lisieux*, trans. John Clarke (Washington, D.C.: ICS Publications, 1996), 248, 26–27.

25. Catherine of Genoa, *Purgation and Purgatory-The Spiritual Dialogue*, trans. Serge Hughes (New York: Paulist Press, 1979), 76–77.

26. Ibid., 130.

27. Kathleen Norris, *The Quotidian Mysteries: Laundry, Liturgy and "Women's Work"* (New York: Paulist Press, 1998), 15.

28. Holly W. Whitcomb, *Feasting with God: Adventures in Table Spirituality* (Cleveland: United Church Press, 1996), 135–36.

29. Sarah Coakley, *Powers and Submissions: Spirituality, Philosophy and Gender* (Oxford: Blackwell, 2002), 36.

30. Weil, *Reader*, 438, 354.

31. Ibid., 426.

Chapter 2

1. Mineke Schipper, *Never Marry a Woman with Big Feet: Women in Proverbs from Around the World* (New Haven: Yale University Press, 2003), 133, 227.

2. Piero Camporesi, *The Magic Harvest: Food, Folklore and Society*, trans. Joan Kracover Hall (Cambridge: Polity Press, 1998), 15.

3. Alan Richter, *Sexual Slang: A Compendium of Offbeat Words and Colorful Phrases from Shakespeare to Today* (New York: HarperPerennial, 1995), 28.

4. Jean Anthelme Brillat-Savarin, *The Physiology of Taste, or Meditations on Transcendental Gastronomy*, trans. M. F. K. Fisher (New York: Harvest/HBJ, 1949), 4.

5. Caroline Oates, "Cheese Gives You Nightmares: Old Hags and Heartburn (Focus on the Nightmare)," *Folklore* 114.2 (August 2003); *Random House Historical Dictionary of American Slang*, ed. J. E. Lighter (New York: Random House, 1994), 1:387–88; Richter, *Sexual Slang*, 42; "If I have to give my *caciotta* to another man, better a Christian than a muslim," http://www.deit.univpm.it/~dragoni/Pensieri/vaccino.html (accessed June 2005).

6. Rosalind Coward, *Female Desires: How They Are Sought, Bought and Packaged* (New York: Grove Press, 1985), 90.

7. *The Passion of Ss. Perpetua and Felicitas*, trans. H. R. Musurillo, in *Medieval Women's Visionary Literature*, ed. Elizabeth Alvilda Petroff (New York: Oxford University Press, 1986), 70–77, 71.

8. Joyce E. Salisbury, *Perpetua's Passion: The Death and Memory of a Young Roman Woman* (New York: Routledge, 1997), 103; Peter Dronke, *Women Writers of the Middle Ages: A Critical Study of Texts from Perpetua to Marguerite Porete* (Cambridge: Cambridge University Press, 1984); William Tabbernee, "'Polluted Sacraments': Augustine's Denunciation of Montanist Eucharistic Meals," available online at http://divinity.library.vanderbilt.edu/burns/chroma/eucharist/euchtabb.html#N_14_ (accessed June 2005).

9. *The Passion of Ss. Perpetua and Felicitas*, 71.

10. Hildegard of Bingen, *On Natural Philosophy and Medicine: Selections from Cause et cure*, ed. and trans. Margret Berger (Cambridge: D. S. Brewer, 1999), 84, 53, 105.

11. Hildegard of Bingen, *Scivias*, trans. Columba Hart and Jane Bishop (New York: Paulist Press, 1990), 81–82.

12. Ibid., 118. The original Latin can be found in *Hildegardis Scivias*, ed. Adelgundis Führkötter and Angela Carlevaris, 2 vols. (Turnhout, Belgium: Brepols, 1978), 1:75–76. Throughout *The Women in God's Kitchen*, emphasis in a quotation indicates emphasis in the original text.

13. Hildegard of Bingen, *On Natural Philosophy*, 44, 62.

14. Marcia Kathleen Chamberlain, "Hildegard of Bingen's *Causes and Cures*: A Radical Feminist Response to the Doctor-Cook Binary," in *Hildegard of Bingen: A Book of Essays*, ed. Maud Burnett McInerney (New York: Garland, 1998), 53–73, 63.

15. Ibid., 65.

16. Hildegard of Bingen, *Scivias*, 152; *Hildegardis Scivias*, 1:116.

17. Hélène Cixous, "The Laugh of the Medusa," trans. Keith Cohen and Paula Cohen, *Signs* 1.4 (Summer 1976): 865–93, 881.

18. Hildegard of Bingen, *On Natural Philosophy*, 50.

19. Margaret Ebner, *Major Works*, trans. Leonard P. Hindsley (New York: Paulist Press, 1993), 125.

20. Hildegard of Bingen, *Scivias*, 222 (206 in the Latin edition).

21. Both poems can be found in *Appetite: Food as Metaphor. An Anthology of Women Poets*, ed. Phyllis Stowell and Jeanne Foster (Rochester: BOA Editions, 2002), 36–38, 43.

22. Hadewijch of Antwerp, *The Complete Works*, trans. Columba Hart, OSB (Ramsey, N.J.: Paulist Press, 1980), 187.

23. Ibid., 353.

Chapter 3

1. More on this topic can be found in Carolyn Korsmeyer, *Making Sense of Taste: Food and Philosophy* (Ithaca: Cornell University Press, 1999)—particularly in chapter 1, "The Hierarchy of the Senses."

2. Hadewijch of Antwerp, *The Complete Works*, trans. Columba Hart, OSB (Ramsey, N.J.: Paulist Press, 1980), 187.79, 344.

3. Margaret Ebner, *Major Works*, trans. Leonard P. Hindsley (New York: Paulist Press, 1993), 91.

4. Angela of Foligno, *Complete Works*, trans. Paul Lachance (New York: Paulist Press, 1993), 129, 140–48.

5. Julian of Norwich, *Showings*, trans. Edmund Colledge and James Walsh (New York: Paulist Press, 1978), 255.

6. Margery Kempe, *The Book of Margery Kempe*, trans. B. A. Windeatt (London: Penguin Books, 1985), 85.

7. Catherine of Genoa, *Purgation and Purgatory—The Spiritual Dialogue*, trans. Serge Hughes (New York: Paulist Press, 1979), 79, 127.

8. Teresa of Avila, *The Life of Saint Teresa of Avila by Herself*, trans. J. M. Cohen (London: Penguin Books, 1987), 209–10.

9. Elizabeth Ann Seton, *Selected Writings*, ed. Ellin Kelly and Annabelle Melville (Mahwah, N.J.: Paulist Press, 1987), 226.

10. Jean Soler, "Biblical Reasons: The Dietary Rules of the Ancient Hebrews," in *Food: A Culinary History from Antiquity to the Present*, ed. Jean-Louis Flandrin and Massimo Montanari, 46–54 (New York: Columbia University Press, 1999).

11. Sidney Mintz, *Sweetness and Power: The Place of Sugar in Modern History* (New York: Viking, 1985), 32; Claude Fischler, "Attitudes towards Sugar and Sweetness in Historical and Social Perspective" and Paul Rozin, "Sweetness, Sensuality, Sin, Safety, and Socialization: Some Speculations," both in *Sweetness*, ed. John Dobbing (London: Springer-Verlag, 1987), 83–98 and 99–111 respectively.

12. Barbara Newman, preface to *The Complete Works*, by Elisabeth of Schönau, trans. Anne L. Clark, xi–xviii (New York: Paulist Press, 2000), xi.

13. Clark, introduction to *The Complete Works*, by Elisabeth of Schönau, trans. Anne L. Clark (New York: Paulist Press, 2000), 1–37, 35.

14. Ibid., 8–9. On the collaboration between holy women and their spiritual directors, see the essays in Catherine M. Mooney, ed., *Gendered Voices: Medieval Saints and Their Interpreters* (Philadelphia: University of Pennsylvania Press, 1999), as well as Anne L. Clark, "Repression or Collaboration? The Case of Elisabeth and Ekbert of Schönau," in *Christendom and Its Discontents: Exclusion, Persecution, and Rebellion, 1000–1500*, ed. Scott L. Waugh and Peter D. Diehl (Cambridge: Cambridge University Press, 1996), 151–67.

15. Elisabeth of Schönau, *The Complete Works*, 249. Subsequent references to this book in this chapter will be given in parentheses.

16. Hildegard of Bingen, *The Letters of Hildegard of Bingen*, ed. Joseph L. Baird and Radd K. Ehrman, 2 vols. (New York: Oxford University Press, 1994), 1:28 (dated 1146–1147).

17. What Clark translates as "bitter justice" might be more exactly translated as "sour justice"—in the original Latin, "*acerbitati justicie.*" Wilhelm Roth, ed., *Die Visionen der hl. Elisabeth und die Schriften der Aebte Ekbert und Emecho von Schönau* (Brünn: Verlag der Studien aus dem Benedictiner- und Cistercienser-Orden, 1884), 82.

18. The first letter to the Abbess of Dietkirchen is found in Roth, ed., *Die Visionen der hl. Elisabeth*, 146, the second in ibid., 146–48.

19. T. Sarah Peterson, *Acquired Taste: The French Origins of Modern Cooking* (Ithaca: Cornell University Press, 1994), 7.

20. Claude Fischler, "La morale degli alimenti: l'esempio dello zucchero," in *Fra tutti i gusti il più soave… Per una storia dello zucchero e del miele in Italia*, ed. Massimo Montanari, Giorgio Mantovani, Silvio Fronzoni, 3–33 (Bologna: CLUEB, 2002), 4, 17; Massimo Montanari, *The Culture of Food*, trans. Carl Ipsen (Oxford: Blackwell, 1994), 60–61.

21. Joyce Carol Oates, "Food Mysteries," *Antaeus* 68 (Spring 1982): 25–37, 25.

22. Martin Versfeld, *Food for Thought: A Philosopher's Cook-Book* (Cape Town: Tafelberg, 1983), 11–12, 60.

Chapter 4

1. The definitive study of literary apples, including a reference to and a reproduction of Grien's woodcut, is Robert Palter, *The Duchess of Malfi's Apricots, and Other Literary Fruits* (Columbia: University of South Carolina Press, 2002), 8–146, 33. An early Christian author to describe as gluttony Adam and Eve's sin was Cassianus (fourth–fifth centuries), and questions about the nature of their sin continued to be asked, both in the monastic and in the popular traditions; see Francesca Rigotti, *La filosofia in cucina. Piccola critica della ragion culinaria* (Bologna: Il Mulino, 1999), 93.

2. Hildegard of Bingen, *Scivias*, trans. Columba Hart and Jane Bishop (New York: Paulist Press, 1990), 83.

3. Virginia S. Jenkins, "Bananas: Women's Food," in *Cooking Lessons: The Politics of Gender and Food*, ed. Sherrie A. Inness (Lanham, Md.: Rowman and Littlefield, 2001), 111–28.

4. Bia Lowe, *Splendored Thing: Love, Roses, and Other Thorny Treasures* (New York: Carroll & Graf, 2002), 160.

5. Piero Camporesi, *The Anatomy of the Senses: Natural Symbols in Medieval and Early Modern Italy*, trans. Allan Cameron (Cambridge: Polity Press, 1994), 6, 9.

6. From *The Jesus Papers* in *The Book of Folly* (1972), in *Selected Poems of Anne Sexton*, ed. Diane Wood Middlebrook and Diana Hume George (Boston: Houghton Mifflin, 1988), 191.

7. Camporesi, *Anatomy*, 14–15.

8. Caitlin Hines, "Rebaking the Pie: The *Woman as Dessert* Metaphor," in *Reinventing Identities: The Gendered Self in Discourse*, ed. Mary Bucholtz, A. C. Liang, and Laurel A. Sutton, 145–62 (New York: Oxford University Press, 1999), 151.

9. Allison James, "The Good, the Bad and the Delicious: The Role of Confectionery in British Society," *Sociological Review* 38.4 (1990): 666–88, 685.

10. Palter, *The Duchess of Malfi's Apricots*, 691–95.

11. Bernard of Clairvaux, *The Works of Bernard of Clairvaux*, vol. 2, *On the Song of Songs I*, trans. Kilian Walsh, OCSO (Spencer, Mass.: Cistercian Publications, 1971), 1.

12. Ibid., 41–42.

13. The versions of the Song of Songs I have consulted can be found in *The New American Bible*, *The New Catholic Translation* (Nashville: Catholic Bible Press, 1987); E. Ann Matter, *The Voice of My Beloved: The Song of Songs in Western Medieval Christianity* (Philadelphia: University of Pennsylvania Press, 1990), xvi–xxxiii; and Nicholas Ayo, *Sacred Marriage: The Wisdom of the Song of Songs* (New York: Continuum, 1997).

14. Ave Appiano, *Bello da mangiare* (Rome: Beltemi, 2000), 34–36.

15. Catherine of Genoa, *Purgation and Purgatory-The Spiritual Dialogue*, trans. Serge Hughes (New York: Paulist Press, 1979), 120.

16. María de San Jerónimo, "Virtues of Our Mother Saint Teresa according to a Report Made by Her Cousin the Venerable Mother María de San Jerónimo," in *The Complete Works of Saint Teresa of Jesus*, trans. and ed. E. Allison Peers, 3 vols. (London: Sheed and Ward, 1946), 3:338–51, 344; Ana de San Bartolomé, "The Last Acts of the Life of Saint Teresa," in ibid., 3:352–62, 357.

17. Margot Schmidt and Leonard P. Hindsley, introduction to *Major Works*, by Margaret Ebner, trans. Leonard P. Hindsley, 9–81 (New York: Paulist Press, 1993), 46.

18. Margaret Ebner, *Major Works*, 91. Subsequent references to this book in this chapter will be given parenthetically.

19. Massimo Montanari, *The Culture of Food*, trans. Carl Ipsen (Oxford: Blackwell, 1994), 91.

20. 1 Enoch 32:6, in *Eve and Adam: Jewish, Christian, and Muslim Readings on Genesis and Gender*, ed. Kristen E. Kvam, Linda S. Schearing, and Valarie H. Ziegler (Bloomington: Indiana University Press, 1999), 48.

21. Camporesi, *Anatomy of the Senses*, 8.

22. Francis de Sales, *Introduction to the Devout Life*, trans. Michael Day (Westminster, Md.: Newman Press, 1956), 12, 82, 110, 124, 190.

23. Ibid., 175, 225–28, 235.

24. Ibid., 150–51.

Chapter 5

1. Brillat-Savarin, *The Physiology of Taste, or Meditations on Transcendental Gastronomy*, trans. M. F. K. Fisher (New York: Harvest/HBJ, 1949), 169. On convents and cooking, see Giovanna Casagrande, *Gola e preghiera nella clausura dell'ultimo '500* (Foligno: Edizioni dell'Arquata, 1989), 9.

2. Felipe Fernández-Armesto, *Near a Thousand Tables: A History of Food* (New York: Free Press, 2002), 33.

3. More on this topic can be found in Angelo D'Ambrosio and Mario Spedicato, *Cibo e clausura: Regimi alimentari e patrimoni monastici nel Mezzogiorno moderno (sec. XVII-XIX)* (Bari: Cacucci, 1998).

4. Alberto Capatti and Massimo Montanari, *Italian Cuisine: A Cultural History*, trans. Aine O'Healy (New York: Columbia University Press, 2003), xvii.

5. Mary Taylor Simeti, *On Persephone's Island: A Sicilian Journal* (New York: Alfed A. Knopf, 1986), 15.

6. Sidney Mintz, *Tasting Food, Tasting Freedom: Excursions into Eating, Culture, and the Past* (Boston: Beacon Press, 1996), 89.

7. Mary Laven, *Virgins of Venice: Broken Vows and Cloistered Lives in the Renaissance Convent* (New York: Viking, 2002), 109–10.

8. In Mario Fanti, *Abiti e lavori delle monache di Bologna in una serie di disegni del secolo XVIII* (Bologna: Tamari, 1972).

9. In Mary Taylor Simeti, *Pomp and Sustenance: Twenty-Five Centuries of Sicilian Food* (Hopewell, N.J.: Ecco Press, 1998), 223.

10. http://www.fondazionemarianostrano.it/Tradizioni%20Gastronomiche .htm (accessed June 2005).

11. Simeti, *On Persephone's Island*, 65.

12. Enrichetta Caracciolo, *Misteri del chiostro napoletano* (Florence: Giunti, 1986), 131–32.

13. Giuseppe di Lampedusa, *The Leopard*, trans. Archibald Colquhoun (New York: Pantheon Books, 1960), 267.

14. Santo D'Arrigo, *Il martirio di S. Agata nel quadro storico del suo tempo*, 2 vols. (Catania, 1988), 1:259–80 (Greek with Italian translation), 1:358–74 (Latin with Italian translation), 1:366–67.

15. Elizabeth Johnson, *Friends of God and Prophets: A Feminist Theological Reading of the Communion of Saints* (New York: Continuum, 1998), 155.

16. I am alluding to Luce Irigaray's theories in *This Sex Which Is Not One*, trans. Catherine Porter and Carolyn Burke (Ithaca: Cornell University Press, 1985).

17. D'Arrigo, *Il martirio di S. Agata*, 1:275.

18. Giuseppe Rossi Taibbi, ed., *Martirio di Santa Lucia—Vita di Santa Marina* (Palermo: Istituto siciliano di studi bizantini e neogreci, 1959).

19. As of 1981, the "Occhietti di Santa Lucia" were also regularly prepared at the Monastero di Santa Lucia e di San Giovanni Evangelista in Leonessa (near Rieti, in central Italy), and a recipe for these raisin and anise studded, eye-shaped cookies can be found in Sebastiana Papa, *La cucina dei monasteri* (Milan: Mondadori, 1981), 62–63.

Chapter 6

1. *Francis and Clare: The Complete Works*, trans. Regis J. Armstrong, OFM CAP, and Ignatius C. Brady, OFM (Ramsey, N.J.: Paulist Press, 1982), 201–2.

2. Ibid., 139, 118, 120. For a charming story of a food miracle performed by Clare of Assisi, see "How St. Clare Miraculously Imprinted the Cross on Some Loaves of Bread," in *The Little Flowers of Saint Francis*, ed. and trans. Raphael Brown (Garden City, N.Y.: Image Books, 1958), 120–22.

3. Important books on medieval women's mysticism include Bernard McGinn, *The Flowering of Mysticism: Men and Women in the New Mysticism— 1200–1350* (New York: Crossroad, 1998); Grace M. Jantzen, *Power, Gender and Christian Mysticism* (Cambridge: Cambridge University Press, 1995); Ulrike Wiethaus, ed., *Maps of Flesh and Light: The Religious Experience of Medieval Women Mystics* (Syracuse, N.Y.: Syracuse University Press, 1993).

4. Jantzen, *Power, Gender and Christian Mysticism*, 169.

5. On the composition of the *Memorial*, see Catherine M. Mooney, "The Authorial Role of Brother A. in the Composition of Angela of Foligno's Revelations," in *Creative Women in Medieval and Early Modern Italy: A Religious and Artistic Renaissance*, ed. E. Ann Matter and John Coakley (Philadelphia: University of Pennsylvania Press, 1994), 34–63.

6. See Terence Scully, "Tempering Medieval Food," in *Food in the Middle Ages: A Book of Essays*, ed. Melitta Weiss Adamson (New York: Garland, 1995), 3–23.

7. Allen J. Grieco, "Food and Social Classes in Late Medieval and Renaissance Italy," in *Food: A Culinary History from Antiquity to the Present*, ed. Jean-Louis Flandrin and Massimo Montanari, 302–12 (New York: Columbia University Press, 1999), 307.

8. Angela of Foligno, *Complete Works*, trans. Paul Lachance (New York: Paulist Press, 1993), 137. All future page references to this book in this chapter will be given in parentheses.

9. Massimo Montanari, *The Culture of Food*, trans. Carl Ipsen (Oxford: Blackwell, 1994), 15.

10. Maria Giuseppina Muzzarelli and Fiorenza Tarozzi, *Donne e cibo. Una relazione nella storia* (Milan: Mondadori, 2003), chapter 9.

11. Massimo Montanari, "Production Structures and Food Systems in the Early Middle Ages," in *Food*, ed. Flandrin and Montanari, 168–77, 172.

12. The Latin version of the *Memorial* can be consulted online at: http://www.sismelfirenze.it/mistica/ita/mistica.htm (accessed June 2005).

13. Terence Scully, *The Art of Cookery in the Middle Ages* (Woodbridge: Boydell Press, 1995), 127, 133.

14. In Alberto Capatti and Massimo Montanari, *Italian Cuisine: A Cultural History*, trans. Aine O'Healy (New York: Columbia University Press, 2003), 38.

15. Giacomo Castelvetro, *The Fruit, Herbs and Vegetables of Italy*, trans. Gillian Riley (London: Viking, 1989), 65–68.

16. On Angela's inedia, see Rudolph Bell, *Holy Anorexia* (Chicago: University of Chicago Press, 1985), 103–13.

17. Margaret Visser, *Much Depends on Dinner: The Extraordinary History and Mythology, Allure and Obsessions, Perils and Taboos, of an Ordinary Meal* (New York: Grove Press, 1986), 221.

18. Ibid., 221.

19. Muzzarelli and Tarozzi, *Donne e cibo*, 19–20.

20. Rowan Williams, "The Passion of My God," in *Women's Spirituality: Resources for Christian Development*, ed. Joann Wolski Conn, 2nd ed. (New York: Paulist Press, 1996), 327–41, 327.

21. I have changed Lachance's translation of "asperum" from "bitter" to its more literal English equivalent, "sour."

22. This episode is found, among other sources, in Thomas of Celano, *Vita prima di San Francesco d'Assisi*, available online at http://www.sanfrancescoassisi .org (accessed June 2005); the kiss to the leper can be found in part 1, chapter 7.

23. Jean Anthelme Brillat-Savarin, *The Physiology of Taste, or Meditations on Transcendental Gastronomy*, trans. M. F. K. Fisher (New York: Harvest/HBJ, 1949), 3.

24. Louis Marin, *Food for Thought*, trans. Mette Hjort (Baltimore: Johns Hopkins University Press, 1989), 121.

Chapter 7

1. Iris Marion Young, "House and Home: Feminist Variations on a Theme," *Intersecting Voices: Dilemmas of Gender, Political Philosophy, and Policy* (Princeton: Princeton University Press, 1997), 134–64, 151.

2. Valerie Lagorio, "*Defensorium Contra Oblectratores*: A 'Discerning Assessment of Margery Kempe," in *Mysticism: Medieval and Modern*, ed. Valerie Lagorio, 29–48 (Salzburg: Institut für Anglistik und Amerikanistik, 1986), 29.

3. Kathy Lavezzo, "Sobs and Sighs between Women: The Homoerotics of Compassion in *The Book of Margery Kempe*," in *Premodern Sexualities*, ed. Louise Fradenburg and Carla Freccero with the assistance of Kathy Lavezzo, 175–98 (New York: Routledge, 1996), 180.

4. Margery Kempe, *The Book of Margery Kempe*, trans. B. A. Windeatt (London: Penguin Books, 1985), 43. All further page references to this book in this chapter will be given in parentheses.

5. Judith M. Bennett, *Ale, Beer, and Brewsters in England: Women's Work in a Changing World, 1300–1600* (New York: Oxford University Press, 1996), 53.

6. On Margery Kempe's identification with Mary, see for example Karma Lochrie, *Margery Kempe and Translations of the Flesh* (Philadelphia: University of Pennsylvania Press, 1991), 193.

7. Caroline Walker Bynum, *Fragmentation and Redemption: Essays on Gender and the Human Body in Medieval Religion* (New York: Zone, 1991), 198.

8. Adrienne Rich, *Of Woman Born: Motherhood as Experience and Institution* (New York: W. W. Norton, 1976); Luce Irigaray, "Each Sex Must Have Its Own Rights," in *Sexes and Genealogies*, trans. Gillian Gill (New York: Columbia University Press, 1993), 1–5.

9. Margaret Ebner, *Major Works*, trans. Leonard P. Hindsley (New York: Paulist Press, 1993), 110.

10. Margaret Visser, "The Sins of the Flesh," *Granta* 52 (December 1995): 111–32, 122.

11. Roland Barthes, *Mythologies*, trans. Annette Lavers (New York: Hill and Wang, 1972), 62.

12. Margery's original Middle English can be found in *The Book of Margery Kempe*, ed. Barry Windeatt (Harlow, England: Longman, 2000), 365.

13. Quoted in Sean French, "First Catch Your Puffin," *Granta* 52 (December 1995): 195–202, 198.

14. Adrian Franklin, "An Unpopular Food? The Distaste for Fish and the Decline of Fish Consumption in Britain," *Food and Foodways* 7.4 (1997): 227–64.

15. *The Book of Margery Kempe*, Middle English edition, 197.

16. Joyce Carol Oates, "Food Mysteries," *Antaeus* 68 (Spring 1992): 25–37, 25.

17. *The Spiral Path: Explorations in Women's Spirituality*, ed. Theresa King (Saint Paul, Minn.: Yes International Publishers, 1992), 159–67, 164.

Chapter 8

1. Teresa of Avila, *Conceptions of the Love of God*, in *The Complete Works of Saint Teresa of Jesus*, trans. and ed. E. Allison Peers, 3 vols. (London: Sheed and Ward, 1946), 2:359–99, 384.

2. Roland Barthes, *Mythologies*, trans. Annette Lavers (New York: Hill and Wang, 1972), 60.

3. Teresa of Avila, *Conceptions of the Love of God*, 391.

4. E. Ann Matter, "Medieval Women Mystics and the Song of Songs," (lecture, Pendle Hill, October 16, 2000) available online at http://www.pendlehill .org/frames%20lectures/Medieval%20Women%20Mystics.htm (accessed June 2005).

5. References and a discussion can be found in Cristina Mazzoni, *Saint Hysteria: Neurosis, Mysticism, and Gender in European Culture* (Ithaca: Cornell University Press, 1996), 37–53.

6. Michel de Certeau, *The Mystic Fable*, vol. 1, *The Sixteenth and Seventeenth Centuries*, trans. Michael B. Smith (Chicago: University of Chicago Press, 1992), 25.

7. Teresa de Jesús, *Obras completas*, ed. Luis Santullano (Madrid: Aguilar, 1957), 751.

8. Teresa of Avila, *Book of the Foundations*, in *Complete Works of Saint Teresa of Jesus*, 3:1–206, 22.

9. María de San Jerónimo, "Virtues of Our Mother Saint Teresa," 338.

10. Kathleen Norris, *The Quotidian Mysteries: Laundry, Liturgy and "Women's Work"* (New York: Paulist Press, 1998), 3, 35, 82.

11. Teresa of Avila, *Book of the Foundations*, 23. Future page references to this book in the next two paragraphs are indicated in parentheses.

12. Carole Slade, *St. Teresa of Avila: Author of a Heroic Life* (Berkeley: University of California Press, 1995), 34.

13. Cathleen Medwick, *Teresa of Avila: The Progress of a Soul* (New York: Knopf, 2000), xii.

14. María de San José Salazar, *Book for the Hour or Recreation*, trans. Amanda Powell, ed. Alison Weber (Chicago: University of Chicago Press, 2002), 134, 41, 139, 141, 146, 142.

15. Teresa of Avila, *The Life of Saint Teresa of Avila by Herself*, trans. J. M. Cohen (London: Penguin Books, 1987), 208–9.

16. Ibid., 92. I have changed Cohen's translation of "manjar" as meats into the more accurate "foods."

17. Ibid., 96, 114, and 149 respectively. Bell describes her use of an olive twig to induce vomiting as an anorexic practice (*Holy Anorexia* [Chicago: University of Chicago Press, 1985], 18).

18. Teresa of Avila, *Constitutions Which the Mother Teresa of Jesus Gave to the Discalced Carmelite Nuns*, in *The Complete Works of Saint Teresa of Jesus*, 3:219–38, 222.

19. Teresa of Avila, *Life*, 94.

20. Teresa of Avila, *The Interior Castle*, trans. Kieran Kavanaugh (New York: Paulist Press, 1979), 34. For the remainder of this chapter, page references to this work will be given in parentheses.

21. The original Spanish can be found in Teresa de Jesús, *Obras completas*, 396.

22. Michel de Certeau, *The Mystic Fable*, vol. 1, *The Sixteenth and Seventeenth Centuries*, trans. Michael B. Smith (Chicago: University of Chicago Press, 1992), 192.

23. Alison Weber, *Teresa of Avila and the Rhetoric of Femininity* (Princeton: Princeton University Press, 1990), 105, 159.

24. Catherine Swietlicki (Connor), "The Problematic Iconography of Teresa of Avila's *Interior Castle*," *Studia Mystica* 11.3 (1988): 37–47, 40.

25. Ibid., 40.

26. De Certeau, *The Mystic Fable*, 195–96.

27. I have changed the translator's "it" to refer to the soul as "she," a more literal translation from the Spanish and a female gendering of the soul that is central to Teresa's and other mystics' conception of it.

28. Ignatius Loyola, *The Autobiography of St. Ignatius Loyola*, trans. Joseph F. O'Callaghan (New York: Fordham University Press, 1974), 37.

29. Barbara Redi, *Choosing the Better Part? Women in the Gospel of Luke* (Collegeville, Minn.: Liturgical Press, 1996), 144.

30. James L. Resseguie, *Spiritual Landscape: Images of the Spiritual Life in the Gospel of Luke* (Peabody, Mass.: Hendrickson Publishers, 2004), 85.

31. On the Martha and Mary story and the paintings it has inspired, see the excellent essays in Jean-Louis Chrétien, Guy Lafon, Étienne Jollet, *Marthe et Marie* (Paris: Desclée de Brouwer, 2002).

32. The other objection is the nuns' alleged inability to draw souls to God, which Teresa undoes by noting that prayer and service to those around us are very effective in achieving this objective.

Chapter 9

1. Carlo Ginzburg, *The Cheese and the Worms: The Cosmos of a Sixteenth-Century Miller*, trans. John and Anne Tedeschi (Baltimore: Johns Hopkins University Press, 1980), 5–6.

2. Ibid., 57–58.

3. Marvin Harris, *Good to Eat: Riddles of Food and Culture* (New York: Simon and Schuster), 13.

4. Claude Lévi-Strauss, "The Culinary Triangle," in *Food and Culture: A Reader*, ed. Carole Counihan and Penny Van Esterik, 28–35 (New York: Routledge, 1997), 29.

5. Piero Camporesi, *The Anatomy of the Senses: Natural Symbols in Medieval and Early Modern Italy*, trans. Allan Cameron (Cambridge: Polity Press, 1994), 38.

6. Ibid., 58.

7. Wendy Gibson, *Women in Seventeenth-Century France* (London: MacMillan, 1989), 209; Elizabeth Rapley, *Women and Church in Seventeenth-Century France* (Montreal: McGill-Queen's University Press, 1990); Raymond Jonas, *France and the Cult of the Sacred Heart: An Epic Tale for Modern Times* (Berkeley: University of California Press, 2000).

8. Sainte Marguerite Marie, *Sa vie par elle-même. Texte authentique* (Paris: Éditions Saint Paul, 1979), 66.

9. Ibid., 65–67. My translation.

10. Julia Kristeva, *Powers of Horror. An Essay on Abjection*, trans. Leon Roudiez (New York: Columbia University Press, 1982), 2.

11. In Camporesi, *Anatomy*, 45.

12. Kristeva, *Powers of Horror*, 3.

13. Camporesi, *Anatomy*, 45.

14. Kristeva, *Powers of Horror*, 4.

15. David Le Breton, "La cuisine du dégoût," *Revue des Sciences Sociales* 27 (2000): 74–80, 79.

16. Kristeva, *Powers of Horror*, 2–3.

17. Mary Douglas, *Purity and Danger: An Analysis of Concepts of Pollution and Taboo* (London: Routledge and Kegan Paul, 1966), 5, 7. On Catherine of Siena and food, see Bell's chapter "I, Catherine," in *Holy Anorexia* (Chicago: University of Chicago Press, 1985), 22–53.

18. Camporesi, *Anatomy*, 59–60.

19. Kristeva, *Powers of Horror*, 5.

20. Kathleen Ann Myers, *Neither Saints Nor Sinners: Writing the Lives of Women in Spanish America* (Oxford: Oxford University Press, 2003), 93.

21. Sor Juana Inés de la Cruz, *The Answer / La Respuesta. Including a Selection of Poems* (New York: The Feminist Press at the City University of New York, 1994), 75 (this is a dual-language edition).

22. Ibid., 83.

23. Ibid., 49; Sor Juana's editors note that the name "Lupercio Leonardo"

should be his brother's, Bernardo Leonardo de Argensola (1562–1631), Spanish poet and satirist who made this claim in his "First Satire" (Sor Juana, *Answer*, 123–24).

24. Francesca Rigotti, *La filosofia in cucina. Piccola critica della ragion culinaria* (Bologna: Il Mulino, 1999), 33.

25. "Am besten kann ich jetzt arbeiten, währen ich Kartoffeln schäle," quoted in Rigotti, *La filosofia in cucina*, 76.

26. Myers, *Neither Saints Nor Sinners*, 105–6.

27. Mónica Lavín, *Sor Juana en la cocina* (Mexico City: Clío, 2000), 25; Sor Juana, *Il libro di cucina di Juana Inés de la Cruz*, Italian trans. Angelo Morino (Palermo: Sellerio, 1999); this volume includes useful short commentaries.

28. Myers, *Neither Saints Nor Sinners*, 114.

29. Michelle A. González, "Seeing Beauty within Torment: Sor Juana Inés de la Cruz and the Baroque in New Spain," in *A Reader in Latina Feminist Theology: Religion and Justice*, ed. María Pilar Aquino, Daisy L. Machado, and Jeanette Rodríguez, 3–22 (Austin: University of Texas Press, 2002), 4.

30. Cecilia Ferrazzi, *Autobiography of an Aspiring Saint*, ed. and trans. Anne Jacobson Schutte (Chicago: University of Chicago Press, 1996), 58. See also Anne Jacobson Schutte, "Un caso di santità affettata: l'autobiografia di Cecilia Ferrazzi," in *Finzione e santità tra medioevo ed età moderna*, ed. Gabriella Zarri, 329–42 (Turin: Rosenberg & Sellier, 1991), 332.

31. Anne Jacobson Schutte, introduction to *Autobiography of an Apsiring Saint*, 3–18, 10.

32. Cecilia Ferrazzi, *Autobiografia di una santa mancata, 1609–1664*, ed. Anne Jacobson Schutte (Bergamo: Pierluigi Lubrina Editore, 1990), 75.

33. Anne Jacobson Schutte, *Aspiring Saints: Pretense of Holiness, Inquisition, and Gender in the Republic of Venice, 1618–1750* (Baltimore: Johns Hopkins University Press, 2001), 138, 274 n. 28.

34. Ferrazzi, *Autobiography*, 67, 68, and 48 respectively.

35. Ibid., 43–44.

36. Schutte, "Un caso," 336.

37. Peter Barnham, *The Science of Cooking* (Berlin: Springer, 2001), 1.

Chapter 10

1. See Maria Giuseppina Muzzarelli and Fiorenza Tarozzi, *Donne e cibo. Una relazione nella storia* (Milan: Mondadori, 2003), chapter 2.

2. Ibid., chapter 3.

3. Elizabeth Ann Seton, *Selected Writings*, ed. Ellin Kelley and Annabelle Melville (Mahwah, N.J.: Paulist Press, 1987), 70, 123, 23, 34. All subsequent references to this book in this chapter will be given in parentheses. I owe much of my knowledge of Elizabeth Ann Seton's biography to Annabelle Melville's thorough introduction to this volume (15–72).

4. Harvey A. Levenstein, "The Perils of Abundance: Food, Health, and Morality in American History," in *Food: A Culinary History from Antiquity to the Present*, ed. Jean-Louis Flandrin and Massimo Montanari, 516–29 (New York: Columbia University Press, 1999), 517.

5. Ibid., 517.

6. Sara Maitland, *A Big-Enough God: A Feminist's Search for a Joyful Theology* (New York: Holt, 1995), 23.

7. Joseph I. Dirvin, CM, *The Soul of Elizabeth Seton* (San Francisco: Ignatius Press, 1990), 18.

8. Caroline Walker Bynum, *Holy Feast and Holy Fast: The Religious Significance of Food to Medieval Women* (Berkeley: University of California Press, 1987), 186.

9. Charles Simic, "On Food and Happiness," *Antaeus* 68 (Spring 1992): 19–24, 24.

Chapter 11

1. Sally Cline, *Just Desserts: Women and Food* (London: André Deutsch, 1990), 2.

2. Massimo Montanari, "Il messaggio tradito: Perfezione cristiana e rifiuto della carne," in *La sacra mensa. Condotte alimentari e pasti rituali nella definizione dell'identità religiosa*, ed. Roberto Alessandrini and Michelina Borsari, 99–130 (Modena: Banca Popolare dell'Emilia Romagna/Fondazione Collegio San Carlo di Modena, 1999).

3. The English translation says "hepatic oil and ground agracio," a transformation into English of the misspelled words "olio apatico et agracio pesto" present in one of the manuscripts; I translated into English the words of the other manuscript provided in the critical edition, which make more sense. See Catherine of Genoa, *Purgation and Purgatory-The Spiritual Dialogue*, 120; Italian edition in P. Umile Bonzi da Genova, *S.Caterina Fieschi Adorno*, vol. 1, *Edizione critica dei manoscritti cateriniani* (Genova: Marietti, 1962), 1:406.

4. Discussions of *Babette's Feast* can be found in Priscilla Parkhurst Ferguson, *Accounting for Taste: The Triumph of French Cuisine* (Chicago: University of Chicago Press, 2004), 187–201; Mary Elizabeth Podles, "Babette's Feast: Feasting with Lutherans," *Antioch Review* 50.3 (Summer 1992):551–67; Wendy Wright, "*Babette's Feast:* A Religious Film," *Journal of Religion and Film* 1.2 (October 1997). I am much indebted to these essays for my understanding of the movie.

5. Gemma Galgani to Father Germano, May 9–13, 1901, in *Lettere* (Rome: Postulazione dei PP. Passionisti, 1941), 163.

6. Gemma Galgani to Father Germano, around June 26, 1902, in *Lettere*, 263.

7. Hans Jurgen Teuteberg and Jean-Louis Flandrin, "The Transformation of the European Diet," in *Food*, ed. Flandrin and Montanari, 442–456, 446; Martin Bruegel, "A Bourgeois Good? Sugar, Norms of Consumption and the Laboring

Classes in Nineteenth-Century France," in *Food, Drink and Identity: Cooking, Eating and Drinking in Europe since the Middle Ages*, ed. Peter Scholliers, 99–118 (Oxford: Berg, 2001).

8. Luce Irigaray, "Divine Women," in *Sexes and Genealogies*, trans. Gillian Gill, 55–72 (New York: Columbia University Press, 1993), 65.

9. This is the criticism leveled at Gemma by the editors of the entry dedicated to Gemma Galgani in the volume *Scrittrici mistiche italiane*, ed. Giovanni Pozzi and Claudio Leonardi (Genova: Marietti, 1989), 637–40.

10. Luce Irigaray, "When Our Lips Speak Together," trans. Carolyn Burke, in *Signs: Journal of Women in Culture and Society* 6.1 (1980):69–79

11. "As long as woman lacks a divine made in her image she cannot establish her subjectivity or achieve a goal of her own," for "having a God and becoming one's gender go hand in hand" (Irigaray, "Divine Women," 63, 67). For a discussion of Gemma's self-sanctification see Rudolph Bell and Cristina Mazzoni, *The Voices of Gemma Galgani: The Life and Afterlife of a Modern Saint* (Chicago: University of Chicago Press, 2003), 260–63.

12. Gemma Galgani, *Lettere*, 263, 267.

13. Rudolph Bell, *Holy Anorexia* (Chicago: University of Chicago Press, 1985), Bell mentions Gemma Galgani on p. 178; Caroline Walker Bynum, *Holy Feast and Holy Fast: The Religious Significance of Food to Medieval Women* (Berkeley: University of California Press, 1987).

14. Gemma Galgani to Father Germano, December 8, 1900, in *Lettere*, 98. On chocolate and religion, see Wolfgang Schivelbusch, "Chocolate, Catholicism, Ancien Régime," in *A Slice of Life: Contemporary Writers on Food*, ed. Bonnie Marranca, 375–78 (Woodstock and New York: Overlook Press, 2003).

15. Gemma Galgani, *Lettere*, 98, 227, 238 respectively.

16. Bell and Mazzoni, *The Voices of Gemma Galgani*, 139.

17. Ibid., 97.

18. Gemma Galgani, *Estasi—Diario—Autobiografia—Scritti vari di S. Gemma Galgani*, ed. the Postulazione dei PP. Passionisti (Rome: Postulazione Generale dei Passionisti, 1958), 160 (ecstasy dated November 20, 1902).

19. Allison James, "Confections, Concoctions and Conceptions," in *Popular Culture: Past and Present*, ed. Bernard Waites, Tony Bennett, and Graham Martin, 294–307 (London: Croom Helm and the Open University Press, 1982), 306.

20. Galgani, *Estasi—Diario—Autobiografia—Scritti vari*, 149 (ecstasy dated toward the end of August 1902).

21. Ibid., 142 (ecstasy dated August 11, 1902, ellipses in the original).

Chapter 12

1. Jean-Jacques Rousseau, *La nouvelle Héloïse*, in *Oeuvres complètes*, ed. Henri Coulet and Bernard Guyon, 5 vols. (Paris: Gallimard, 1961), 1:452–53 (part 4, letter 10). My translation.

2. Brillat-Savarin, *Physiology of Taste*, 104.

3. In Jane Dusselier, "Bonbons, Lemon Drops, and Oh Henry! Bars: Candy, Consumer Culture, and the Construction of Gender, 1895–1920," in *Kitchen Culture in America: Popular Representations of Food, Gender, and Race*, ed. Sherrie A. Inness, 13–49 (Philadelphia: University of Pennsylvania Press, 2001), 17.

4. John Thorne with Matt Lewis Thorne, *Outlaw Cook* (New York: Farrar, Straus and Giroux, 1992), xix.

5. Andrew Weil and Winifred Rosen, *From Chocolate to Morphine: Everything You Need to Know about Mind-Altering Drugs* (Boston: Houghton Mifflin, 1993), 43; a simple navigation on the web will find many anecdotal and scientific discussions of this connection between chocolate and menstrual periods.

6. Caitlin Hines, "Rebaking the Pie: The *Woman as Dessert* Metaphor," in *Reinventing Identities: The Gendered Self in Discourse*, ed. Mary Bucholtz, A. C. Liang, and Laurel A. Sutton, 145–62 (New York: Oxford University Press, 1999). On the association of men with meat, see Carol J. Adams, *The Sexual Politics of Meat: A Feminist-Vegetarian Critical Theory* (New York: Continuum, 1990).

7. Celsus, *On the True Doctrine: A Discourse against the Christians* (New York: Oxford University Press, 1987), 73; Lynn Abrams, *The Making of Modern Woman: Europe 1789–1918* (London: Pearson, 2002), 34–40; Michela De Giorgio, "The Catholic Model," in *A History of Women in the West*, vol. 4, *Emerging Feminism From Revolution to World War*, ed. Geneviève Fraisse and Michelle Perrot, 166–97 (Cambridge, Mass.: The Belknap Press of Harvard University Press, 1993).

8. Vita Sackville-West, *The Eagle and the Dove* (1943) (London: Quartet Books, 1973), 146; Ida Friederike Görres, *The Hidden Face: A Study of St. Thérèse of Lisieux* (New York: Pantheon Books, 1959), 14, 13; Louis Bouyer, *Women Mystics: Hadewijch of Antwerp, Teresa of Avila, Thérèse of Lisieux, Elizabeth of the Trinity, Edith Stein*, trans. Anne Englund Nash (San Francisco: Ignatius Press, 1993), 135–36.

9. Dorothy Day, *Thérèse* (Springfield, Ill.: Templegate Publishers, 1960), 174.

10. Görres, *The Hidden Face*, 10.

11. On this topic see Richard Burton, *Holy Tears, Holy Blood: Women, Catholicism, and the Culture of Suffering in France, 1840–1970* (Ithaca: Cornell University Press, 2004); and Cristina Mazzoni, *Saint Hysteria: Neurosis, Mysticism, and Gender in European Culture* (Ithaca: Cornell University Press, 1996).

12. An extensive discussion of this question may be found in Mary Frohlich, "Christian Mysticism in Postmodernity: Thérèse of Lisieux as a Case Study," in *Women Christian Mystics Speak to Our Times*, ed. David B. Perrin, OMI (Franklin, Wis.: Sheed and Ward, 2001), 157–71.

13. Hans Urs von Balthasar, *Two Sisters in the Spirit: Thérèse of Lisieux and Elizabeth of the Trinity*, trans. Donald Nichols, Anne Elizabeth Englund, Dennis Martin (San Francisco: Ignatius Press, 1992), 305.

14. Ida Magli, *Santa Teresa di Lisieux* (Milan: Rizzoli, 1984), 108.

15. Thérèse of Lisieux, *Story of a Soul: The Autobiography of Saint Thérèse of Lisieux*, trans. John Clarke (Washington, D.C.: ICS Publications, 1996), 211. All subsequent references to this book in this chapter will be given in parentheses. The original French edition can be found in Sainte Thérèse de l'Enfant-Jésus et de la Sainte-Face (Thérèse of Lisieux), *Histoire d'une âme. Manuscrits autobiographiques* (Paris: Cerf, 1973).

16. "Don't you see that God is going to take me at an age when I would not have had the time to become a priest. If I had been able to become a priest, it would have been in this month of June, at this ordination that I would have received holy orders. So in order that I may regret nothing, God is allowing me to be sick; I wouldn't have been able to present myself for ordination, and I would have died before having exercised my ministry." St. Thérèse of Lisieux, *Her Last Conversations*, trans. John Clarke, OCD (Washington, D.C.: Institute of Carmelite Studies, 1977), 260.

17. Thérèse of Lisieux, *General Correspondence*, vol. 1 (1877–1890), trans. John Clarke, OCD (Washington, D.C.: ICS Publications, 1982), 461.

18. Letter dated August 13, 1893, in *Correspondance Générale*, by Sainte Thérèse de l'Enfant-Jésus et de la Sainte-Face (Thérèse of Lisieux), 2 vols. (Paris: Cerf, 1992), 2:790.

19. Thérèse of Lisieux, *Her Last Conversations*, 108 (July 22, 1897).

20. Ibid., 110–11.

21. The original French of this passage may be found in Thérèse of Lisieux, *Histoire d'une âme*, 30.

22. Elisabetta Rasy, *La prima estasi* (Milan: Mondadori, 1985), 24. Thérèse again compares herself to Petit Poucet when she is on her deathbed; *Last Conversations*, 180 (September 2, 1897).

23. Day, *Thérèse*, 74.

24. Wolfgang Schivelbusch, "Chocolate, Catholicism, Ancien Régime," in *A Slice of Life: Contemporary Writers on Food*, ed. Bonnie Marranca, 375–78 (Woodstock and New York: Overlook Press, 2003), 377.

25. Letter to Mme Guérin, July 20, 1895, in *Correspondance Générale*, 2:811.

26. Letter to Léonie, July 17, 1897, in ibid., 2:1036.

27. Letter to P. Roulland, July 14, 1897, in ibid., 2:1029. A note reminds the reader that Thérèse had been on a milk diet since the week before Pentecost.

28. Thérèse of Lisieux, *Her Last Conversations*, 148 (August 12, 1897), 176 (August 31, 1897).

29. Ibid., 192–93.

30. Luisa Muraro, *Lingua e verità in Emily Dickinson, Teresa di Lisieux, Ivy Compton-Burnett* (Milan: Libreria delle donne, 1995), 42.

31. Thérèse of Lisieux, *Histoire d'une âme*, 226.

32. Thérèse of Lisieux, *Her Last Conversations*, 155 (August 20, 1897).

33. Ibid., 291.

34. Pierre Bourdieu, *Distinction: A Social Critique of the Judgment of Taste*, trans. Richard Nice (Cambridge, Mass.: Harvard University Press, 1984).

Conclusion

1. Ernst Schuegraf, *Cooking with the Saints: An Illustrated Treasury of Authentic Recipes Old and Modern* (San Francisco: Ignatius Press, 2001); Evelyn Vitz, *A*

Continual Feast: A Cookbook to Celebrate the Joys of Family and Faith throughout the Christian Year (San Francisco: Ignatius Press, 1985); Miriam Feinberg Vamosh, *Food at the Time of the Bible: From Adam's Apple to the Last Supper* (Nashville: Abingdon Press, 2004).

2. *Dialogues of Alfred North Whitehead*, ed. Lucien Price (Boston: Little, Brown, 1954), 250 (July 27, 1943); Martin Versfeld, *Food for Thought: A Philosopher's Cook-Book* (Cape Town: Tafelberg, 1983), 29.

3. Hildegard of Bingen, *The Letters of Hildegard of Bingen*, ed. Joseph L. Baird and Radd K. Ehrman, 2 vols. (New York: Oxford University Press, 1994), 1:107.

4. Wendell Berry, "The Pleasures of Eating," in *What Are People For? Essays by Wendell Berry* (San Francisco: North Point Press, 1990), 145–152, 149.

5. Simone Weil, *The Simone Weil Reader*, ed. George A. Panichas (New York: David McKay Company, 1977), 428.

Index